JEWS AND CHRISTIANS
GETTING OUR STORIES STRAIGHT

JEWS AND CHRISTIANS

GETTING OUR STORIES STRAIGHT

THE EXODUS AND THE PASSION-RESURRECTION

MICHAEL GOLDBERG

Abingdon Press

Nashville

Jews and Christians, Getting Our Stories Straight

Copyright © 1985 by Abingdon Press

Library of Congress Cataloging in Publication Data

GOLDBERG, MICHAEL, 1950–
  Jews and Christians, getting our stories straight.
  1. Exodus, The. 2. Paschal mystery. 3. Identification (Religion) 4.
Narration in the Bible. I. Title.
      BS1245.5.G64   1985   220.6   84-14450

ISBN 0-687-20330-9

MANUFACTURED BY THE PARTHENON PRESS AT
NASHVILLE, TENNESSEE, UNITED STATES OF AMERICA

For Myrna
for her faith

FOREWORD

Near the beginning of *Theology and Narrative,* I wrote that while that work was not itself a piece of constructive theology, one day I hoped to write a book that was. That day has now arrived sooner than I imagined. But whether sooner or later, I am certain that the writing of this book would never have been possible without the nuturing that it—and I—received from all those whose care for the enterprise showed them to be not only kind, but also kindred.

As always, James McClendon has provided a sympathetic ear and a critical eye enabling me to hear and see more clearly which matters truly matter. Additionally, Stanley Hauerwas's repeated contributions to the whole field of narrative theology as well as to this one corner of it have proved invariably invaluable. For the several penetrating suggestions Nancey Murphy has offered and for the encouragement generously given by David Burrell, Harold Schulweis, and Rachel Adler, I am genuinely thankful. Finally, a very special debt is owed my students at Temple Isaiah in Lafayette, California, and at Saint John's University in Collegeville, Minnesota, for affording me the opportunity to sound out my earliest and most recent thoughts on the storied relationship between Jews and Christians.

Hence, my saying that this book about that relationship exists only due to so many others being related to it is no *pro forma* author's statement, but instead a straightforward statement of the facts. Such facts ought to remind us that as Jews and Christians, giving our own story a proper telling may well depend on giving the other's story a decent hearing so that we finally may come to know why our lives, which are the embodiments of our stories, have taken one shape rather than another. Clearly, being attentive to our communal story lines may prove at times a bit disturbing, as we note those points at which our core narratives, like our lives, diverge. However, it will do no good to gloss over those points and in fact do lots of bad by implying that Jews and Christians cannot bear simple honesty with one another. But failing to live truthfully in each other's presence, how then can we possibly make good our claims—and hopes—to live truthfully in that Other's presence?

As for those who might disagree with my reading of these formative Jewish and Christian narratives, I invite them to come forward with their own interpretations and know that they are welcome; indeed, if those of us engaged in narrative theology are to have any credibility, how could we wish things otherwise? Interpretation thus elicited helps prove our theological endeavor justified and our stories still provocatively alive. And yet, each fresh piece of exegesis may serve an even more important function. For in the last analysis, every added insight may not simply spur us to get our respective communal narratives clearer still, but ultimately, to get God's own story straight at last.

Note to reader: In this book, double quotes (" ") are used for all quotations except for quotes within quotes (" ' ' ") and 'scare' quotes.

CONTENTS

JEWS AND CHRISTIANS
GETTING OUR STORIES STRAIGHT

PROLOGUE

In an earlier book, I put forth the thesis held by several 'narrative theologians' that as human beings, virtually all of our rock-ribbed beliefs about our lives are grounded in some bedrock story, and consequently, our more serious convictional disputes with one another frequently reflect rival narrative accounts.[1]

In *this* book, I propose to back up that general claim with a concrete example. I suggest that the age-old doctrinal dispute between Jews and Christians has its source in a clash of interpretations centered around two specific stories—Israel's Exodus from Egypt on the one hand, and Christ's passion and resurrection on the other. I call such narratives as these *master stories*, for they offer us both a model for understanding the world and a guide for acting in it.[2] By providing us with a paradigm for making sense of our existence, master stories furnish us with a basis for answering some of the most fundamental questions that we human beings can have: Who are we? What is our world like? And given who we are and what our world is like, what then is the best way for us to respond to such a world as this? The answers to those questions often constitute our most deep-seated convictions about our identity, responsibility, and destiny over the course of our existence. Hence, master stories not only *inform* us, but more crucially, they *form* us.[3]

Clearly, the Exodus narrative and the narrative of Christ's

death and resurrection are two such master stories, because in speaking to their respective communities of their epic pasts, they tell each one how it came to be the community that it most distinctly is. In the process, they implicitly relate how our individual life stories figure in their overarching story lines. In short, for Jews and Christians, such narratives provide a basic orientation to the world.[4]

Now it is obviously true that Jewish and Christian Scriptures contain many narratives besides these two, and it is also patently true that each of these master stories is itself contained within the structure of a broader narrative framework, e.g., Israel's round-trip trek between Canaan and Egypt in the one case, and the life of Jesus in the other. However, it is undeniably true as well that these particular narratives are the *key* stories of each canon, because they are the ones depicting those singular events in human history through which we are to get our bearings for the rest of Scripture, and hence, for the rest of history itself.[5]

Thus, for Christians, the narration of the events surrounding Jesus' crucifixion is the biblical account that most plainly illuminates the Bible's other portions—including the saga of Israel's deliverance from Egypt. The church takes that part of Christ's story as its formative *Christian master story* and sees it as following from the Exodus by being its natural follow up, decisive climax, and ultimate fulfillment. And what do Jews say for their part? 'No! That's not the way at all to take the Exodus, our *Jewish master story.*' What the Christian story represents, say Jews, is not a true interpretation or working out of the Exodus narrative, but instead a serious misreading and profound distortion of it.

That very bone of contention forms the backbone of this inquiry. In the past, Christians and Jews have far too often viewed the differences between them as turning on such creedal statements as: The Jews are/are not the distinctive bearers of God's promise to the world; Jesus is/is not God incarnate; Jesus is/is not the Messiah; the world has/has not been saved. Yet if, in fact, such convictional claims all find their origin and intelligibility in each community's central narrative,

14

then being a Christian or a Jew is not so much a matter of subscribing to one community's core doctrine as of affirming its core story. Hence, Jews and Christians cannot even begin investigating their convictional dispute without first investigating their master stories, and that is exactly what this book aims to do.

I propose to draw attention to these foundational narratives through a literary-theological commentary that forces us to attend closely to what the stories themselves portray. I call the commentary 'literary-theological' in order to make a crucial point—namely, there is no issue of theological substance detachable from the stories' substance. That is, these recountings of the Exodus and the Christ are not fables, such that once their 'point' or 'moral' has been gleaned, the actual narratives can be then discarded. To take the Jewish and Christian master stories as mere fables is to mis-take them terribly, for their truth and meaning are neither extrinsic nor incidental to them, but can only be gotten in and through the narratives themselves as we follow how each one cumulatively builds, develops, and renders its own particular themes.

The formation and justification of our theological convictions hinge, therefore, on our remaining constantly attentive to such literary matters as the unfolding of story line and the depiction of character. For instance, before we start debating theologically whether Jesus Christ signifies the fulfillment of God's promise to Israel, we need to discuss something else: whether—and how—the Christian story line picks up where the Jewish one leaves off, or whether—and how—it veers off from that one altogether. Or again, before we launch into our arguments about Jesus' divinity, we need to consider how the *character called God* is himself portrayed in each narrative. In other words, through the way we read each story, do we, along with Christians, find in the work and person of Jesus Christ the character we have previously met in Israel's chronicle? Or does our reading instead lead us to agree with Jews, concluding that the work and person attributed to Jesus are completely out of character for the One we have earlier come to know as the Lord of the Exodus? Naturally, I cannot promise that an in-depth study of both their master stories will *necessarily* lead Jews and Christians to reach agreement on topics as profound as these. One thing I can, however, guarantee without any hesitation. Lacking such a read-through, Jews and Christians will lack as well *the very possibility* of any agreement between them, because the true ground and nature of their disagreement will continue to remain obscure and enigmatic.

Typically—and understandably—only Christians have been interested in investigating the story-bound relationship between the two traditions.[6] However, in undertaking this enterprise as a Jew, my purpose is not apologetics. My goal is not, for instance, to show that Judaism is somehow 'better' than Christianity. Although I shall spend a bit more time dealing with the Jewish master story than with the Christian, it is only because comprehension of the latter presupposes knowledge of the former—as the church itself has traditionally confessed. Therefore, through my mode of presentation, I in no way mean to slant the issue(s), but on the contrary, I only intend to be better able to present *both* stories as clearly and as compellingly as I can and consequently show with *equal* clarity and power what precisely is at stake in being a Jew or a Christian. In sum, the project has a twofold aim: (1) to get Jews and Christians to understand where their stories and their lives run on track together, and (2) to have them also comprehend where—and why—their stories and their lives critically diverge.

In mapping out the course of any such exploration, there are generally many possible routes to follow, and so it is in this case, too, for while Jewish Scriptures offer only one full-scale rendition of Israel's Exodus from Egypt, the Gospels give several portraits of Christ and his crucifixion and resurrection. Nevertheless, I have chosen Matthew's account of the Christian master story for what I believe to be extremely cogent reasons given the objectives of our investigation. For Matthew draws the sharpest lines, both of comparison and contrast, between the Jewish and Christian core narratives; no wonder that his Gospel has been readily described as the one "which has the strongest Jewish flavour.'"[7] At bottom, Matthew wants to show that the story of the Christ grows directly out of Israel's preceding story. And yet he also means to show that outgrowth occurring in a decisively new and unexpected way, resulting in a new and unexpected life, not only for Israel, but for all the world. Jews, of course, would dispute that notion, arguing that it is Exodus alone which most distinctly displays life's true course and character. But in any case, when during the course of our inquiry I use the locution "the Christian master story," I shall be using it as shorthand for the more cumbersome expression, 'Matthew's *version* of the Christian master story.'

Before we embark on our journey through the narratives themselves, I want to say something about my commentary meant to help us chart our way. First with Exodus, then with Matthew, I intend to take a few verses at a time and make comments aimed at calling attention to the relationship between what these passages *have to say* and what they *have to say to us*—that is, between what they *mean to the stories* and what they might therefore *mean to our lives*. In general, I shall attempt to explain the sense and significance of these storied texts in the clearest, most concise, and technically uncluttered way possible, so that while making use of the fruits of both classical and modern biblical scholarship when needed, I shall in the end require of the reader only the capacity to follow a story with sensitivity and openness.

Indeed, that requirement has guided my choice of scriptural texts for comment as well as my selection of supplemental commentaries for assistance. In the first place, neither our study nor my remarks will run continuously through the entirety of either Exodus or Matthew. Instead, we will tend to focus on those sections of each story that are primarily *narrative in structure*. Such passages, in highlighting the basic story line of each account, not only signal how we ought rightfully to understand the various non-narrative segments they bracket; but by displaying the narrative flow driving each work forward, they also suggest how we ought properly to envision our convictions *flowing from* our master stories.

Hence, in the second place, I have made extensive use of other commentators whose own work shows them well attuned to just such literary/theological concerns as these. Too often, modern and traditional critics alike have distorted the Bible's narrative texts—and themes—through analyses that wrenched them out of the *con*texts of their larger story settings. Brevard Childs, whose writing has consistently avoided this kind of error and upon which I have therefore heavily relied in my writing here, has skillfully laid out the base line for the task before us: "It is the final text, the composite narrative, in its present shape which the church, following the lead of the synagogue, accepted as canonical and thus the vehicle of revelation and instruction."[8]

In an effort to remain faithful to Childs's dictum and to stay close to both these stories, I have tried to keep my remarks in the same simple, straightforward style of the narratives themselves. While I am well aware that such a mode of expression tends (sadly) to be rare among works of serious theology, I must caution against anyone's equating such simplicity of expression with simplemindedness of thought, even though I confess that such a style may seem a bit unusual in a work of serious theology. For those wishing a more detailed theoretical exposition of some of the topics covered, I suggest my notes at each chapter's end, and naturally, my discussion of these subjects in *Theology and Narrative*.

Finally, I would issue an additional caveat here—namely, against dismissing the commentary's rather bare-boned approach as 'mere' midrash. For if midrash is rightly seen as exegesis that draws from the text and not as eisegesis that tends to draw away from it, then I admittedly—and unrepentantly—stand convicted. Indeed, considering the root meaning of *midrash*—"seek from"—what better way for us as Jews and Christians to seek the ground of our convictions than by *seeking it from the foundation provided by our master stories?* Hence, if we are not to lose our way with either our scriptural interpretations or our thelogical convictions, we must keep a constant eye on those wider narrative frameworks from which our varied claims draw whatever meaning, power, and validity they might ultimately possess.

For some time now, many have been trumpeting the promise of narrative theology. I believe the time has come at last to deliver on that promise. And what more hopeful way for us to do that than by listening to two stories that are themselves so richly promise-laden?

Notes

1. Michael Goldberg, *Theology and Narrative* (Nashville: Abingdon Press, 1982), p. 36; cf. also Stanley Hauerwas, with David Burrell and Richard Bondi, *Truthfulness and Tragedy* (Notre Dame, Ind.: University of Notre Dame Press, 1977), p. 15.

2. The notion of a "master story" first occurred to me while reading David Harned's book, *Images for Self-Recognition* (New York: The Seabury Press, 1977). Harned speaks of "master images" which, he says, "furnish the self with the perspectives from which it must judge and seek to understand other selves and its world" (p. xvii). While intrigued by Harned's insight, I nevertheless felt that his idea of dominant images was far too limited, for such images depend for their status and power on the underlying, formative narratives in which they occur. Consequently, my own view is that more fundamentally significant than various master images are certain master stories.

3. I am indebted to Professor Hans Frei for this perceptive observation.

4. For a short account of the Exodus as an "orienting experience," see Irving Greenberg's "Judaism and History: Historical Events and Religious Change," in *Perspectives in Jewish Learning*, vol. 1, eds. Stanley Kazan and Nathaniel Stampfer (Chicago: Spertus College Press, 1977). Building on Greenberg's suggestive concept, Emil Fackenheim has written briefly about the Exodus as "root-experience"; see his *God's Presence in History* (New York: Harper Torchbooks, 1970).

5. Thus, for instance, even though Jesus' birth and subsequent ministry are significant for making sense of the story of Christ, the crucifixion and resurrection are *decisively revelatory* for grasping the meaning and truth of *the narrative as a whole*. Drawing from H. Richard Niebuhr's *The Meaning of Revelation* (New York: Macmillan, 1967), we might say that the passion and resurrection constitute those "intelligible event[s] which [make] all other events intelligible."

Moreover, notice how these revealingly key stories of the Exodus and the Christ run as key motifs through various aspects of Jewish and Christian tradition. Thus, note, for example, Rabbinic Judaism's recurrent references to "the going out from Egypt" in its tripartite fashioning of the *Shema,* in all its varied formulations of the *Kiddush,* and in its historically oriented reformulations of the Pilgrimage Festivals' rationale. And for the church, consider, for instance, its repeated traditional emphasis on the cross, the Eucharist, and Easter. Hence, at a deeper level, both Judaism and Christianity seem constantly to retell their master stories by continually reenacting them though ritual and liturgy.

6. Paul van Buren, the author of *Discerning the Way: A Theology of the Jewish-Christian Reality* (New York: The Seabury Press, 1982), stands as perhaps the most recent example.

7. Stendahl, "Matthew," in *Peake's Commentary on the Bible*, eds. Matthew Black and H. H. Rowley (London: Thomas Nelson and Sons, 1962), s. 673 f.

8. Brevard Childs, *The Book of Exodus: A Critical, Theological Commentary* (Philadelphia: The Westminster Press, 1974), p. xv.

THE JEWISH
MASTER STORY

I
EXODUS 1

¹These are the names of the sons of Israel who came to Egypt with Jacob, each coming with his household: ²Reuben, Simeon, Levi, and Judah; ³Issachar, Zebulun, and Benjamin; ⁴Dan and Naphtali, Gad and Asher. ⁵The total number of persons that were of Jacob's issue came to seventy, Joseph being already in Egypt. ⁶Joseph died, and all his brothers, and all that generation. ⁷But the Israelites were fertile and prolific; they multiplied and increased very greatly so that the land was filled with them.

As a master story, the Exodus narrative holds out a model of human existence intended not only as a paradigm for explaining the nature and the realities of our lives, but intended as well as a guide for sustaining and transforming those lives. In so doing, this one particular narrative thus becomes a story of universal import, and indeed, the opening passage of the narrative makes known to us that that is exactly the kind of story we shall hear.

Despite its brevity, this introductory passage, functioning as a prologue for the story to follow, pointedly directs our attention to elements in that story whose significance will be far-reaching. The verses here train our vision on what will be the focal point of the narrative as a whole. Importantly, that focus is not an individual, but a community: the household of Israel. At the very outset, we learn that the bearer of the story is not a person, but a people—Israel. Therefore, from this master story's vantage point, the key for understanding the meaning of human experience lies in the aggregate experience of a whole human community and not in the individual experiences of some random human being.

The story also tells us right from the start that it is more than just a story about Israel; as a *master story*, it is about all humankind. Its opening lines express that idea in a variety of ways. We hear, for instance, that Jacob's offspring numbered "seventy" people. The number seventy, however, stands for much more than the tally of Jacob's issue. According to a biblical conception, it is also a number that corresponds to the number of peoples that make up the world.[1] In other words, this story about the people Israel stands as and for a story about all peoples everywhere.

The words of verse 7 carry through this theme with even greater force; they help us see that in reality this is a story about the world told in and through Israel's story. The words we find in this verse—"fertile" (Heb.: *paru*), "prolific" (Heb.: *vayishretsu*), "multiplied" (Heb.: *vayirbu*)—all first appear in the Genesis narratives telling of the world's creation. Such words repeated in the present narrative skillfully remind us that the One who began the work of creation 'back then' is still at work on his creation even now. As before, so too now, God devotedly works to bring life to that creation. Life continually comes into the world as both the expression and the result of the Creator's continuing commitment to his handiwork. It is a commitment that quite literally spells the promise of life for all his creatures: for the animals on the fifth day (Gen. 1:22), for man and woman on the sixth (Gen. 1:28), for the survivors in the ark after the Flood subsides (Gen. 8:17; 9:7)—and for Abraham a long time after that (Gen. 12:2-3; 17:6; 22:17-18). And now we hear that that same commitment to life is still being kept alive through Abraham's descendants in Egypt: "The children of Israel proliferated, swarmed, multiplied and grew more and more."[2] Through words and verses such as these, the core story of the Jewish people thus becomes set within a larger story set in motion at the dawn of time. And hence, the stage is set for Exodus as a master story, that is, as a story for all time.

However, before the narrative moves forward with Israel's story—and the world's story—it takes one short look backward, mentioning laconically the migration of Jacob and his sons to Egypt. Now someone who had just come in on the story at this point might naturally be led to wonder, 'Well, what got them all down to Egypt in the first place?' The simplest way to answer that question would be to go back and look at the narrative that has come before. Nevertheless, the answer itself remains far from simple. Many people, perhaps most, would respond by citing Genesis 42:1 ff., answering that famine caused the children of Israel to leave Canaan in search of more favorable economic conditions in Egypt. Others, however, might answer by referring to Genesis 15:13-16, where God tells Abra[ha]m:

> Know well that your offspring shall be strangers in a land not theirs, and they shall be enslaved and oppressed four hundred years; but I will pass judgment on the nation they shall serve, and in the end they shall go free with great wealth. As for you,
> You shall go to your fathers in peace;
> You shall be buried at a ripe old age.
> And they shall return here in the fourth generation, for the iniquity of the Amorites will not be fulfilled[3] until then.

Whatever problems concerning justice these verses may pose, their basic thrust nevertheless remains clear enough. In short, Israel's going into Egypt is part of some larger plan of God—a plan yet to be revealed.

So now, in addition to our original question about the reason for Israel's journey into Egypt, we have one more: Which of our two narrative-grounded responses is correct? And our answer to *that* question may just be: both. Certainly, the second explanation—i.e., God's plan—does not necessarily preclude the first—economic factors—and in fact may even encompass it. And just as certainly, the answer of economic factors alone may not necessarily be incorrect. But crucially, while it may not be totally incorrect, it still may not be totally complete either. For although it may be true to say that what led Israel to come to Egypt was famine in the land, it may be truer still to say that *through the famine, God led Israel to Egypt.*

How then to answer and decide what is going on?[4]

That riddle about our existence in the world is one that we human beings puzzle over all our lives. Of all the possible ways of linking together and accounting for the events that make up our experience, which one offers us the fullest description and the most adequate explanation *of* and *for* our lives? That is certainly an issue we would expect a master story to address, and it surely is an issue Exodus will confront time and time again. Throughout the narrative, both the story's characters and the story's hearers will be faced with having to choose between alternative ways of accounting for the events of which the story speaks. Again and again, Exodus will ask both its characters and us to make up our minds about what is going on.

> [8]Now a new king arose over Egypt, who did not know Joseph. [9]And he said to his people, "Look, the Israelite people are much too numerous for us. [10]Let us, then, deal shrewdly with them, lest they increase and, in the event of war, join our enemies in fighting against us and gain ascendancy over[a] the country." [11] So they set taskmasters over them to oppress them with forced labor; and they built garrison cities[b] for Pharaoh: Pithom and Raamses. [12]But the more they were oppressed, the more they increased and spread out, so that the [Egyptians] came to dread the Israelites.
>
> [a]Others "get them up out of"[5]
> [b]Others "store cities"

With these verses, the story's focus shifts from past events to more current news. We receive tidings of a new Egyptian king who had no firsthand experience of the now dead Joseph and the good he had done for Egypt.[6] Moreover, something else has changed as well. Suddenly, somehow, God's blessing has become Israel's curse. For it is nothing other than Israel's sheer fruitfulness that apparently arouses both the king's suspicion and his people's dread.

But why? Why should the mere numbers of Israel cause such fear? Verses 9 and 10 provide an answer: "And [the king] said to *his people*, 'Look, *the Israelite people* are much too numerous *for us*. Let *us*, then, deal shrewdly with *them*, lest *they* increase, and in the event of war, *join our enemies* in fighting *against us*' "(italics added). From the perspective of these verses, what at bottom underlies Egypt's fear of Israel is Egypt's perception of a fundamental dichotomy between the two peoples—between 'us' and 'them.' At the most fundamental level, Egypt's dread of Israel rests on her seeing Israel as 'other,' as those in the world 'not us.' With that, the oppression begins.

Yet notice what has happened. Egypt's plan to thwart the other's growth represents nothing less than a scheme to thwart the plan of God. All along, from Genesis until now, we have repeatedly heard that whoever else this God may be, he is none other than the Creator of the world and all life in it. Consequently, he is the Creator whose creatures' lives are all necessarily bound one to the other as part and parcel of the same creation, whose prime directive God gave at its inception: be fruitful in bringing forth new life and thus ensure that creation's work goes on. Hence, to divide that creation into two irreconcilable camps of 'us' and 'them,' and then to try to snuff out the spark of life in 'them' entirely, is ultimately to deny what this particular master story portrays the world as being—a creation made by One Creator, who made all of it "very good." In the end, to deny that storied claim is to claim instead another kind of world altogether. It is in fact to argue for an altogether different story.

Exactly that kind of clash between two stories will provide part of the dramatic tension in this Exodus narrative. Which story will prevail? Which view of the world, *which plan for the world*, will win out? That of God, or that of someone else? Furthermore, with what power and determination will each plan and purpose be pursued? Although we do not yet possess the answers to any of these questions, we still do have a hint of sorts: "But the more they were oppressed, the more they increased." As we latch on to this clue, we cannot help but start to wonder about the chances for success of the Egyptians' scheme when pitted against the scheme of God for his creation. And in pondering that, we may also begin to reflect on just how "shrewd" or wise the Egyptian plan really is. Is it truly a smart 'life plan'? Indeed, throughout the rest of the

"story" becoming too difuse a term?

narrative to follow, not only the Egyptians, but all of us, will continually be asked to judge the prudence of our proposed life projects.

But first, before we continue with the narrative, we need to stop and make a critical observation about what kind of narrative Exodus is meant to be. We recall that at the beginning of the story, its characters were referred to only as "the Israelite people," "the Egyptians," "the king."[7] The story may thus have initially called to mind a fairy tale, i.e., the kind of story that typically starts out, 'Once upon a time, there was an evil king who said to his people. . . .' Such a tale is, *by definition*, a fiction. It is is not intended in any way as a historical portrayal of what actually happened, and the events it depicts are not to be construed as having occurred within the framework of any set historical place or time. By contrast, this Exodus narrative, with its specific references to the historical sites Pithom and Raamses, now shows us that it is not that kind of story at all. Unlike fairy tales, fictions, and fantasies, the truth of this story will lie not only in its ability to *ring true* to some common features of human experience, but also in its capacity to *be true* to certain historical occurrences. That is *not* to say that *every* event mentioned in the Exodus narrative needs actually to have taken place. But it *is* to say that if *none* of the events portrayed in Exodus ever happened, then any claims to truth or significance that we might make on its behalf will go simply unsupported—and rightly unbelieved.

> [13]The Egyptians imposed tasks upon the Israelites ruthlessly: [14]they embittered their lives with harsh labor at mortar and brick and in all sorts of work in the fields, with all the tasks that they ruthlessly imposed upon them.

In these two lines, with their fivefold use of the Hebrew root '*vd*—"serve"—the stress is squarely on Israel's forced servitude to Egypt. And here, we need to ask something which at first glance might appear to need no asking at all: Just what is so bad about such servitude? As children of the Enlightenment and as heirs to the American Revolution, we would probably be quick to reply that what makes that kind of servitude, that slavery, so horrible is that it doesn't leave you at liberty to do what you yourself want to do as your own free and independent lord and master. Perhaps so. To be sure, that kind of response makes good sense in light of the Enlightenment's master story that depicts history as the progressive liberation of the individual. However, when set within the context of the master story of the Exodus, such a response makes no sense at all. For this is a story, after all, whose climax is not a Declaration of Independence at Philadelphia, but a binding covenant at Sinai. In this narrative, being liberated from Egypt does not result in your being left free to your own devices. Instead, down the road in the Exodus, the Israelites go from being the servants of the Egyptians to being the servants of God.

Thus, let us ask again within the context of the Exodus story: What does it mean for Israel to be enslaved to Egypt, and where lies the essential wrongness of such servitude? In the first place, for one people or person to enslave another is, by that very act, to claim the other as *one's own*; it is in a fundamental sense to claim another's life as *belonging* to oneself. Such a claim, however, flies in the face of the biblical story that we have heard thus far. If the creation narratives of Genesis tell us anything, they tell us that the sovereign source and lord of life is God—and God alone. It is in just that sense that to God—and God alone—all life ultimately belongs. Therefore, from the perspective of these biblical narratives, anyone besides God laying such ultimate claim to another's life would in effect be arrogating to himself prerogatives not his. In essence, such a one would be making the most presumptuous claim any human being could make—the claim to be God. And in the framework of this story at least, that is part of what is most plainly wrong about Egypt's enslaving Israel. Such enslavement reflects a profound misunderstanding of the truth about who God is, about who humanity is, and about what the proper relationship is between the two in the great order of creation.

But there is something else wrong about the bondage, and, as before, it too reflects a distorted notion of the truth of our existence. The repetition of the root *'vd*—"serve"—five times in the space of two verses is no mere rhetorical effect. Its effect on us is something altogether different. When these words and verses underscore the origins and nature of Israel's forced servitude to Egypt, they force us in turn to consider *in whose service* our own lives are. The question these verses raise—the question this whole story raises—starkly put, is this: What purpose does our living serve? And now we have just asked something central to every master story: What is the purpose of life? Importantly, this particular master story's conflict will center on two diametrically opposed cross purposes: God's on the one hand versus Pharaoh's on the other. Against the background of this narrative, whatever else may be wrong about Pharaoh's enslaving Israel, what is most fundamentally mistaken about it is that it is terribly mistaken about the true ends and purposes of our lives—about the true ends and purposes of God and his creation.

> [15]The king of Egypt spoke to the Hebrew midwives, one of whom was named Shiphrah and the other Puah, [16]saying, "When you deliver the Hebrew women, look at the birthstool: if it is a boy, kill him; if it is a girl, let her live." [17]The midwives, fearing God, did not do as the king of Egypt had told them; they let the boys live. [18]So the king of Egypt summoned the midwives and said to them, "Why have you done this thing, letting the boys live?" [19]The midwives said to Pharaoh, "Because the Hebrew women are not like the Egyptian women: they are vigorous. Before the midwife can come to them, they have given birth." [20]And God dealt well with the midwives; and the people multiplied and increased greatly. [21]And because the midwives feared God, He established households[c] for them. [22]Then Pharaoh charged all his people, saying, "Every boy that is born you shall throw into the Nile, but let every girl live."

> [c]Meaning of Heb. *batim* uncertain

Egypt's oppression of Israel now intensifies. The enslavement intended to check Israel's numbers has been ineffective, and a policy of genocide is therefore instituted. And as with the policy of bondage before it, it likewise comes in a two-stage process. Initially, the king of Egypt had sought to control the

Israelite population's growth through a program of corvée; the Israelites were to build some store cities under the direction of taskmasters especially appointed for that purpose. However, when that program failed to achieve its aims ("the more they were oppressed, the more they increased"), the king stepped up the oppression with a more systematic and comprehensive policy of total enslavement whose implementation involved the Egyptian people as a whole. Now as well, in carrying out his plan of mass extermination, Pharaoh follows a similar course of action. At first, he enjoins only the midwives to see to the killing of the Hebrew babies. But later, when his goals fail to materialize (v. 20), Pharaoh again resorts to a more systematically comprehensive approach which, as before, involves—and implicates—all Egypt: "Then Pharaoh charged all his people saying, 'Every boy that is born you shall throw into the Nile.'"

In any event, Pharaoh's policy of genocide, like that of enslavement, seems flawed—and not only practically, but logically as well. After all, if Pharaoh is anxious about Israel's growing population, what sense does it make for him to have all the males killed while sparing all the females, the ones who are literally the bearers of life for Israel? We note this incoherency in the Egyptian plan, and we go back and remember that its original objective was to enable Egypt to "deal shrewdly" with 'the Israelite problem.' Once again, we start to wonder about the judiciousness of such a program. And we begin to doubt as well the wisdom of a king who can be so easily deceived by a couple of simple midwives' rather far-fetched ploy: 'O Great Pharaoh! Somehow all those Hebrew babies just keep on being born before we manage to get there!'

And exactly who are these midwives anyway? Although the masoretic text identifies them as Hebrews, nevertheless, many commentators, on the basis of the internal logic of the story, have instead identified them as Egyptian women who are midwives *to the Hebrews*.[8] What grounds are there for such a reading?

First, throughout the course of the entire narrative—and

especially up to now—Pharaoh's commands are addressed solely to Egyptians. And surely, orders calling for the murder of Hebrew infants would not be the kind we would expect Hebrew women either to receive or to obey.

However, a second and even more persuasive reason for identifying the midwives as Egyptians lies in the source of their refusal to comply with Pharaoh's wishes. Their disobedience is not due, for example, to any feelings of detest for Pharaoh or sympathy for Israel. Instead, that disobedience, we learn, stems from the fact that "the midwives feared God."

Those who maintain that the midwives were Hebrews rather than Egyptians use this bit of data as the chief ground of their argument, for they argue that only Hebrews could rightly be expected to be 'God-fearing' people. However, reverence and loyalty to God are qualities this narrative expects and demands of all people, all of whom, according to this story's beginnings, have been created in the image of God.[9] It is precisely such faithful reverence to God the creator of all that undergirds a similar attitude toward all God's creation. In fact, that kind of faithfulness sets the standard the story uses for judging the behavior of non-Israelites (cf. Gen. 20:11 and Deut. 25:18). As Nehama Leibowitz, for instance, has so correctly seen, whether a Gentile "is praised for being godfearing or condemned for lacking that quality [depends on his] attitude towards the minority, to the defenseless outsider or stranger."[10] In the last analysis, to be God-fearing means to see the other not as other—i.e., not as stranger or outsider—but as fellow creature who is also part of the whole of God's wholly good creation.

Of course, it is that sort of vision that the Egyptian policies of enslavement and genocide deny. Slavery, for its part, tears apart the fabric of creation by making divisions between master and slave, owner and owned, 'valuable lives' and lives that are valued less. Yet while slavery is thus bad enough, genocide is even worse. For by seeking to kill off some life altogether, genocide literally attempts to stop creation dead in its tracks.

In the context of the biblical narrative, what therefore

justifies the midwives' disloyalty to Pharaoh is *not* their loyalty to some abstract moral principle or rule, such as, 'Killing babies is always wrong.' Instead, their actions grow out of their loyalty to God the Creator and his plans and purposes for all his creatures. Significantly, when Pharaoh orders the mid-wives to kill the Israelite baby boys, he uses a word for the first time which will later be all-important to this master story as a whole: *tsav*—"command." Equally significant, therefore, is the midwives' disobedience. Refusing to comply with Pharaoh's latest command issued to his subjects, the women follow instead God's first commandment given his creation: be fruitful and multiply. Clearly, that is exactly what we should expect from *midwives*, i.e., from those whose primary charge is to help bring forth life and who can thus be counted on as God's partners in creation. Hence, the reward given these women makes perfect sense: "And because the midwives feared God, He established households [literally: 'houses'] for them." In short, a commitment to life brings life. Despite Pharaoh's wishes, God's wishes for his creatures and his world inexorably reach fulfillment: "And God dealt well with the midwives; and the people multiplied and increased greatly."

Notes

1. See Deut. 32:8; cf. also Gen. 46:27. In particular, see the 'Table of Nations' given in Gen. 10 where seventy peoples are traced back to the three sons of Noah.

2. Nehama Leibowitz, *Studies in Shemot (Exodus)*, trans. Aryeh Newman, part 1 (Jerusalem: World Zionist Organization, 1981), p. 13.

3. Better: "complete"; Hebrew: *shaleim*.

4. This, of course, is the central issue addressed by H. Richard Niebuhr in his classic study, *The Responsible Self* (New York: Harper & Row, 1978).

5. NJPS translates this part of Exod. 1:10 as "gain ascendancy over the country." Clearly, such a translation seems to make good sense in terms of the narrative's dramatic movement and tension. However, as Childs quite correctly notes, such a rendering nevertheless lacks, philologically speaking, "adequate warrant from the text" (*Book of Exodus*, p. 15).

6. A primary sense of the Hebrew *yd'* is 'to know through intimate and personal experience'; hence, the use of the word in passages such as Gen. 4:1: "And the man knew [*yada*] Eve his wife, and she conceived."

At any rate, this word will reappear later in the narrative, and its appearance at that juncture will mark a critical turning point in the story.

7. Or 'Pharaoh'—literally: 'Great House.' 'Pharaoh' is thus a metonym for 'the leader.' Our use of 'White House' functions in much the same way, e.g., 'The White House announced today. . . '

8. Cf., e.g., Philo, Josephus, Luzzato, Malbim.

9. The Hebrew used for "God" in verse 21 is *elohim*. It is the same generic term used in Gen. 1:27 which speaks of the creation of *all* human beings "in the image of God" (*betselem elohim*).

10. Leibowitz, *Studies in Shemot*, p. 36.

II
EXODUS 2

¹A certain man of the house of Levi went and married a Levite woman. ²The woman conceived and bore a son; and when she saw how beautiful he was, she hid him for three months. ³When she could hide him no longer, she got a wicker basket for him and calked it with bitumen and pitch. She put the child into it and placed it among the reeds by the bank of the Nile. ⁴And his sister stationed herself at a distance, to learn what would befall him.

Suddenly, the story's focus shifts. Up to now, the drama of the narrative has revolved around the large-scale conflict between two peoples. Now, however, the action centers on the life of an individual family. Strikingly, this Israelite family, belonging to the clan of Levi, is caught in the crosscurrents of such awesome happenings. On the one hand, as a Hebrew family, it has probably been subjected to Egyptian thralldom and pressed into Pharaoh's service. But on the other hand, as a Levite family, it consists of those who one day will be specially designated to perform the service of the Lord. And even if we leave aside the family's levitical strain, its members still remain poised at the vortex of a fateful clash between two opposing wills. As members of Israel, they are the vassals of Pharaoh who have received word that their children are destined to die. Yet as members of Israel, they are also the seed of Abraham who have received a promise of life for their children, assuring that one day their offspring will grow as numerous "as the stars of the sky and as the sands by the seashore" (Cf. Gen. 22:17).

What the Israelite mother does with her infant son reflects the tension inherent in the collision between these two very different master plans. For in her attempt to save her baby's life, where does she put him but in what seems the most life-threatening place of all: the Nile—the Egyptians' killing ground! Moreover, the ambiguity of her act is further deepened if we stop to think about the nature of water itself. In a quite literal sense, water is both life-giving and life-ending. Taken one way, it can refresh us and give us life; taken another, it can drown us and so end our lives. We already know a story that reminds us of that very fact: the story of the Flood. We recall how the life-giving waters of the heavens and the seas were turned into instruments of chaos and destruction. And now we remember that in the Flood story—as in this one—those to be saved from death are put into a *teiva:* literally, a chest or box having neither rudder nor sail nor any other sort of navigational device. In that story of the Flood, as in this one of the Exodus, riding out the waters of destruction crucially depends on the guidance given by an unseen providence.[1] Before this narrative is over, water will again appear at crucial junctures of the story. Each time, its appearance will carry in its wake and signify an issue of salvation or destruction—a matter of life or death.

But for now, we, along with the infant's sister, must simply position ourselves to see what will transpire. Nevertheless, we ought be clear about the narrative ahead. That master story will repeatedly put all of us in the position of having to consider what truly lies in store for us as human beings. What power is it that really guides our lives? One like Pharaoh? Or that of God?

[5]The daughter of Pharaoh came down to bathe in the Nile, while her handmaids walked along the Nile. She spied the basket among the reeds and sent her slave girl to fetch it. [6]When she opened it, she saw that it was a child, a boy crying. She took pity on it and said, "This must be a Hebrew child." [7]Then his sister said to Pharaoh's daughter, "Shall I go and call you a

Hebrew nurse to suckle the child for you?" [8]And Pharaoh's daughter answered, "Yes." So the girl went and called the child's mother. [9]And Pharaoh's daughter said to her, "Take this child and nurse it for me, and I will pay your wages." So the woman took the child and nursed it. [10]When the child grew up, she brought him to Pharaoh's daughter, and she made him her son. She named him Moses,[a] saying, "It means: I drew him out of the water."

[a]Heb. *Mosheh* from Egyptian for "born of"; here associated with *mashah* "draw out"

Once again, we witness the confrontation between the power of Pharaoh and that of God. What the story has intimated to us before, it makes even more explicit now: the contest between God and Pharaoh is really no contest at all. For all his reputed power, Pharaoh lacks even sufficient power to get his own daughter to comply with his decrees. First, she saves the Hebrew baby instead of killing it. Then, instead of treating the baby's mother as one of the lowly Hebrew slaves, she offers *to pay* the woman *for her services*. Last, and perhaps most significant of all, rather than follow her father's policies placing a complete and utter barrier between Hebrew and Egyptian, the Egyptian princess adopts the Hebrew infant as her own.[2]

Importantly, Pharaoh's daughter, like the midwives before her, is a Gentile whose actions here at the story's outset are absolutely essential if Israel's story is to go on at all. Although the princess and the midwives are members of the same people who initiated Israel's oppression, their acts nevertheless show that neither cruelty nor kindness is an inherent ethnic trait. On the contrary, their deeds testify to a story-based conviction that above and beyond any distinction between Egyptian and Israelite, between Jew and Gentile—between 'us' and 'them'— there is ultimately only *one* creation and *one* world of which *all* of us are indivisibly a part.

[11]Some time after that, when Moses had grown up, he went out to his kinsfolk and witnessed their toil. He saw an Egyptian beating a Hebrew, one of his kinsmen. [12]He turned this way and that and, seeing no one about, he struck down the Egyptian and hid him in the sand.

The story now skips abruptly forward; Moses has grown up. No doubt, some may feel that the story has moved *too* abruptly. In their eyes, it has skipped over a very important issue. They want to know how Moses came to identify with the Hebrews, how he came to learn they were "his kinsmen" in the first place.

Although we can venture guesses of our own (maybe his nurse/mother revealed these things to him?), the narrative itself remains unconcerned about the matter and passes over it in silence. We might perhaps think back to the account of Abraham's leading Isaac to the sacrificial altar[3] and notice that there, too, the matrix of concern is not the realm of the hero's private, subjective feelings. Instead, it is the arena of his actions manifest for all to see. Hence, for Exodus as well, the primary locus of significance is not some individual's psychic world. Rather, the site for its events of saving meaning is our shared, common world: *the* world.

In this passage, we see Moses in action for the first time, and his actions are indeed directed to—and for—his people in the world 'out there.' Yet despite all the apparent straightforwardness of Moses' acts, they still seem in some way rather odd. The 'man of action' that we meet in these verses is not just a 'man of few words'; he is a man of *no words*. Moreover, though Moses strikes with strength and boldness once he decides to act, he nonetheless seems somehow uncertain and even sneaky both prior to and following the deed. Finally, Moses' actions here give the narrative an unexpected twist. According to many story lines, the protagonist is born into a ruling family, grows up among the masses, then returns upon maturity to the royal household to claim his rightful place.[4] However, in this narrative, that story line has been reversed. Moses is born into the lower class and then raised by the master class; when he grows up, he turns on the Egyptians to take his place and stand with Israel.

These three elements—the importance of the spoken word, the efficacy of acts, and the reversal of expectations—will play a vital role in the narrative to follow. However, we are not yet far enough along in the story to be able to expand on their meaning any further. But as they reappear, we shall have to pause and ponder their significance.

> [13]When he went out the next day, he found two Hebrews fighting; so he said to the offender, "Why do you strike your fellow?" [14]He retorted, "Who made you chief and ruler over us? Do you mean to kill me as you killed the Egyptian?" Moses was frightened, and thought: Then the matter is known! [15]When Pharaoh learned of the matter, he sought to have Moses killed; but Moses fled from Pharaoh. He arrived[b] in the land of Midian, and sat down beside a well.

[b]Lit. "sat" or "settled"

In certain key respects, Moses' intervention here between two Hebrews illuminates his previous intervention between an Egyptian and a Hebrew. In verse 13, the Hebrew word translated as "offender" is *rasha*; it is a technical, judicial term meaning 'the one who is in the wrong.' Thus, when Moses interjects himself between the fighting Hebrews, he does so out of a basic concern for justice and not, e.g., out of some sense of pity or empathy for the one who is getting the worse of it. In other words, both here and in the previous case involving the Egyptian taskmaster, Moses is moved to act not because he feels sorry for the Israelites. Instead, Moses intervenes both times simply in order *to set things right*.

There is, however, still another illuminating parallel between the two incidents. In both episodes, Moses' actions are a good deal less than totally effective, and on each occasion, their efficacy is undermined for the exact same reason. The offending Hebrew's response to Moses—"Who made you chief and ruler over us?"—constitutes a pointed challenge to Moses' authority. But, of course, Moses has no authority. Consequently, though having just now managed to blurt out his first words of the story, Moses is quickly reduced again to total silence. The Hebrew's contemptuous reply has laid bare the flaw in Moses' action, both here and in the incident before: Moses simply has no authority for what he undertakes to do. Hence, having no authority, Moses has no choice but to act in stealth and secrecy both before and after killing the Egyptian. That same lack of authority now forces him to flee Egypt in terror. And finally, as the story at this point makes crystal clear, without any authority Moses can never effect any deliverance or salvation for his people.

If we fail to follow the narrative closely here as it raises the issue of authority, we can all too easily lose track of its meaning at this juncture. For example, we might wrongly conclude that we are to learn from Moses' frustrated efforts the lesson that 'violence never solves anything.' And yet, this is a story in which later on, we will hear of all kinds of violence being quite effective in achieving Israel's release from Egypt. Alternatively, we might mistakenly conclude that Moses' mistake lay in his overreacting in the Hebrew/Egyptian incident. Although the taskmaster was 'merely' *striking* the slave, Moses went too far by *striking the Egyptian dead*. To be sure, the Hebrew text of verse 11 might even theoretically permit that sort of linguistic nicety. However, in terms of *the context of the narrative* itself, there simply is no warrant for drawing such a fine—and finally erroneous—distinction. Instead, our concern with the rightness of Moses' acts must be the same as that of the Hebrew, who asks Moses in effect, '*What gives you the right* to tell me what to do?' That concern with the question of authority is one that we will meet time and time again in this master story. For now, Moses must become a fugitive. And from the viewpoint of the narrative, he will never be able to work any deliverance or justice for his people until he can return to them fully authorized to take up and press their cause.

> [16]Now the priest of Midian had seven daughters. They came to draw water, and filled the troughs to water their father's flock; [17]but shepherds came and drove them off. Moses rose to their defense, and he watered their flock. [18]When they returned to their father Reuel, he said, "How is it that you have come back so soon today?" [19]They answered, "An Egyptian rescued us from the shepherds; what is more, he drew water for us and watered the flock." [20]He said to his daughters, "Where is he

then? Why did you leave the man? Ask him in to break bread."
²¹Moses consented to stay with the man, and he gave Moses his
daughter Zipporah as wife. ²²She bore a son whom he named
Gershom,ᶜ for he said, "I have been a stranger in a foreign
land."

ᶜAssociated with *ger sham* "a stranger there"

When we compare this section with the one that preceded it,
we find that it is loaded with ironic reversals. Previously,
Moses had been completely unable to deliver his own people;
they, for their part, had utterly rejected him and even had a
hand in causing him to go into exile. Now, however, he
successfully comes to the rescue of non-Jews; even while
mistaking him for an Egyptian(!), these strangers end up
warmly accepting him and giving him a home.

And yet despite the rather strange turn the story has taken
here, it still has not turned away from its basic motifs and
themes. Even though Moses is now in out-of-the-way Midian,
his actions there show him nonetheless to be the sort of man
who remains close to the story's fundamental concerns and
interests. The words used to describe Moses' defense of
Reuel's daughters are laden with meaning: *veyoshian*—"and he
saved them"—and *hitsilanu*—"and he *rescued* us" (author's
translation). Moses is thus still portrayed as someone whose
acts are thoroughly and intrinsically connected to deliverance.
As if this reminder provided by Moses' actions were not
enough, the story further calls attention to this thematic strand
by pointedly reintroducing its water motif. After all, where
does this act of rescue happen but at a well, that is, at a site
where there is water! In fact, the daughters' very description of
Moses' activity on their behalf—"he drew water for us"—reminds us of Moses' original deliverance when he himself was
drawn up and saved from water.[5] But most relevant and
instructive of all, Moses' actions here reveal him to be a man
whose care and concern for other people is not limited to his
own people. He is a man whose regard for others extends even
to those who are most distinctively 'other'—strangers. He is
therefore just the kind of man this story needs to realize its

fulfillment; he is just the kind of man that God needs to realize his original plan of creation and overcome the perverted plan of Pharaoh. Thus, though Moses is presently an outcast, exiled to the wilderness of Midian, he nevertheless remains at the very center of this story.

> [23]A long time after that, the king of Egypt died. The Israelites were groaning under the bondage and cried out; and their cry for help from the bondage rose up to God. [24]God heard their moaning, and God remembered his covenant with Abraham and Isaac and Jacob. [25]God looked upon the Israelites, and God took notice of them.

The fourfold repetition of "God" in the last two verses is charged with meaning and significance.[6] These few lines represent *the* critical turning point of the story where God actively enters into story for the first time to set in motion the chain of events that will eventually lead to his people's deliverance. To be sure, God has been somewhere in the story's background all along, as, for example, in the earlier incident with the midwives. With these verses, however, God now makes his first appearance in the narrative on center stage.

And thus, we need to stop and ask: Why now? After all, there have been other places in the narrative prior to this one where we might have expected God to intervene, e.g., the time Moses struck the Egyptian who in turn had been beating the Hebrew slave. But God, we remember, did not come to anyone's aid there, and as a result, the people go unsaved, and Moses has to 'take it on the lam.' So why does God start to come to the rescue here?

As these few lines quite simply but quite pointedly suggest, God comes into the story at this point to deliver his people, because it is exactly at this point in the story that his people call on him to deliver on the covenantal promise he made to Abraham, Isaac, and Jacob. While it is neither the object of the narrative's concern—nor of our knowledge—why God made such a covenant in the first place or why the people waited so long before calling out to God,[7] the objective and point of these verses nevertheless remain unmistakable. According to the

plain sense of the story here, God comes to save his people not
because he feels sorry for them, nor because he takes pity on
them, nor even because he necessarily likes or loves them.
Rather, God comes to save because of the binding obligations
and commitments that are at the heart of the covenant to which
he is a partner. Whatever salvation is in store for Israel is not
essentially the result of some gracious or loving act of charity
on the part of God. Instead, it is the result of an act of justice by
God, done when God comes forward to honor and meet the
demands of the binding pact between himself and Israel. And
reading these verses, we can't help but somehow have the
feeling that had Israel not called out to God—i.e., had not
'called in the chits' and called on God to live up to his
obligations—Israel's salvation and deliverance would never
have been forthcoming.

Without doubt, some will take this last remark to be
altogether blasphemous—as though any human being could
put any kind of claim on God! And yet, that is still what we
must say—precisely because that is what the narrative is
saying. From the time of Abraham up in Haran to the time of
Abraham's descendants down in Egypt, this story has
continually portrayed the relationship between God and Israel
as a covenant. As such, it is the kind of relationship most truly
characterized by the making and keeping of mutually binding
promises and commitments. The final working out of this
story will critically depend on how well the two covenant
partners, God and Israel, can mutually work together, with
each side's coming through to do its respective part. Of all the
various convictional claims that spring from this master story
of the Exodus, perhaps the most rock-ribbed, rock-bottom one
is simply this: the promise of this world will be realized and
fulfilled only if all of us—God included—first fulfill and keep
our promises to one another. Conversely, no salvation can or
will be wrought by any of us alone—not by a morally outraged
Moses, not even by an equally impassioned God. The
deliverance of the people in this story—as well as of all people
in the larger story of humankind—ultimately awaits the action
of God and human beings in partnership together.

Notes

1. Cf. Nahum Sarna, *Understanding Genesis* (New York: Schocken Books, 1970), p. 49.

2. Despite the etiology given in the Torah text, the basic etymology of the name "Moses" comes from an Egyptian word broadly meaning "son." In other words, Pharaoh's daughter took the baby in and called him "Sonny."

3. See Erich Auerbach's now-classic work, *Mimesis* (trans. Willard R. Trask [Princeton: Princeton University Press, 1953]), in which he provides a superb analysis of this powerfully dramatic story, which he perceptively describes as "fraught with background."

4. Cf., e.g., the stories of Cyrus and Sleeping Beauty to name but two that fit this type.

5. For an extremely sensitive exposition of this particular water-drawing "type-scene" as well as others given in the Pentateuch, see Robert Alter's remarkable book, *The Art of Biblical Narrative* (New York: Basic Books, 1981), pp. 50-58.

6. See Leibowitz's remarks about the highly unusual Hebrew grammar and syntax here consisting of a "fourfold repetition of subject by name rather than by pronominal reference" (*Studies in Shemot*, p. 19). See also her cogent observations comparing various Jewish and non-Jewish translations of this text, ibid., pp. 22-23, n. 8.

7. Perhaps the people believed that the oppression instituted by the previous Pharaoh would pass away once he died. However, when it happened that "the king of Egypt died" and *still* the oppression remained in force under the direction of his successor, the situation, appearing virtually hopeless, became too much for the people to bear, and hence, they cried out to God both in desperation and as a last resort.

For the root *z'k* specifically meant as outcry of distress to God, see Judg. 3:9, 15; 6:6,7; I Sam. 7:8; Mic. 3:4. For the same use and sense of the older form of *z'k*—i.e., *ts'k*—see especially, Exod. 3:7, and in addition, Exod. 14:10 and Num. 20:16.

III
EXODUS 3:1–4:17

3:1Now Moses, tending the flock of his father-in-law Jethro, the priest of Midian, drove the flock into the wilderness, and came to Horeb, the mountain of God. 2An angel of the LORD appeared to him in a blazing fire out of a bush. He gazed, and there was a bush all aflame, yet the bush was not consumed. 3Moses said, "I must turn aside to look at this marvelous sight; why is the bush not burnt?" 4When the LORD saw that he had turned aside to look, God called to him out of the bush: "Moses! Moses!" He answered, "Here I am."

Today we are used to having the biblical text divided into chapter and verse for the sake of easy reference. Originally, however, the biblical narrative stood without any such divisions. It unfolded instead as one continuous, ongoing story.

And at this juncture in the story, that point is crucial. Otherwise, what now appears as the end of chapter 2 and the beginning of chapter 3 cannot help but seem to be terribly disjointed. Chapter 2 has just concluded with an abrupt shift of scene—from Moses with his new life in Midian to God with His people back in Egypt. Then chapter 3 starts with another change every bit as sudden—and this time from Egypt back again to Midian! What ties these scenes together? How are we to follow a narrative that moves by such fitful leaps and bounds?

Following the story here means following closely its

story line, for even though the locales in Egypt and Midian are far removed from each other, the plot and action of the narrative remain as tightly knit as ever. Just as the last episode of chapter 2 told of a response made in answer to a call, so too the episode here at the beginning of chapter 3 portrays the same kind of circumstance. There, in Exodus 2:23-25, God became involved as a central actor in this master story when he responded to the call of Israel. Here, in Exodus 3:1-4 ff., Moses will become actively involved in the narrative by responding to the call of God.

And yet, despite their strong thematic similarities, the two incidents differ from each other in certain key respects. God's involvement comes in direct response to the justice demanded of him by his covenant with Israel and her ancestors. But Moses' response is evoked by something else entirely—simple curiosity: 'I have to turn aside to look at this great marvel; *why* doesn't the bush burn up?' Moses is drawn by a sense of wonder when, out in the middle of nowhere and out of nowhere, something extraordinary unexpectedly breaks in on the ordinary course of his life. Moses' encountering God—and encountering his own role in Israel's story—are not predicated on his having some deep sense of 'religious awe.' Nor are they dependent on his possessing some rare power of intellectual genius or mystical insight. Instead, all depends on his ability to be amazed and astonished. Everything hinges on his capacity to be open to the possibility that in the midst of the commonplace—an ordinary life, a typical day, a nondescript bush[1]—the uncommon may burst in at any time. As the story tells it, that kind of simple (but not simpleminded) openness is what forms the ground for meeting God: "When the LORD saw *that [Moses] had turned aside to look, God called* to him out of the bush."

Back in chapter 2, Israel's call and God's response had moved the narrative forward at a crucial juncture. Now in chapter 3, call-and-response also drives the story on. Throughout this master story of God and Israel, the promise of the story—which is the promise of the world—will repeatedly turn on one very simple (but again not simpleminded) question: Who is willing to respond when called upon to act?

But for now at least, God's first approach has been met with a reply from Moses. Thus the way is clear to continue the encounter with yet another overture seeking yet another answer. Hence the call: "Moses, Moses!"; hence the response: "Here I am." Once more, the way is open to proceed.

> ⁵And He said, "Do not come closer. Remove your sandals from your feet, for the place on which you stand is holy ground. ⁶I am," He said, "the God of your father, the God of Abraham, the God of Isaac, and the God of Jacob." And Moses hid his face, for he was afraid to look at God.
> ⁷And the LORD continued, "I have marked well the plight of My people in Egypt and have heeded their outcry because of their taskmasters; yes, I am mindful of their sufferings. ⁸I have come down to rescue them from the Egyptians and to bring them out of that land to a good and spacious land, a land flowing with milk and honey, the home of the Canaanites, the Hittites, the Amorites, the Perizzites, the Hivites, and the Jebusites. ⁹Now the cry of the Israelites has reached Me; moreover, I have seen how the Egyptians oppress them. ¹⁰Come, therefore, I will send you to Pharaoh, and you shall free My people, the Israelites, from Egypt."
> ¹¹But Moses said to God, "Who am I that I should go to Pharaoh and free the Israelites from Egypt?"

The preliminary niceties now out of the way, God comes straight to the point of the call: 'Moses, I am the God of your forebears and of your people; it is time for me to deliver on my promises to those forebears by delivering that people safely out of Egypt and to their promised land. And *you*, Moses, are going to help me do it!'

And Moses' response to God's urgent, pressing call? 'Who, *me*?' Above, we saw that both Moses and God initially got involved in the story due to a response each of them felt compelled to make. We also noticed, however, a marked dissimilarity in the reasons spurring those responses. God responded out of simple justice, Moses out of simple curiosity. Not surprisingly, that difference in *why* each of them first reacted is now reflected in *how* each one begins to act. God appears as determined, decisive, and direct; Moses by contrast is anything but unflinching. Although he may have given in to his curiosity at first, Moses now seems to have second thoughts about satisfying it: after all, that's what killed the cat! He turns away, afraid to look. As a response to God's impassioned 'call to arms,' Moses' answer is at best an excuse and at worst an evasion.

Nevertheless, for all its weakness and fearfulness, Moses' answer to God is still not a flat statement of rejection; it is still not an outright no. Instead, it is a question waiting for a reply—a *response* left open to response from the other side. As before, God employs even this narrowest of openings to pursue the broader ends he has in mind:

> [12]And He said, "I will be with you, and it shall be your sign that it was I who sent you. And when you have freed the people from Egypt, you shall worship God at this mountain."

Moses has tried to resist God's summons to return to Egypt and free the Israelites by pointing to his own lack of stature and status. From bitter experience in the now distant past, he knows full well that he has neither the position nor the authority to release Israel from bondage. And what is God's response to these self-doubts? "I will be with you." It is a reply that implicitly grants the validity of Moses' reservations while seeking to overcome them nonetheless: 'True—by yourself and on your own, you would be unable to accomplish the mission I have described, and your efforts at liberation would meet with the same kind of failure they encountered before. *But* this time things will be different. *This time* you will not be by yourself and on your own. This time *I will be with you.*' Then, as if to give that pledge some backing, God gives Moses a 'token of good faith.' "And this will be the sign for you that I have sent you: when you have brought the Israelites out of Egypt, you shall serve God on this mountain" (Childs's translation, *Book of Exodus*, p. 48).

But just what kind of token is this? Rather than offering some *prior* confirmation of his promise, God indicates that the real assurances of his pledge will come only *after* the mission has been accomplished. In effect, God is telling Moses that if he manages to lead Israel back to the same spot for another rendezvous, then that will be the clearest sign that God really *has* been with him all along. In other words, if everything works out, then God's promise will be borne out; if not, God's word will be discredited. Therefore, the one for whom this token most genuinely signifies an act of good faith is not God at all: it's Moses. So just how good *is* Moses' faith in God?

In the context of this narrative, that sort of faith is not to be equated with belief in some abstract religious doctrine, such as, 'God exists.' Instead, this story likens faith to the kind of trust we put in someone else to keep his or her promises to us. Thus, for this saga of the Exodus, the question of faith is identical with the question of whether God can be trusted to keep his word. That question, like all such questions, can finally only be answered in the light of the *character* of the promise-maker. How reliably has he acted in the past? And moreover, how will he act to keep faith with us in the future too?[2]

Questions just like these form the basis for Moses' next exchange with God:

> [13]Moses said to God, "When I come to the Israelites and say to them 'The God of your fathers has sent me to you,' and they ask me, 'What is his name?' what shall I say to them?" [14]And God said to Moses, "Ehyeh-Asher-Ehyeh.[a]" He continued, "Thus shall you say to the Israelites, 'Ehyeh[b] sent me to you.'" [15]And God said further to Moses, "Thus shall you speak to the Israelites: The LORD,[c] the God of your fathers, the God of Abraham, the God of Isaac, and the God of Jacob, has sent me to you:
>
>   This shall be My name forever,
>   This My appellation for all eternity."
>
> [a]Meaning of Heb. uncertain; variously translated: 'I Am That I Am"; "I Am Who I Am"; "I Will Be What I Will Be"; etc.
> [b]Others "I Am" or "I Will Be"
> [c]The name YHWH (traditionally read *Adonai*—"the Lord") is here associated with the root *hayah* "to be"

What is Moses asking for? How can knowing God's name possibly answer the question of whether God will act faithfully in the future to keep his promises of the past? Can it be that so much actually depends on "what's in a name"?

The answer, according to many of the Bible's stories, is very often yes. In these narratives, one's name does not merely designate some person, but more pointedly, it designates that person's *character* besides.[3] Indeed, our contemporary English idiom still retains some sense of that connection; preserving one's good *name* is synonymous with protecting one's *reputation*. Consequently, the people's query about God's name makes perfect sense and amounts to asking this: 'Even if you are the God of our ancestors—the Promise-Maker of the Past—what will it be like for us, their descendants, to work with you now and in the future? While it's one thing to make a promise, it's quite another to keep it. So it all comes down to a matter of your character, a matter of how dependable and trustworthy you really are.'

God's response addresses that issue head-on. His answer for the people takes virtually the same form as the one he had before for Moses: Be assured, I will be with you.[4] Whatever future will be held in store for Israel, Israel's God will be there with her; wherever she will be, he, her Lord, will be there too. That is what makes God's identity of eternal significance for Israel, and that is what makes Israel's recollection of that revelatory designation imperative for all time to come. For the time being, however, Israel, like Moses, has no choice but to wait for this God and his character to be most fully revealed through the events—the *experiences*—that lie ahead. It is through those future events and experiences that God will most distinctively make a name for himself and thereby firmly establish his reputation.[5]

To that future, God now directs his attention—and ours as well:

> [16]"Go and assemble the elders of Israel and say to them: the LORD, the God of your fathers, the God of Abraham, Isaac and Jacob, has appeared to me and said, 'I have taken note of you and of what is being done to you in Egypt, [17]and I have declared: I will take you out of the misery of Egypt to the land of the Canaanites, the Hittites, the Amorites, the Perizzites, the Hivites, and the Jebusites, to a land flowing with milk and honey.' [18]They will listen to you; then you shall go with the

elders of Israel to the king of Egypt and you shall say to him, 'The LORD, the God of the Hebrews, manifested Himself to us. Now therefore, let us go a distance of three days into the wilderness to sacrifice to the LORD our God.' ¹⁹Yet I know that the king of Egypt will not let you go except by force. ²⁰So I will stretch out My hand and smite Egypt with various wonders which I will work upon them; after that he shall let you go. ²¹And I will dispose the Egyptians favorably toward this people, so that when you go, you will not go away empty-handed. ²²Each woman shall borrow from her neighbor and the lodger in her house objects of silver and gold, and clothing, and you shall put these on your sons and daughters, thus stripping the Egyptians."

While Moses may be unsure about how things will turn out, God for his part shows no uncertainty at all about the end result. His reply constitutes a brief précis of the story to unfold. Obviously, though, several elements in the story still need further explication: Why is Moses instructed to ask Pharaoh's permission for a three-day holiday out in the wilderness when the actual objective is a one-way trek across the wilderness to a "land flowing with milk and honey"? Moreover, if God already knows that only force will free Israel from Pharaoh's grasp, why should he have Moses even bother *asking* Pharaoh in the first place? And finally, if these first two matters seem to cast some doubt on God's honesty and candor, what moral qualms are raised by his last instructions, where Israel's asking to borrow[6] items of value will ultimately result in Egypt's plunder?

But in any case, no matter how muddled God's words may leave these issues, they nonetheless leave something else altogether clear: the Lord's steadfast resolve to implement his plan and see it through to its completion. Nothing will soon deter him from his purposes—neither the prospect of a Pharaoh who will be unyielding in the future, nor even of a Moses who is still unwilling now:

⁴:¹But Moses spoke up and said, "What if they do not believe me and do not listen to me, but say: The LORD did not appear to you?" ²The LORD said to him, "What is that in your hand?" And he replied, "A rod." ³He said, "Cast it on the ground." He cast it on the ground and it became a snake; and Moses recoiled from it.

Then the Lᴏʀᴅ said to Moses, "Put out your hand and grasp it by the tail"—he put out his hand and seized it, and it became a rod in his hand—⁵"that they may believe that the Lᴏʀᴅ, the God of their fathers, the God of Abraham, the God of Isaac, and the God of Jacob, did appear to you."

⁶The Lᴏʀᴅ said to him further, "Put your hand into your bosom." He put his hand into his bosom; and when he took it out, his hand was encrusted with snowy scalesᵃ! ⁷And He said, "Put your hand back into your bosom."—He put his hand back into his bosom; and when he took it out from his bosom, there it was again like the rest of his body.—⁸"And if they do not believe you or pay heed to the first sign, they will believe the second. ⁹But if they do not believe these two signs and do not heed you, you shall take some water from the Nile and pour it on the dry ground; and the water that you have taken from the Nile will turn to blood on the dry ground."

ᵃCf. Lev. 13:2-3

Once again, Moses remains unconvinced, and once again, God seeks to reassure him. As before, God tries to bolster the promise "I will be with you"—and Moses' faith in it—by talk of what will happen in the future. And likewise as before, God's words anticipate some key events in the narrative to follow: a-rod-turned-serpent and the-Nile-turned-blood.

Thus, the Lord's commitment to the project seems as firm as ever. And as for Moses? His resistance to committing seems just as resolute:

¹⁰But Moses said to the Lᴏʀᴅ, "Please, O Lord, I have never been a man of words, either in times past or now that You have spoken to your servant; I am slow of speech and slow of tongue." ¹¹And the Lᴏʀᴅ said to him, "Who gives man speech? Who makes him dumb or deaf, seeing or blind? Is it not I, the Lᴏʀᴅ? ¹²Now go, and I will be with you as you speak and will tell you what to say." ¹³But he said, "Please, O Lord, make someone else Your agent.ᵇ"

ᵇLit. "send through whomever You will send"

Compared to God's lengthy speeches reflecting a steady confidence, Moses' brief outbursts betray a rising desperation. In fact, those outbursts seem to prove the truth of his objection: he really *isn't* very good with words.[7] Confronted by the

Lord's majestically poetic answer—he is not only the Redeemer of the future; he is Creator of the past as well—Moses is reduced to blurting out, 'Oh, please, sir! Just send somebody else!'

Perhaps God *has* erred in his judgment. After all, what kind of messenger is this to choose for delivering words of such importance? Indeed, it looks as if God's patience has just about run out:

> [14]The LORD became angry with Moses, and He said, "There is your brother Aaron the Levite. He, I know, speaks readily. Even now he is setting out to meet you, and he will be happy to see you. [15]You shall speak to him and put the words in his mouth—I will be with you and with him as you speak, and tell both of you what to do—[16]and he shall speak for you to the people. Thus he shall be your spokesman, and you shall be an oracle[c] to him. [17]And take with you this rod, with which you shall perform the signs."

[c]Lit. "god"; cf. 7:1

Although God may have lost some of his patience, it ought by now to come as no surprise that he has lost none of his determination to achieve his final aims.

What *is* surprising, however, is the way he chooses to accomplish them. In his previous attempt at rebuttal, God has eloquently reminded Moses that as Author of creation, He has the power to empower others to speak with that same kind of facility. Hence, what might Moses justifiably expect from God to put his fears (and arguments) to rest? A miracle!—something from his Creator to recreate his mouth anew and thus eliminate his speech impediment.

Yet astonishingly, God does not offer to do that at all. Instead, he implicitly acknowledges the legitimacy of Moses' doubts: 'All right, then, take your brother Aaron; let him be your mouthpiece.' Instead of reworking things to work to his advantage, God works with things *as they are*. Instead of remaking Moses into a gifted orator, God accepts him *as he is*. Although he is unwilling to be turned aside from his stated goals, God is nevertheless still willing to let this human being *be human*.

JEWS AND CHRISTIANS

And that is precisely how it should be if we have been at all correct in characterizing the interaction of call-and-response, of mutual give-and-take, as being the dynamic that drives the story forward. In such a case, *each* party to the meeting must be truly and freely able to contribute—or to refuse to contribute—something to the exchange. Of course, that involves a risk to the success of the proceedings as a whole: one of the parties may unilaterally decide to break off the talks. Despite all God's determination to bring Israel out of Egypt, his resolve would ultimately have gone for nothing had Israel for her part *not* decided to cry out to him for help,[8] or had Moses for his part *not* decided to investigate the burning bush. And were Moses simply to decide, at any point and for whatever reason, to discontinue the conversation, then all God's steadfast reassurances and promptings would finally be to no avail.

According to the Bible's story, part of what it means to be human is to be fashioned in God's image; it is to be a creature that bears a certain likeness to its Creator, possessing in ways analogous to his a capacity for free, creative acts. But another part of what it means to be human—and again according to that selfsame story—is to be a limited, imperfect being who is most certainly *not* God. What this current chapter of that story stresses is that even God himself must be able to live with both these 'facts' about human beings—and apparently so must we. By sending Aaron to go along with Moses, God makes a compromise that in some very basic sense squarely faces facts. In just this sense, God, the supreme source of the reality of all, becomes God, the supreme realist of all. Thus, as God stands to Moses, so Moses shall stand to Aaron, and through that roundabout, almost jerry-built connection, God shall try to place his most important call of all—the call sent out to Egypt and to Israel, the one awaiting their responses.

And as for the current call? It ends with a reminder to Moses to take his rod; it shall be his staff of office, empowering him to work great acts on behalf of God. Long ago, Moses, lacking any such authority, was forced to flee Egypt for his life. Now fully authorized, he is fully armed for his return. Hence, it seems that the promise of "I will be with you" is already being kept.

Notes

1. The Hebrew word *sneh* is just a common word for "bush"; cf. Deut. 33:16. *"Thorn*bush" may already be too much of a description. The midrash (Shemot Rabbah 2:7) pointedly reflects this notion when in answer to its own question about why God chose such a location for his theophany, it replies, "To teach you that there is no place without God's presence—not even a bush."

2. See I Sam. 2:34 and Jer. 44:29 for parallel instances of the credibility of God's word being established by a 'sign-event' that will occur at some future date.

See also, however, Childs's learned discussion (*Book of Exodus*, pp. 56-60) of this admittedly difficult passage. Though in partial agreement with my interpretation of the nature of the sign to Moses, Childs nevertheless claims that such an interpretation is not wholly consistent with the biblical definition of a sign, namely, something that "ordinarily . . . takes the form of a concrete guarantee which follows the promise and yet precedes the fulfillment." Childs's own solution is that the sign to which God is referring is the bush itself, and that therefore, a "typological relation [is formed] between the burning bush on the holy mountain and the devouring fire at Sinai."

Yet even if Childs's understanding of the significance of the bush is correct (and there are those who like Cassuto would take exception to that understanding), the fact nonetheless remains that the credibility of God's promise in any case rests on certain events yet to transpire.

3. See, for example, the significant name changes given to Abram and Sarai in Gen. 17, and in particular, that given to Jacob in Gen. 32.

4. God's answer to the people given in v. 14 uses the same Hebrew word—*ehyeh*—that has just appeared in the Lord's reply to Moses in v. 12. This same word signifying God's continuing commitment will appear again at the end of this section in chap. 4, vv. 12 and 15.

5. Without doubt, the proper understanding of Exod. 3:14 and the true meaning of the Divine Name continue to be among the most hotly disputed subjects concerning biblical scholars. Proposals have ranged from textual emendations (cf., e.g., Wellhausen, Noth, Cross) to philosophical interpretations (e.g., Haupt, Albright, Freedman).

Of these latter sort of suggestions, one of the most interesting is that of Moshe Greenberg (*Understanding Exodus*). He argues (1) that Moses' question is aimed at discovering God's name for a future, absolutely crucial use in the cult, and (2) that God's reply, "I am who I am" (or: "I will be who I will be") is in fact no answer at all, but instead a *refusal* to answer, indicating the total freedom of this God to stand above any attempts at cultic (or magical) manipulation.

One can certainly sympathize and even agree with the underlying assumptions of Greenberg's hypothesis. A large part of what makes

God truly God is that, unlike the impostor deities worshiped by Israel's neighbors, he is a completely and radically free being. This notion clearly seems to lie at the heart of the creation narrative related in Gen. 1–2:4*a* (cf. the comments of Speiser, Sarna, and Kaufmann *ad loc*).

Nevertheless, *in the context of this stage of this story*, Greenberg's interpretation is simply out of place. Moses' question seems to have nothing at all to do with any cultic concerns. Instead, the concern addressed by Moses and the people here—and the one addressed by God both here and later in chap. 6 where the issue of the Divine Name is raised once more—is quite clearly this: What is the relation, *the significance*, between the promises of the past and the promise of the future? In other words, at this point in the narrative, both Moses and Israel are asking God, 'Can you be counted on to keep those promises made previously to the Fathers and made now again to us?' Importantly, much of what will transpire during the rest of the story will happen so that God might make a *name* for himself, i.e., so that Egypt and Israel—and all the world—might come to know who he really is and what he is really like (cf. e.g., Exod. 9:16).

6. The Hebrew word in v. 22 can take the meaning of either 'ask' or 'borrow'; the narrative context there can obviously bear either meaning.

7. And of course, we also remember the incident back in Egypt with the two quarreling Hebrew slaves when words failed Moses at that crucial moment, too. Cf. Exod. 2:13-14.

8. Cf. Exod. 2:23-25, and my comments *ad loc*.

IV
EXODUS 4:18–6:1

---

^{4:18}Moses went back to his father-in-law Jethr ^d and said to him, "Let me go back to my kinsmen in Egypt and see how they are faring."^e And Jethro said to Moses, "Go in peace."

¹⁹The Lord said to Moses in Midian, "Go back to Egypt, for all the men who sought to kill you are dead." ²⁰So Moses took his wife and sons, mounted them on an ass, and went back to the land of Egypt; and Moses took the rod of God in his hand.

²¹And the Lord said to Moses, "When you return to Egypt, see that you perform before Pharaoh all the marvels that I have put within your power. I, however, will stiffen his heart so that he will not let the people go. ²²Then you shall say to Pharaoh, 'Thus says the Lord: Israel is My first-born son. ²³I have said to you, "Let My son go, that he may worship Me," yet you refuse to let him go. Hence, I will slay your first-born son.'"

^di.e., Jethro
^eLit. "whether they are still alive"

Appearing five different times in the space of these five verses, the Hebrew root *shuv*—"return"—squarely puts the emphasis on getting Moses from Midian back again to Egypt. Hence, a series of short transition scenes meant to do just that now moves the drama forward from the preceding major act's rendering of God's initiatory call to the next fateful episode's account of Pharoah's initial confrontation. First comes a brief allusion to Moses' lingering reservations about fully committing himself to the enterprise—'Nothing special, Jethro; just going back home to see how my family is.' There then follows

59

an equally brief hint at God's continued efforts to overcome those reservations through added reassurance: "All the men who sought to kill you are dead." Omitting any detail that might slow the action's pace, the narrative relates in quick succession how Moses takes his leave from Jethro, learns from God the coast is clear, packs up his family, and heads back. The only detail to be stressed at all is once again the rod. Previously designated at the burning bush as the sign of God's power and authority, it now goes with Moses to work God's signs and wonders before the king of Egypt.

One more item gets some special notice, and it too anticipates a significant event to occur in Egypt—the killing of the firstborn. As yet another "marvel," its purpose is to draw attention to enslaved Israel's true and rightful status as the one destined from birth to be enlisted in the sacred service of the Lord.[1] Pharaoh's continuing conscription of Israel for *his* service is thus at bottom an act of ongoing desecration. As such, it is a dreadful act of sacrilege; as such, it invites consequences that are every bit as dire.[2]

> [24]At a night encampment on the way, the LORD encountered him and sought to kill him. [25]*f*So Zipporah took a flint and cut off her son's foreskin, and touched his legs with it, saying, "You are truly a bridegroom of blood to me!" [26]And when He let him alone, she added, "A bridegroom of blood because of the circumcision."

f Vv. 25-26 obscure

These three verses constitute one of the Torah's great enigmas: Why should God suddenly turn on his own and try to kill one of them? And just *which* "him" is attacked—Moses, or one of Moses' sons? Similarly, why does the foreskin's touching "his legs" ward off the attack, and again, exactly *whose* legs are touched? Finally, what is the meaning of the phrase "bridegroom of blood"? Attempts at answering such questions have typically sought to get 'behind the text' in a search for explanations with roots in earlier, pre-Israelite pagan practices. In the last analysis, however, none of the proposed solutions proves terribly persuasive.[3]

But worse than being unconvincing, such proposals seem largely misguided, if not totally irrelevant, for any kind of illumination of our current text. For as both traditional Bible scholars and modern form critics would agree, whatever meaning can be gotten from this passage must be gotten out of / the framework of its present narrative setting. What thematic links are there between the passage and the larger story? First, this section also forms one of the transition scenes relating the journey back to Egypt. Second, there is a conceptual connection between this part of the story and the piece immediately preceding it; as the dramatic foci of verses 21-23 were 'son' and 'killing,' those same two motifs dominate this segment, too.[4]

Yet the clearest and most important tie between this passage and the narrative surrounding it lies in the role played here by the act of circumcision. Despite all the obscurities lodged within this admittedly puzzling incident, circumcision is nevertheless plainly allied with something that safeguards life, and that idea rings strong and true with the rest of Israel's story. As the story tells it, circumcision is the visible sign of the pact between God and Abraham pledging Abraham and his descendants fruitfulness and fertility. It is a covenant, in other words, that promises *life itself*.[5] It is that covenant that the Egyptian oppression stands to thwart,[6] but that simultaneously holds out Israel's sole hope for surviving that oppression.[7] Analogously here in verses 24-26 as well, circumcision, the covenant sign, provides the only real hope for preserving life in the face of another life-threatening menace.[8] Circumcision, the covenant, and Israel's hopes are thus inextricably bound to one another. Keeping the rite of circumcision is a way of keeping the covenant between God and Israel, and keeping that covenant alive keeps Israel alive in the bargain. That theme, woven so delicately into the narrative fabric here, is a unifying thread that runs vividly throughout the whole of Israel's epic saga.

[27]The LORD said to Aaron, "Go to meet Moses in the wilderness." He went and met him at the mountain of God, and he kissed him. [28]Moses told Aaron about all the things that the

LORD had committed to him and all the signs about which He had instructed him. [29]Then Moses and Aaron went and assembled all the elders of the Israelites. [30]Aaron repeated all the words that the LORD had spoken to Moses, and he performed the signs in the sight of the people, [31]and the people were convinced. When they heard that the LORD had taken note of the Israelites and that He had seen their plight, they bowed low in homage.

So far, everything seems to be going splendidly. Starting back to Egypt, Moses meets Aaron in the wilderness. When they arrive, Aaron, following Moses' instructions, repeats all God's words to the elders of the people. Then the people see the marvels for themselves, are convinced, and bow down reverently in acknowledgment and worship. Yes, everything is going just like clockwork, exactly the way that God had predicted.

And yet, there is something else the Lord has foretold as well: "The king of Egypt will not let you go except by force." What now of that ominous prediction? How solid will the people's confidence remain in God and Moses when countered by staunch opposition from Pharaoh? If Israel's belief must ultimately rest on the firm conviction that the Lord can be trusted to keep his long-term promises, a few 'parlor tricks' would hardly seem to provide the grounds necessary to warrant or sustain that kind of faith. What will happen to the people's strength of purpose—and God's—if subsequent events fail to be similarly crowned with such immediate success?

[5:1]Afterward Moses and Aaron went and said to Pharaoh, "Thus says the LORD, the God of Israel: Let My people go that they may celebrate a festival for Me in the wilderness." [2]But Pharaoh said, "Who is the LORD that I should heed Him and let Israel go? I do not know the LORD, nor will I let Israel go."

Now comes the moment everyone has been anxiously awaiting. Cloaked in the confidence gained from their previous triumph with the Israelites, Moses and Aaron move to confront Pharaoh in grand, prophetic style: "Thus says the LORD! . . ."

Pharaoh's response abruptly disabuses them of any illusions they might have for attaining swift or easy victory: 'The Lord, you say? Who's *he*?' Singularly unimpressed, the king of Egypt disdainfully informs the brothers that just as he knows nothing of their God, he similarly knows no reason why he should care about, much less obey, their God's wishes.

Nevertheless, Pharaoh in his arrogance has managed to hit upon something that the Israelites, perhaps too easily impressed by a few magic tricks, still have fully to comprehend: knowing the Lord, *this* God, is like knowing another person. It is not like knowing an idea, a concept, or a formula. Indeed if, as we have heard earlier, so much really *does* depend on this God's *proper name*,[9] how could knowing him possibly involve anything less than *coming to know* him in ways analogous to those we have for getting acquainted with other persons—namely, through our *experiences of them over time*? Pharaoh's haughty retort thus unintentionally invites the kind of experiences that will provide him with such intimate knowledge of God firsthand.[10] If Pharaoh's lack of personal contact with the Lord is the basis for his question about what gives God the right or power to tell him what to do, then perhaps all those signs and marvels that we've heard so much about will soon remedy that ignorance.

For now, however, there are no "mighty acts"—only more words from Moses and Aaron, who, though initially rebuffed, continue on their errand:

> [3]They answered, "The God of the Hebrews has manifested Himself to us. Let us go, we pray, a distance of three days into the wilderness to sacrifice to the Lord our God, lest He strike us with pestilence or sword." [4]But the king of Egypt said to them, "Moses and Aaron, why do you distract the people from their tasks? Get to your labors!" [5]And Pharaoh continued," ᵃ⁻The people of the land are already so numerous,⁻ᵃ and you would have them cease from their labors!"

> ᵃ⁻ᵃSamaritan "Even now they are more numerous than the people of the land," i.e., than the native population (cf. Gen. 23:7)

Moses and Aaron seem stunned by Pharaoh's brusque

rejection. Earlier, they boldly presented Egypt's king with the demand, "Thus says the LORD . . ., 'Let My people go!'"; now they meekly petition him with a request, 'Let us go, please,[11] on a three-day trip.' Previously, they confronted Pharaoh with the sheer, unadulterated call of God; now, however, they implore him with a feeble plea for mercy: 'Look! He'll kill us if you don't let us go!'[12]

Pharaoh remains unmoved. In his eyes, no matter Moses and Aaron's reasons—whether the command of God or the fear of God—their words can only serve to divert the people from their work. Even if this Lord of theirs strikes them dead for their disobedience, what is it to him? After all, the original purpose behind enslaving Israel was to control the people's growth, and yet, despite all Egypt's determined efforts, the Israelites *still* outnumber the native population.[13] Hence, the request for even a temporary respite from their labor is denied. And as for Moses and Aaron, why are *they* standing around wasting time? Those two also ought to be hard at work.

And with that, Pharaoh summarily ends the audience. To his mind, the only cause for all this idle talk about time off is that the Israelites already have too much idle time to sit around and dream up such harebrained schemes. Wasting no time, the king of Egypt sets out to correct that situation.

[6]That same day Pharaoh charged the taskmasters and foremen of the people saying, [7]"You shall no longer provide the people with straw for making bricks as heretofore; let them go and gather straw for themselves. [8]But impose upon them the same quota of bricks as they have been making heretofore; do not reduce it, for they are shirkers; that is why they cry, 'Let us go and sacrifice to our God!' [9]Let heavier work be laid upon the men, and let them keep at it and not pay attention to idle chatter."

[10]So the taskmasters and foremen of the people went out and said to the people, "Thus says Pharaoh: I will not give you any straw. [11]You must go and get the straw yourselves wherever you can find it; but there shall be no decrease whatever in your work." [12]Then the people scattered through the land of Egypt to gather stubble for straw. [13]And the taskmasters pressed them, saying, "You must complete the same work assignment each day as when you had straw." [14]And the foremen of the

Israelites, whom Pharaoh's taskmasters had set over them, were beaten. "Why," they were asked, "did you not complete the prescribed amount of bricks either yesterday or today?" [15]Then the Israelite foremen came to Pharaoh and cried: "Why do you deal thus with your servants? [16]No straw is issued to your servants, yet they demand of us: Make bricks! Thus your servants are being beaten, when the fault is with your own people." [17]He replied, "You are shirkers, shirkers! That is why you say, 'Let us go and sacrifice to the LORD.' [18]Be off now to your work! No straw shall be issued to you, but you must produce your quota of bricks!"

With consummate literary skill, Pharaoh's plan of action is portrayed as the direct obverse of what the Lord desires. Egypt's king contemptuously answers the Lord's command by issuing orders of his own (v. 6). Moses has begged him to let the people go out to sacrifice in the wilderness (v. 3); Pharaoh will let them go all right—out to collect their own straw for making brick (v. 7).[14] And if Israel has cried out asking for a brief respite (v. 8), he'll really give them something now to cry out about (v. 15):[15] there shall be no diminishment of Israel's servitude (vv. 8, 11), but instead an intensification of it (v. 9). The call, "Thus says the LORD . . ." (v. 1), has been met with the response, "Thus says Pharaoh . . ." (v. 10).

And evidently, Pharaoh's policy is working. If God's aim had been to have the Israelites released to be his servants (4:23),[16] just the opposite is happening—their words show them to be Pharaoh's servants more than ever: "Why do you deal thus with *your servants*?" (v. 15, italics added). What more could go wrong with God's master plan?

[19]Now the foremen of the Israelites found themselves in trouble because of the order, "You must not reduce your daily quantity of bricks." [20]As they left Pharaoh's presence, they came upon Moses and Aaron standing in their path, [21]and they said to them, "May the LORD look upon you and punish you for making us objectionable to Pharaoh and his courtiers—putting a sword in their hands to slay us." [22]Then Moses returned to the LORD and said, "O Lord, why did you ever bring harm upon this people? Why did you select me? [23]Ever since I came to Pharaoh

to speak in Your name, it has gone worse with this people; yet
You have not delivered Your people at all."

Things have indeed gone from bad to worse. At least before,
the Israelites were united, if only in virtue of their common
bondage. But now since their suffering has been heightened,
they have turned on one another: work gangs at odds with
foremen, foremen—and probably everybody else—against
Moses and Aaron. The chances of Israel's ever getting out of
Egypt look extremely bleak, if not altogether nonexistent.
Three major obstacles stand in the way of God's realizing his
goals—and keeping his promises.

First, there is Moses. It seems as though God has picked the
worst possible messenger for his purposes. Not only is Moses
tongue-tied, he is mealymouthed besides. How can someone
apparently so weak ever have the strength to deliver the word
of God with any force or faithfulness?

Second, there is Israel. What kind of people has God chosen
to be the bearer of his promise? At first easily persuaded of
God's concern for them, and later just as easily dissuaded from
wholeheartedly trusting him, this people hardly looks like the
ideal choice for a dependable covenant partner. How can such
a fickle band of slaves ever be transformed into the reliable
servants of the Lord?

Last, of course, there is Pharaoh. If God has appeared
determined to get his way, then Pharaoh surely seems to be no
less resolute. The Egyptian king will not tolerate anything that
might remotely threaten to diminish his power or control.
Consequently, he has refused a request for even three days'
leave, let alone a demand to let Israel leave forever. Indeed,
even that minimal request has served only to amplify the
harshness of the bondage. True to God's prediction, Pharaoh
has acted obdurately hardhearted; thus far, it seems to be
paying off. How can the Lord prevail against an adversary so
unrelenting?

At this point, we can readily appreciate Moses' outburst
reminding the Lord that despite all his fine words, he has so far
done nothing to deliver the Israelites. While God may talk a

good game, he certainly has yet to show that he can play to win the game. Instead, he appears to have met his match in a team of formidable problems stubbornly confronting him—the least qualified leader, the most inconstant people, the sternest opponent. It's simply inconceivable how the Lord could possibly have chosen to start the contest with the cards more heavily stacked against him.

And that just may be God's point. To be able to overcome such awful odds, the Lord's powers must themselves be very awesome. To achieve victory in this struggle, God must prove himself to be more powerful and more determined than all those arrayed against him. Only thus can he show Pharaoh and Moses, Egypt and Israel, us and all the world, who is truly in power and finally in command. Moses, Israel, Pharaoh— each has thrown down the gauntlet in one way or another. The time has come for God to take up the challenge.

And so he does:

6:1Then the LORD said to Moses, "You shall soon see what I will do to Pharaoh: he shall let them go because of a greater might; indeed, because of a greater might he shall drive them from his land."

Notes

1. In the Ancient Near East, the firstborn was designated from birth as the child to be consecrated to the god, either through his performance of the deity's cultic service—as was the case in Israel—or through his being the sacrificial victim of that service—as was the case with many of Israel's pagan neighbors; cf. Exod. 13:2, 22:28, 34:19, and Num. 8:17. Cf., also, Matt. 2:15 and my comments *ad loc*.

2. God's threat to kill Pharaoh's firstborn might not unreasonably be seen as a retaliatory blow directed at the heart of Egyptian religious life. For if Pharaoh himself were considered to be a god, then striking down his firstborn, the prime heir to that title, would upset not only the continuity of the ruling house, but of the cult as well.

3. Cf. Childs, *Book of Exodus*, pp. 95-101.

4. In addition, the relatively rare word *encountered* (*yifgesheihu*), which appears in v. 24 of the present section, occurs again in v. 27 of the next section.

5. See Gen. 17:1-14.

6. See my comments to Exod. 1:8-12, above.

7. Cf. Exod. 2:23-25; 6:2-7.

8. Interestingly, just as the courageous acts of certain women—i.e., the midwives, Moses' mother and sister, Pharaoh's daughters—have heretofore proved absolutely essential in preserving Moses' life and destiny (and ultimately Israel's as well), so too another of those death-defying acts is now performed by yet another woman, Zipporah—i.e., by yet another *bearer of life*.

9. 'Proper name,' that is, in two senses: (1) of appropriate designation, and (2) of specific reference to a particular person. Stanley Hauerwas has quite forcefully put the matter another way: "The grammar of God is not that of an indefinite noun, but rather of a proper name. . . . Put starkly, God is not a concept, but a name like Stanley Hauerwas" (*Truthfulness and Tragedy*, p. 79). Furthermore, Hauerwas's note to this instructive observation is highly suggestive for our work here: "This, of course, raises great difficulty for if God is an agent who must be known like other agents—that is, through his story—it must also be a story told from his point of view. But we know of no such story and must learn of God through others' stories of their relationship with him. Perhaps this is the grammatical context for the claim that some people are his chosen ones" (ibid., p. 225, n. 29).

10. See Gen. 4:1, 25, and my comments to Exod. 1:8, above.

11. The Hebrew word *na'* carries the connotative force of courteous and even deferential request.

12. Leibowitz has aptly noted (*Studies in Shemot*, p. 89) that biblical dialogues are more properly "duologues," and as such, they typically follow the pattern: request—refusal; repetition of the request—

refusal (or acceptance). She points out that "the second request invariably attempts to achieve by other means what the first one has failed to do. The second request is either more modest, the quid pro quo offered is greater or the argument advanced in its support more convincing." Hence, as the earlier encounter between God and Moses at the burning bush evidenced some sort of negotiation, these subsequent encounters with Pharaoh will also display a mutual give-and-take. There is, of course, one important difference. While God strikes a compromise with Moses (he gives him Aaron as a mouthpiece), in Pharaoh's case, the give-and-take is finally aimed at having the Egyptian king totally give in.

13. Cf. Exod. 1:9. The masoretic text of 5:5 is somewhat difficult to understand; the Samaritan reading (which is supported by the sense of the LXX) is to be preferred.

14. The same Hebrew root *hlch* is used in each verse.

15. Cf., also, the same root *ts'k*—"cry out"—in Exod. 3:7, 9. Once more, the antithetical contrast between God and Pharaoh is expressed. To whom will Israel cry out for relief from their oppression?

16. See also 5:3, where the word *nizbecha*—"sacrifice"—has the more limited sense of *'cultic* service.'

7:8The LORD said to Moses and Aaron, 9"When Pharaoh speaks to you and says, 'Produce your marvel,' you shall say to Aaron, 'Take your rod and cast it down before Pharaoh.' It shall turn into a serpent." 10So Moses and Aaron came before Pharaoh and did just as the LORD had commanded: Aaron cast down his rod in the presence of Pharaoh and his courtiers, and it turned into a serpent. 11Then Pharaoh, for his part, summoned the wise men and the sorcerers; and the Egyptian magicians, in turn, did the same with their spells: 12each cast down his rod, and they turned into serpents. But Aaron's rod swallowed their rods. 13Yet Pharaoh's heart stiffened and he did not heed them, as the LORD had spoken.

The struggle between God and Pharaoh begins in earnest. "Marvel," "rod," "hardened heart"—narrative elements and motifs that have previously foreshadowed the coming battle now grimly reappear. Soon Egypt's king will come face-to-face with all the signs pointing to the powerful presence of Israel's Lord.

Yet the Lord's first signal seems somewhat garbled, leaving its message equally distorted. As God has bid him earlier, Aaron lets loose his wonder: he throws down his rod, and behold, it is transformed into a serpent. Surely *now* Pharaoh will take notice, pay heed, and let Israel go! Instead, however, Pharaoh simply bids his own magicians to do the same; at his command, each one duplicates the 'wonder' of turning a rod into a serpent. For Pharaoh, such reproducibility suffices to make the "marvel" not really so marvelous after all. Even Aaron's serpent devouring the magicians' serpents[1] fails to get the king's attention: "He did not heed them." While slick stunts may work well enough to convince a bunch of gullible Israelites, to more 'sophisticated' types, they prove totally unpersuasive. The aim of God's first sign seems to be badly off the mark.

Or is it? "Pharaoh's heart stiffened, and he did not heed them—*as the* Lord *had spoken*" (italics added). In the same way that the Lord has 'called the shot' instructing Aaron which sign to perform, he has similarly called the outcome of the act as well. Just what kind of signal is God sending? On the one hand, this easily duplicated act seems to fail to signify anything important; on the other, its very failure seems to trumpet the urgent message 'Attention—God at work!' How can one sign be so ambiguous?

But then, how can one sign—i.e., any *single* sign—help but be ambiguous? For a sign to function *as a sign,* that is, for it to *signify* or *designate,* it has to point to something beyond itself. As such, it does not carry its own meaning; it does not itself say how it is to be read or understood. Instead, a sign's significance issues from the context in which it is set. Hence, Pharaoh quite rightly ascribes no meaning to Aaron's isolated trick. Whatever slim chance Pharaoh has of correctly reading God's 'sign language' depends on his learning to read individual events as part of a larger *pattern of events.*

Therefore, an event's being uniquely supernatural or mundanely commonplace seems quite beside the point.[2] Despite all Pharaoh's magicians being able to copy Aaron's feat, the fact nevertheless remains that Aaron's action really does signify the activity of God. Consequently, for such activity to become more evident, still more signs are needed; more than that, a narrative is needed that relates such signs to one another and thereby sets the appropriate framework for their accurate interpretation. Only thus can the meaning of all these events—from the transformation of Aaron's rod to the hardening of Pharaoh's heart—properly be grasped. At a very basic level, learning to recognize the signs of God's active presence is bound up with learning to read the story that speaks of it.

> ¹⁴And the LORD said to Moses, "Pharaoh's heart is hard; he refuses to let the people go. ¹⁵Go to Pharaoh in the morning, as he is coming out to the water, and station yourself before him at the edge of the Nile, taking with you the rod that turned into a snake. ¹⁶And say to him 'The LORD, the God of the Hebrews, sent me to you to say, "Let My people go that they may worship Me in the wilderness." But you have paid no heed until now. ¹⁷Thus says the LORD, "By this you shall know that I am the LORD." See, I shall strike the water in the Nile with the rod that is in my hand, and it will be turned into blood; ¹⁸and the fish in the Nile will die. The Nile will stink so that the Egyptians will find it impossible to drink the water of the Nile.'"
>
> ¹⁹And the LORD said to Moses, "Say to Aaron: Take your rod and hold out your arm over the waters of Egypt—its rivers, its canals, its ponds, all its bodies of water—that they may turn to blood; there shall be blood throughout the land of Egypt, even in vessels of wood and stone." ²⁰Moses and Aaron did just as the LORD commanded: he lifted up the rod and struck the water in the Nile in the sight of Pharaoh and his courtiers, and all the water in the Nile was turned into blood ²¹and the fish in the Nile died. The Nile stank so that the Egyptians could not drink water from the Nile; and there was blood throughout the land of Egypt. ²²But when the Egyptian magicians did the same with their spells, Pharaoh's heart was stiffened and he did not heed them—as the LORD had spoken. ²³Pharaoh turned and went into his palace, paying no regard even to this. ²⁴And all the Egyptians had to dig round about the Nile for drinking water, because they could not drink the water of the Nile.

More signs are in store—but with a difference: tricks have given way to plagues. No longer aimed at impressing detached observers, they are directed at morally implicated oppressors and are meant to strike home and get results. The words expressing Pharaoh's initial resistance hauntingly come to mind: "I do not know the LORD, nor will I let Israel go." As we saw, the king's indifference *to* God and his inexperience *of* God go hand in hand. How then to get him *personally involved* with the Lord? How to do something that will *strike* him with the magnitude of God's authority and might? Hence a proposal to try to solve the problem: "Thus says the Lord, 'By this you shall know that I am the Lord.' See, [Aaron] shall strike the water in the Nile . . . , and it will be turned into blood."

And now notice where the first of these solutions—these *plagues*—shall occur: in front of Pharaoh, "as he is coming out *to the water*" (italics added). Water has appeared elsewhere in the story at another such crucial moment, namely, when the infant Moses was set adrift in his tiny wicker basket. We recall that his mother's act of placing him in the water was fraught with ambiguity; not simply or unequivocally life-giving, it could just as easily have been death-dealing as well.[3] With the first plague, that kind of ambiguity surfaces again. Here are the waters of the Nile, normally Egypt's source of life—its *lifeblood*. But now, the Nile's waters flow red with blood that kills every living thing in it, leaving the stench of death in its wake. Water and blood, two signs of life, easily transformed into tokens of death. What is the Nile really, then? A fountain of life and salvation? Or a reservoir of death and destruction? And *for whom*? Such ambiguity implicit in the plague suggests a question of explicit concern for all involved: What shall its import be for us—life or death?

But in any case, the first plague leaves Pharaoh totally unaffected, both physically and mentally. He will simply get his water from somewhere else, and consequently, the sign is easy to ignore. It has failed to get his attention—much less his compliance. "Pharaoh turned and went into his palace, paying no regard even to this." Clearly, the king still does not see himself involved. As before, his magicians can duplicate the act, and even if all Egypt's rivers, canals, and ponds are full of blood, so what? For Pharaoh, his courtiers, and his people, it is only a temporary inconvenience; for seven days, they will simply dig their water instead of drawing it. If that is the best—or worst—that this "God of the Hebrews" can do, there really is no cause for worry—and certainly no reason to let his people go.

[25]When seven days had passed after the Lord struck the Nile, [26]the Lord said to Moses, "Go to Pharaoh and say to him, 'Thus says the Lord: Let My people go that they may worship Me. [27]If

you refuse to let them go, then I will plague your whole country with frogs. [28]The Nile shall swarm with frogs, and they shall come up and enter your palace, your bedchamber and your bed, the houses of your courtiers and your people, and your ovens and your kneading bowls. [29]The frogs shall come upon you and on your people and on all your courtiers.'"

[8:1]And the Lord said to Moses, "Say to Aaron: Hold out your arm with the rod over the rivers, the canals, and the ponds, and bring up the frogs on the land of Egypt." [2]Aaron held out his arm over the waters of Egypt, and the frogs came up and covered the land of Egypt. [3]But the magicians did the same with their spells, and brought frogs upon the land of Egypt.

[4]Then Pharaoh summoned Moses and Aaron and said, "Plead with the Lord to remove the frogs from me and my people, and I will let the people go to sacrifice to the Lord." [5]And Moses said to Pharaoh, "You may have this triumph over me: for what time shall I plead in behalf of you and your courtiers and your people, that the frogs be cut off from you and your houses, to remain only in the Nile?" [6]"For tomorrow," he replied. And [Moses] said, "As you say—that you may know that there is none like the Lord our God; [7]the frogs shall retreat from you and your courtiers and your people; they shall remain only in the Nile." [8]Then Moses and Aaron left Pharaoh's presence, and Moses cried out to the Lord in the matter of the frogs which He had inflicted upon Pharaoh. [9]And the Lord did as Moses asked; the frogs died out in the houses, the courtyards, and the fields. [10]And they piled them up in heaps, till the land stank. [11]But when Pharaoh saw that there was relief, he hardened his heart and would not heed them, as the Lord had spoken.

At its start, the second plague resembles the first in several ways: as before, the Lord's ultimatum is announced to Pharaoh; the rod is stretched out over all of Egypt's waters; a 'nuisance plague' is produced;[4] and the feat is then reproduced through the magicians' spells.

Nevertheless, other things have changed. The first plague was easy for Pharaoh to ignore. He could literally turn his back on it by leaving the Nile and returning to his palace. With the plague of frogs, however, that route of escape has been cut off, for as Moses warns him, this new plague will "come up and enter your palace, your bedchamber and your bed."

No longer is Pharaoh personally unaffected. No longer can he remain oblivious to events around him—or to the power of the Lord. For the first time, even if but minimally, he *has* to *acknowledge* God: "Plead with the LORD to remove the frogs from me."

And also for the first time, Moses appears as a man who is *not* at a total loss for words. Seizing this initial indication of Pharaoh's weakness, he seeks to exploit it and expose it further. He quick-wittedly gives Pharaoh the advantage of placing him under a time constraint for the plague's removal, thus gaining the opportunity to underscore God's power even more. When Pharaoh takes the bait, Moses nimbly closes the trap, declaring that *all* of this will happen so that Egypt's lord "may know that *there is none like the* LORD *our God*" (italics added).

In the end, however, Pharaoh's quick change of heart remains just that—brief and fleeting. Once more, his own magicians can duplicate the act, and once the plague has been removed, he abruptly changes his heart—and tune—again: "he hardened his heart and would not heed them."

> [12]Then the LORD said to Moses, "Say to Aaron: Hold out your rod and strike the dust of the earth, and it shall to turn to lice throughout the land of Egypt." [13]And they did so. Aaron held out his arm with the rod and struck the dust of the earth, and vermin came upon man and beast; all the dust of the earth turned to lice throughout the land of Egypt. [14]The magicians did the like with their spells to produce lice, but they could not. The vermin remained upon man and beast; [15]and the magicians said to Pharaoh, "This is the finger of God!" But Pharaoh's heart stiffened and he would not heed them, as the LORD had spoken.

The third plague—lice[5]—signals a sudden and dramatic departure from the narrative pattern established heretofore. Pharaoh receives neither the opportunity to be warned nor the chance to concede. More significantly, however, this is the first time the magicians lack the capacity to duplicate Aaron's action. They can instead only confess and witness to the truth: "This is the finger of God!"

The narrative has alluded to God's "hand" before. Earlier, in Exodus 6:1, the Lord predicted that his "strong hand" will eventually loose Pharaoh's grasp on Israel; indeed, such great power shall ultimately force the king of Egypt to *drive* the Israelites from his land. At this point, however, the Egyptians are facing only a relatively small display of that power. And what happens when they confront this plague of lice, the most minute of creatures—a mere "finger" of God's might? The magicians, the 'greats of Egypt,' are compelled to acknowledge that they have been rendered completely impotent. If such is God's power and such is their own lack of power, the magicians would be well advised to withdraw from the contest, and following this plague, they will, in fact, appear no more. Ironically, the magicians, those who might be considered the ones most 'in the know' in Egypt, are the first in Egypt to start to know the truth about the Lord.[6]

[16]And the Lord said to Moses, "Early in the morning present yourself to Pharaoh, as he is coming out to the water, and say to him, 'Thus says the Lord: Let My people go that they may worship Me. [17]For if you do not let My people go, I will let loose *-swarms of insects-ᵃ against you and your courtiers and your people and your houses; the houses of the Egyptians, and the very ground they stand on, shall be filled with swarms of insects. [18]But on that day I will set apart the region of Goshen, where My people dwell, so that no swarms of insects shall be there, that you may know that I the Lord am in the midst of the land. [19]And I will make a distinctionᵇ between My people and your people. Tomorrow this sign shall come to pass.'" [20]And the Lord did so. Heavy swarms of insects invaded Pharaoh's palace and the houses of his courtiers; throughout the country of Egypt the land was ruined because of the swarms of insects.

[21]Then Pharaoh summoned Moses and Aaron and said, "Go and sacrifice to your God within the land." [22]But Moses replied, "It would not be right to do this, for what we sacrifice to the Lord our God is untouchable to the Egyptians. If we sacrifice that which is untouchable to the Egyptians before their very eyes, will they not stone us! [23]So we must go a distance of three days into the wilderness and sacrifice to the Lord our God as He may command us." [24]Pharaoh said, "I will let you go to sacrifice to the Lord your God in the wilderness; but do not go very far. Plead, then, for me." [25]And Moses said, "As I leave your presence, I will plead with the Lord that the swarms of insects depart tomorrow from Pharaoh and his courtiers and his people; but let not Pharaoh act deceitfully, not letting the people go to sacrifice to the Lord."

[26]So Moses left Pharaoh's presence and pleaded with the
LORD. [27]And the LORD did as Moses asked: He removed the
swarms of insects from Pharaoh, from his courtiers, and from
his people; not one remained. [28]But Pharaoh hardened his heart
this time also, and would not let the people go.

[a-a]Others "wild beasts"
[b]Meaning of *peduth* uncertain

The fourth plague marks the reintroduction of various
stylistic features that have appeared before:[7] a warning at the
water, the land invaded by teeming pests, an entreaty to God
to remove the plague—all followed by Pharaoh's reneging on
his promise to let the people go.

Yet also as before, there is more here than the idle repetition
of previous events. With the fourth plague, too, new elements
are injected that significantly extend the implications of earlier
ones. Thus, this 'plague narrative' develops like all narratives
do: what follows in the narrative does not follow along the
lines of a well-constructed syllogism, but instead follows from
the way the story itself *cumulatively* builds, takes shape, and
unfolds.[8] Up to now, all of the plagues have presumably struck
Egyptian and Israelite alike. But the fourth plague adds a novel
wrinkle; it shall not fall on Israel as it does on Egypt. If, on one
level, the plagues function as signs meant to attract attention,
what expanded message is God trying to communicate?

The issue is no longer merely a question of whether Pharaoh
will deign to release God's people. Rather, the issue has
become compounded, for it is now a question of whether
Pharaoh, like God, can protect his people while the ensuing
battle rages. By making a *distinction* between the Israelite
people and the rest of the population, the Lord accomplishes
two things. First, he *distinctively* shows his active presence in
Pharaoh's realm. But second, and more significantly, by
marking Israel as immune from the plague and Egypt as its
target, God has clearly begun to *mark himself* as the true ruler of
the land. Hence, by modifying his tactics slightly, the Lord has
raised the stakes immensely.

In fact, the negotiations between Moses and Pharaoh testify

to the increased ante. As the narrative has developed God's message further, so too it has reflected a further development in its characterization of these two human adversaries. Although Pharaoh has been put on the defensive, he is far from finished. He shows himself to be more than just a heavy-handed tyrant who relies on brute strength alone. Instead, he is a sly and skilled opponent seeking to exploit every possible opening to his advantage. During the initial stage of the negotiations prior to the removal of the swarms, he appears to relent: "Go and sacrifice to your God." However, he quickly moves to add a nullifying countermeasure: Israel's service—*the Lord's service*—must be performed "within the land." Even when the king eventually seemingly concedes in order to have the plague called off, he still stops short of total capitulation: 'But don't go very far!'

For his part, Moses displays a similar growth in debating skill and shrewdness. He is, it seems, becoming better with words all the time, thus simultaneously becoming an increasingly artful advocate. Hence, when Pharaoh adds his countermeasure requiring the Israelites to remain in Egypt to perform their service to the Lord, Moses swiftly and effectively counters that requirement. Next, when Pharaoh apparently relents while nonetheless trying to reassert his authority through his stipulation that the Israelites must not venture too far away, it is *Moses* who has the last word, handily trumping Pharaoh with a condition of his own: '*This* time, don't try anything funny.'

In sum, the fourth plague witnesses a further broadening of Moses' and Pharaoh's personalities, a further heightening of the drama between Israel and Egypt, and a further amplifying of God's call.

> [9:1]The Lord said to Moses, "Go to Pharaoh and say to him, 'Thus says the Lord, the God of the Hebrews: Let My people go to worship Me. [2]For if you refuse to let them go, and continue to hold them, [3]then the hand of the Lord will strike your livestock in the fields—the horses, the asses, the camels, the cattle, and the sheep—with a very severe pestilence. [4]But the Lord will make a distinction between the livestock of Israel and the

livestock of the Egyptians, so that nothing shall die of all that belongs to the Israelites. ⁵The Lord has fixed the time: tomorrow the Lord will do this thing in the land.'" ⁶And the Lord did so the next day: all the livestock of the Egyptians died, but of the livestock of the Israelites not a beast died. ⁷When Pharaoh inquired, he found that not a head of the livestock of Israel had died; yet Pharaoh's heart hardened, and he would not let the people go.

The Lord strikes again, and this time he strikes with greater force than at any time previously. This time living creatures *die* as a result of the plague of pestilence that afflicts the land. But of course, not just *any* livestock dies—only that belonging to the Egyptians perishes; the Israelites' animals remain untouched—as Pharaoh, upon making inquiry, quickly learns. God's sign has begun to serve its purpose: Pharaoh has begun to *take heed* of what is happening.

And see what else has begun to happen too. The community of Israel has itself begun to be a sign of God—and one that is growing more distinct and distinctive all the time. In fact, it is the people Israel *as a whole* that is fast becoming the Lord's most vivid ensign. Now, and from this time forward, the clearest indication of God's activity in the world will be what happens to his people Israel in the world. Israel's ongoing presence, its continued *life* in the face of overwhelming odds, will serve as the surest evidence that the Lord himself is still alive in the midst of all creation, having neither abandoned nor abjured it, no matter how great that creation's inhumanity or ungodliness may be. From the vantage point of this Jewish master story, the truest way in the future to answer questions about whether God exists shall be to make inquiry about whether his people still exists. Forever after, Israel's fate and his—and indeed all the world's—will be inextricably bound up with one another.

⁸Then the Lord said to Moses and Aaron, "Each of you take handfuls of soot from the kiln, and let Moses throw it toward the sky in the sight of Pharaoh. ⁹It shall become a fine dust all over the land of Egypt, and cause an inflammation breaking out in boils on man and beast throughout the land of Egypt." ¹⁰So they took soot of the kiln and appeared before Pharaoh; Moses

threw it toward the sky, and it caused an inflammation breaking out in boils on man and beast. [11]The magicians were unable to confront Moses because of the inflammation, for the inflammation afflicted the magicians as well as all the other Egyptians. [12]But the LORD stiffened the heart of Pharaoh, and he would not heed them, just as the LORD had told Moses.

God steps up the pressure just a bit. Although the plague of boils is not deadly like the pestilence that preceded it, its impact is nevertheless more far-reaching. Perhaps some Egyptians managed to escape the fifth plague's brunt, namely, those who owned no livestock. Moreover, all the previous plagues have not been much more than irritating nuisances; striking crops and/or animals, they have at most affected people only *indirectly*. But the plague of boils breaks out not only on Egypt's beasts, but on her people too. It literally touches every Egyptian *bodily*; it literally *pains* each one personally. Importantly, this plague signals a new stage in the conflict with the Egyptians, because for the most part, the Egyptian people themselves will cease playing any active role in the contest. Indeed, their most active participants to this point—the magicians—are notable here only for their absence. Earlier, the plague of lice had neutralized their *power*; now, the plague of boils has neutralized *them*. From here on in, virtually the only Egyptian left with any heart for continuing the fight will be Pharaoh, and his heart will remain as hard as ever.

To be sure, Pharaoh's heart has attracted considerable attention from commentators, particularly as it is mentioned in this sixth plague. For the passage here that speaks of his heart-hardening reads somewhat differently from the verses that have referred to it in the five preceding plagues. In conjunction with those plagues, the text typically reads, "Pharaoh's heart hardened"[9] or "Pharaoh hardened his heart."[10] Following the plague of boils, however, the text displays a change of wording: *"the LORD hardened Pharaoh's heart"* (author's translation).

Some writers have attached great significance to this word change. Scripture, they say, indicates that through the first five plagues, Pharaoh was responsible for his own unyieldingness—and for the continuing troubles that befell Egypt as a result. But, say these same interpreters, from the sixth plague onward, the narrative declares God to be the one actually responsible for Pharaoh's unwillingness to yield—and for all the subsequent suffering in Egypt. However, this reading, if correct, leads these commentators into a perplexing ethical and theological impasse, i.e., how morally to justify God's punishing those who could not possibly have acted otherwise. And furthermore, if God's freedom of action is really so extensive, what room is finally left for talking about human freedom with any degree of seriousness? Proposed solutions have generally sought to 'soften' the dilemma by taking a pseudo-psychological approach, suggesting, for example, that Pharaoh's initial, self-willed acts led him to be entrapped later, not by God's will, but by his own compulsive willfulness.[11]

And yet, despite the change in formulation between plague six and the other five there is nevertheless one expression that remains constant throughout them all: *"just as the LORD had spoken"* (author's translation). In other words, although the specific language of 'hardening' differs among the various plagues, the basic *meaning* stays the same, namely, that Pharaoh's continuing resistance is itself another manifestation, another *sign*, of God's powerful presence at Egypt's very core—its own king's heart of hearts! While certain parts of the narrative may describe Pharaoh's hardheartedness as the *cause* for additional plagues befalling Egypt, and while other parts may characterize that hardness as the *result* of such occurrences,[12] the 'event' of God's plaguing Pharaoh's heart is, in any case, like the other plagues, another 'sign event' meant to point beyond itself to God, the ultimate *source* of *all* these *signals*.

So much, then, for the proposed psychological interpretation of the hardening motif. But what to do with the moral/theological problems concerning the issues of divine justice and human freedom? While we could dismiss all the various psychological proposals as lacking warrant from the text itself, that selfsame text is precisely what warrants, indeed *necessitates*, our facing these difficulties head-on. For Jewish

Scripture itself has set the background context against which these episodes of God's hardening Pharaoh's heart seem so entirely out of place. After all, the beginning of that Scripture informs us that we human beings are created "in God's image," i.e., that each of us has a capacity, resembling our maker's, to freely fashion a world that we can call our own. Moreover, that same Scripture then goes on to tell us of the teachings, the commands, the *choices* that God holds out to us, and clearly, all those things presuppose that we possess the freedom either to take heed or remain unheedful. Hence, in the light of recurring biblical themes such as these, God's repeated hardening of Pharaoh's heart unavoidably stands out. Childs has succinctly put the matter this way: "The problem of hardening is unique in Exodus. It emerges as if from nowhere and then vanishes."[13] Obviously, the uniqueness of hardening to the plague tradition makes finding a solution an especially tough task. At the same time, however, if any solution *is* possible, it will have to take that uniqueness into account and attempt to relate it to the larger biblical narrative to give it any intelligibility or force. Just what is it about Pharaoh that singles him out for such individual treatment by the story—and by the Lord?

As a starting point, we might do well to notice that at least some of the plagues are attended by certain 'illuminators' of their rationale. The tenth plague, of course, stands as the one whose meaning is most plainly given. Calling to mind Exodus 4:22-23, we remember the Lord's explicit justification of that plague: "Israel is My first-born son. I have said to you, 'Let My son go that he may worship me,' yet you refuse to let him go. Hence, I will slay your first-born son." We might additionally recall other, more subtle clues accompanying some of God's other blows at Egypt, e.g., the water-motif occurring at various critical turning points in the narrative. Thus, the first plague is struck at the water's edge—the place where the Egyptians had previously struck first when they attempted to kill the Hebrew babies. Water will also ominously later reappear to mark the spot of God's last strike at Egypt. Noticing that, an ancient midrash perceptively remarks: "With the same means by which they planned to destroy Israel, I [the Lord] shall judge them; just as they planned to destroy my children by water, so I shall not punish them save through water."[14] In short, it would seem that the tenth plague functions explicitly, and some of the other plagues implicitly, as the Lord's just reprisal against Egypt, taken with all fairness measure for measure.

Can God's hardening of Pharaoh's heart be understood in a similar way? In effect, it plainly deprives Pharaoh of his free will;[15] in essence, it makes him a puppet instead of a human being. If this transformation whereby God makes Pharaoh somehow *less than human*[16] is seen as a plague taken as an act of retaliatory justice, the question becomes: What crime has Pharaoh committed to merit it? The most obvious answer would seem to be that he somehow attempted to act *more than human.* But precisely how? Does the biblical narrative provide other instances of such crimes—such *sins*?

Indeed it does provide them, relating them in its very first chapters. In both the story of Adam and Eve with the forbidden fruit and the story of the people of Babel with the tower, we hear of those who overreach themselves as human beings in order to try to put divinity within their grasp. Not satisfied with being created in God's *mere* likeness, they instead attempt to be *exactly like* him, that is, gods themselves.[17]

And Pharaoh? While the transgression in the garden and that at the tower were each committed only once, Egypt's, by contrast, has been repeated for years and years. By continuing their hold on Israel, this Pharaoh *and his predecessor*[18] have continually reasserted that Israel's lives are at bottom in *their* keeping, such that ultimately, Pharaoh and Pharaoh alone is the Israelites' true lord, determining what and whom their lives shall serve. Therefore, who ought to be surprised by the autocratic response first given to the Lord's impassioned call to let his people go? '*The Lord,* you say? *What lord?* What impostor, what *pretender,* dares presume to tell *me* what to do!' Hence, could there be any clearer indication that Pharaoh has gravely overstepped himself? In the end, he is only human, yet he has usurped dominion which in the end is only God's. One would be hard pressed to find any other figure(s) in the whole of Jewish Scripture who perpetrated crimes of such magnitude or with such perseverance.

As a result, God's hardening Pharaoh's heart is a perfect punishment. Because Pharaoh would not rest content with his rightful human status, instead presumptuously claiming God's prerogatives as his own, the Lord in turn fittingly reduced his standing to something far beneath the human. And yet as horrible as that punishment undeniably is, even worse perhaps is its final irony. No doubt Pharaoh sees his stubbornness as a testament to his own will power. In reality, however, his compulsive willfulness is nothing more than testimony to the true power of the will of God.

[13]The Lord said to Moses, "Early in the morning station yourself before Pharaoh and say to him, 'Thus says the Lord, the God of the Hebrews: Let My people go to worship Me. [14]For this time I will send all My plagues upon your person, and your courtiers, and your people, in order that you may know that there is none like Me in all the world. [15]I could have stretched forth My hand and stricken you and your people with pestilence, and you would have been effaced from the earth. [16]Nevertheless I have spared you for this purpose: in order to show you My power, and in order that My fame may resound throughout the world. [17]Yet you continue to thwart My people, not letting them go! [18]This time tomorrow I will rain down a very heavy hail, such as has not been in Egypt from the day it was founded until now. [19]Therefore, order your livestock and everything you have in the open brought under shelter; every man and beast that is found outside, not having been brought indoors, shall perish when the hail comes down upon them!" [20]Those among Pharaoh's courtiers who feared the Lord's word brought their slaves and livestock indoors to safety; [21]but those who paid no regard to the word of the Lord left their slaves and livestock in the open.

[22]The Lord said to Moses, "Hold out your arm toward the sky that hail may fall on all the land of Egypt, upon man and beast and all the grasses of the field in the land of Egypt." [23]So Moses held out his rod toward the sky, and the Lord sent thunder and hail, and fire streamed down to the ground. As the Lord rained down hail upon the land of Egypt, [24]the hail was very heavy—fire flashing in the midst of the hail—such as had not fallen on the land of Egypt since it had become a nation.

[25]Throughout the land of Egypt the hail struck down all that were in the open, both man and beast; the hail also struck down all the grasses of the field and shattered all the trees of the field. [26]Only in the region of Goshen, where the Israelites were, there was no hail.

[27]Thereupon Pharaoh sent for Moses and Aaron and said to them, "I stand guilty this time. The LORD is in the right, and I and my people are in the wrong. [28]Plead with the LORD; there has been enough of God's thunder and hail. I will let you go; you need stay no longer." [29]Moses said to him, "As I go out of the city, I shall spread out my hands to the LORD: the thunder will cease and the hail will fall no more, so that you may know that the earth is the LORD's. [30]But I know that you and your courtiers do not yet fear the LORD God."—[31]Now the flax and barley were ruined, for the barley was in the ear and the flax was in bud; [32]but the wheat and the millet were not hurt, for they ripen late. [33]—Leaving Pharaoh, Moses went outside the city and spread out his hands to the LORD: the thunder and the hail ceased, and no rain came pouring down upon the earth. [34]But when Pharaoh saw that the rain and the hail and the thunder had ceased, he reverted to his guilty ways, as did his courtiers. [35]So Pharaoh's heart stiffened and he would not let the Israelites go, just as the LORD had foretold through Moses.

ªOthers "exalt yourself over"

With an ever-greater intensity, the narrative moves forward. Earlier motifs of plot and action are relentlessly broadened, sharpened, deepened. Hence, for example, the previous plague of boils only pained people; this plague of hail *kills* them. And while prior plagues witnessed some wavering by certain segments of the Egyptian population,[19] this new plague brings on the first mass defection from its ranks: "Those among Pharaoh's courtiers who feared the LORD's word brought their slaves and livestock indoors." Israel, of course, continues to be spared. For the first time, the narrative expressly accentuates that point, setting it off in sharp counterpoint to the fate of most Egyptians: "Only in the land of Goshen, where the Israelites were, there was no hail."

Expanded also are the story's themes. Issues implicitly underlying the narrative from the beginning now explicitly surface, and their appearance helps answer a question that has been lurking in the background all along: 'If this God really *is* so powerful, why doesn't he simply smash the Egyptians and put an end to the matter once and for all?' However, as the Lord himself informs us, his objective here is far more than simply routing Egypt in order to win Israel's release. Instead, his purposes are on a grander scale, a *worldwide* scale: to let the whole world know that in all the world there is none like him! None whose power can be compared to his, none whose reputation matches his, none whose right to be called 'god' even approaches his. He is not simply the little clan-god of the Hebrews, but YHWH—God of all the earth.[20] We think back to the burning bush when so much apparently hinged on knowing God's true name. Although God divulged that 'information,' its whole significance was yet to be revealed. And later, though Pharaoh had learned of that name from Moses, his arrogant rebuff—'Who is YHWH? I do not know YHWH'—indicated that God's full identity still awaited recognition. Thus, the real import of these plagues—of all these events connected with Israel's Exodus from Egypt—is to give the Lord the recognition he deserves. At a fundamental level, the Exodus itself is one great sign-event, forever pointing out to all the world who is its authentic god and lord.

Lastly, as we might have come to expect by now, the characters of Pharaoh and Moses also receive further elaboration. Pharaoh, though still unbeaten, has nevertheless been somewhat humbled, admitting, "This time I have *sinned; the* LORD is in the right, I and my people in the wrong" (author's translation). With that confession, he has grudgingly acknowledged both the Lord and the righteousness of His decree that Israel should be let go. The Egyptian king has thereby implicitly conceded that there is some standard other than his own—*someone* other than himself—by which and by whom his actions might legitimately be judged.

Moses comes to make a first significant acknowledgment for himself too. When he tells Pharaoh that he knows "that it will be a while before [the king] and [his] courtiers will fear the LORD" (author's translation), Moses virtually admits that God has been right from the start, for despite all the appearances to the contrary, Pharaoh's heart will continually harden to prevent Israel's departure. And sure enough, when the hail stops, Pharaoh—and his courtiers—start up again. The king changes his mind, and thus *sins* again.[21] "So the heart of Pharaoh was hardened and he would not let the Israelites go—*just as the* LORD *had said through Moses*" (author's translation).

[10:1]Then the LORD said to Moses, "Go to Pharaoh. For I have hardened his heart and the heart of his courtiers, in order that I may display these My signs among them, [2]and that you may recount in the hearing of your sons and of your sons' sons how I made a mockery of the Egyptians and how I displayed My signs among them—in order that you may know that I am the LORD." [3]So Moses and Aaron went to Pharaoh and said to him, "Thus says the LORD, the God of the Hebrews, 'How long will you refuse to humble yourself before Me? Let My people go that they may worship Me. [4]For if you refuse to let My people go, tomorrow I will bring locusts on your territory. [5]They shall cover the surface of the land, so that no one will be able to see the land. They shall devour the surviving remnant that was left to you after the hail; and they shall eat away all your trees that grow in the field. [6]Moreover, they shall fill your palaces and the houses of all your courtiers and of all the Egyptians—something that neither your fathers nor your fathers' fathers have seen from the day they appeared on earth to this day.'" With that he turned and left Pharaoh's presence.

[7]Pharaoh's courtiers said to him, "How long shall this one be a snare to us? Let the men go to worship with the LORD their God! Are you not yet aware that Egypt is lost?" [8]So Moses and Aaron were brought back to Pharaoh and he said to them, "Go, worship the LORD your God! Who are the ones to go?" [9]Moses replied, "We will all go, young and old: we will go with our sons and daughters, our flocks and herds; for we must observe the LORD's pilgrimage.[a]" [10]But he said to them, "The LORD be with you the same as I mean to let your children go with you! Clearly, you are bent on mischief. [11]No! You menfolk go and worship the LORD, since that is what you want." And they were expelled from Pharaoh's presence.

[12]Then the LORD said to Moses, "Hold out your arm over the land of Egypt for the locusts, that they may come upon the land of Egypt and eat up all the plants in the land, whatever the hail has left." [13]So Moses held out his rod over the land of Egypt, and the LORD drove an east wind over the land all that day and all night; and when morning came, the east wind had brought

the locusts. [14]Locusts invaded all the land of Egypt and settled within all the territory of Egypt in thick mass; never before had there been so many, nor will there ever be so many again. [15]They hid the surface of the whole land until the land was black; and they ate up all the grasses of the field and all the fruit of the trees which the hail had left, so that nothing green was left, of tree or grass of the field, in all the land of Egypt.

[16]Pharaoh hurriedly summoned Moses and Aaron and said, "I stand guilty before the Lord your God and before you. [17]Forgive, then, my offense just this once, and plead with the Lord your God that he but remove this death from me." [18]So he left Pharaoh's presence and pleaded with the Lord. [19]The Lord caused a shift to a very strong west wind, which lifted the locusts and hurled them into the Sea of Reeds [b]; not a single locust remained in all the territory of Egypt. [20]But the Lord stiffened Pharaoh's heart, and he would not let the Israelites go.

[a]Heb. [ch]ag; others "festival"
[b]Traditionally, but incorrectly, "Red Sea"

The narration of the eighth plague—locusts—is chock-full of irony, with the tables turned on Pharaoh and his remaining followers. Originally, Egypt's motivation for holding Israel in bondage had been to prevent some sort of misfortune from ravaging the land; now, however, Pharaoh's courtiers are appealing desperately to him, 'Let the Israelites go! Can't you see that *they're* the ones who've got *us* trapped? Can't you see the land is *ruined*?' Moreover, when the oppression started, the Egyptians had drowned the Hebrew children in order to be rid of them. But currently, when Moses includes Israel's young among those to make the trek out to the desert, Pharaoh insists on keeping them in Egypt. And as for *children* and *descendants*, it will be Israel's offspring who shall ultimately live to recount what is transpiring during these momentous times—events that have not previously occurred in all the long history of Egypt's *elders* and *ancestors*. Finally, we recall that during the plague of swarms, Moses had warned Pharaoh not to trifle with the Lord.[22] Yet it's abundantly clear that at present, it's the Lord who is toying with all Egypt.[23]

The narrative's irony, however, transcends events that have already come to pass. Key words and phrases point toward future events as well: "the land was black," "remove this death," "I would wish the Lord's blessing,"[24] "they were expelled from Pharaoh's presence," "an east wind," "hurled them into the Sea of Reeds." As the plagues move inexorably toward their climactic fulfillment, such words and phrases will uncannily return, and as they do, the story's irony will turn increasingly grim and bitter.

But for now, two other kinds of turns in the narrative are of more immediate concern. The first is another modest shift in Pharaoh's attitude. When Moses first brought him God's message regarding Israel, the Egyptian monarch was singularly unresponsive. Furthermore, when the Israelite foremen later complained of the king's new quota system for making bricks, Pharaoh met their protests with callous indifference. But this plague of locusts has apparently gotten Pharaoh involved with what is going on around him. Indeed, his words show that he knows himself to be deeply *implicated* in and by everything that is taking place in Egypt: "I have *sinned against the* LORD . . . and *against you*. . . . Now *forgive* my offenses" (author's translation). If part of God's rationale behind the plagues was gradually to force the tyrant to pay regard both to the Lord and to his people, then certainly by this stage in the narrative, the plagues seem to have done their work.

The second twist taken by the story here is likewise full of meaning. Up to now, virtually every time the phrase "that you may know that I am the LORD" has appeared in the narrative, its object has been either Pharaoh or, more broadly, the entire Egyptian people. But now in 10:2, God's words are directed to the Israelites; they, too, must come to know and acknowledge him. For if the Exodus experience fails to persuade Israel that ultimately the Lord is the one whom they must serve and in whom they ought to put their trust, then all of God's works in Egypt, no matter how mighty or marvelous, will have been for nothing. As the plagues enter their final phase, the Lord shall increasingly give Israel additional good reason to believe.

[21]Then the LORD said to Moses, "Hold out your arm toward the sky that there may be darkness upon the land of Egypt, a darkness that can be touched." [22]Moses held out his arm

toward the sky and thick darkness descended upon all of Egypt for three days. [23]People could not see one another, and for three days no one could get up from where he was; but all the Israelites enjoyed light in their dwellings.

[24]Pharaoh then summoned Moses and said, "Go, worship the Lord! Only your flocks and your herds shall be left behind; even your children may go with you." [25]But Moses said, "You yourself must provide us with sacrifices and burnt offerings to offer up to the Lord our God; [26]our own livestock, too, shall go along with us—not a hoof shall remain behind: for we must select from it for the worship of the Lord our God; and we shall not know with what we are to worship the Lord until we arrive there." [27]But the Lord stiffened Pharaoh's heart and he would not consent to let them go. [28]Pharaoh said to them, "Be gone from me! Take care not to see me again, for the moment you look upon my face you shall die." [29]And Moses replied, "You have spoken rightly. I shall not see your face again!"

For those who have attempted to understand the story's movement from one plague to the next in terms of each successive blow's becoming progressively more severe, plague nine presents a problem. Why should darkness be worse than rapacious locusts or killing hail or deadly pestilence? Let us repeat, therefore, what we have been saying all during this plague account, and indeed, all through the course of this master story as a whole: comprehending the narrative's structure lies not so much in looking for strict *logical* connections as for tight *literary* ones. Precisely those sorts of ties make clear how the ninth plague fits in to the rest of the story framework. Thus, as Childs has so nicely seen:

> The plague of darkness is not inappropriate for the last plague but one, in that it *foreshadows* the ultimate judgment when the first-born [is] slain at night. But there is also a certain *contrast* between the deathly silence within a darkness which can be touched and the "great cry" which [is] soon to break forth.[25]

Furthermore, the ninth plague contains yet another literary nexus that binds it to the rest of the plague account. Once again, it is the continuing portrayal of the changing characters of Moses and Pharaoh. In the interval between their first meeting and their encounter following this latest plague, we

have witnessed a full-scale reversal in their personalities as
negotiators, advocates, and leaders. When Moses initially
approached Pharaoh, the king appeared arrogant, unbending,
and totally in control, while Moses himself seemed timid,
ineffectual, and weak.[26] But as Moses and Pharaoh face each
other now, they have apparently switched roles. This time, it's
Pharaoh who looks impotent as he feebly grasps to retain at
least some semblance of power: 'All right, you can go, and you
can even take your children. But you just better make sure you
leave your livestock *here.'* By contrast, Moses' response plainly
reveals him to be the one presently in charge, self-assured and
uncompromising. He tells the tottering despot that he will take
everyone *and* everything, all Israel's people and all her animals
besides. And what's more, the Egyptians will even contribute
to Israel's performance of God's service by providing some of
their own livestock too! In one last frantic outburst, Pharaoh
issues one more idle threat: 'Get out of here! And the next time
you see me, it's death for you!' Moses is not intimidated. The
man who once repeatedly complained that he was slow of
speech now quickly counters with a masterful repartee: 'Just as
you say! The next time you see me, it shall indeed be "death for
you," and that's when you'll get your wish, for *then* I'll be
gone!'

The stage is set for the final confrontation.

Notes

1. Although the text literally reads "Aaron's *rod* swallowed their *rods*," their new form as serpents is nonetheless clearly what is meant.

2. Thus, the many attempts to 'explain' all the succeeding signs and plagues in purely 'naturalistic' terms are, even if valid, totally irrelevant. For the basic question still remains: Is it God working *through* these occurrences, and do these events, therefore, point beyond themselves to him? See my comments, below, pertaining to the crossing of the Sea of Reeds.

3. See the commentary, above, on Exod. 2:1-4.

4. Moshe Greenberg has appropriately categorized the first few plagues as "nuisances." Unlike the later plagues, they cause no real harm or damage.

5. The meaning of the Hebrew word *kinim* is uncertain; it has been variously taken to mean "gnats" or "mosquitoes."

6. It is not insignificant that in the Ancient Near East, magicians were frequently regarded as belonging to the class of the 'educated' or 'enlightened.' Hence, in the present story, the first to come to some realization about the true state of affairs—God at work!—are not the ignorant or uninformed masses, but instead, the 'learned elite.'

7. Some, noticing this recurrence in style and motif, have tried to formulate a cyclical order in the plagues, following the pattern: 1:4:7; 2:5:8; 3:6:9; the tenth plague then provides the capstone for the entire sequence. Nevertheless, I myself tend to be persuaded by Childs's argument that "while this principle of ordering the plagues is useful, it remains questionable to what extent it is more accidental than intentional. But perhaps the decisive question is not that of intentionality, but in what way this structural observation aids in illuminating the final composition. In my judgment, the major themes are not brought into any sharper focus by recognizing this pattern" (*Book of Exodus*, p. 150).

8. As my remarks concerning the preceding plagues have tried to show—and as they will continue to try to indicate with the subsequent ones as well—the striking quality of the succession of these occurrences does not lie in their following some strict logical arrangement such that, e.g., the *effect* of each of God's blows on the Egyptians is, by the same precise degree, harsher than the one before it. (How is darkness [plague nine], for example, worse than a deadly pestilence [plague five]?) Instead, the plagues are arranged so that they *cumulatively* work to *affect* Pharaoh, gradually wearing down his resistance to acknowledging the Lord and to letting God's

people go. Cf. as well my comments in *Theology and Narrative*, pp. 201-2.

9. Following the blood (7:22), the lice (8:15), and the pestilence (9:7).

10. Following the frogs (8:11) and the swarms (8:28).

11. Cf., e.g., Leibowitz's comments in *Studies in Shemot*, pp. 156-57.

12. See Childs, *Book of Exodus*, p. 174, where the former description is attributed to a P source while the latter characterization is traced back to J.

13. Ibid., p. 170.

14. *Mechilta d'Rabbi Ishmael*, Beshallach, chap. 7.

15. In biblical physiology, the heart was, among other things, the seat of the intellect and will. In the context of the plague account, it is clear that God's hardening of Pharaoh's heart refers to his impeding or even blocking the king's ability to act of his own volition.

16. See the discussion above, where the capacity to act freely is singled out as one of the Torah's most basic distinguishing marks for indicating what it means to be human.

17. Notice how the endings of both stories implicitly reflect this idea. Thus see Gen. 3:22-23: "And the Lord God said, 'Now that the man has become like one of us, knowing good and bad, what if he should stretch out his hand and take also from the tree of life and eat, and live forever!' So the Lord God banished him from the garden of Eden." And see as well Gen. 11:6-7: "And the Lord said, "If, as one people with one language for all, this is how they have begun to act, then nothing that they may propose to do will be out of their reach. Let Me, then, go down and confound their speech."

18. I.e., the Egyptian monarch who first instigated Israel's bondage *at his own will and pleasure*.

19. Most notably the magicians, who were unable to reproduce the plague of lice, confessed it to be the "finger of God," and who later, when stricken by the boils, were unable even to appear before Moses and Aaron to do battle with them.

20. Cf. Moses' parting words to Pharaoh as he takes his leave to end the plague (v. 29): "in order that you may know that *the earth is the Lord's*"—or, in other words, the world *belongs* to God, who is therefore its sole rightful master.

21. Cf. v. 34, where the Hebrew is *veyosef lachto*.

22. Cf. Exod. 8:25.

23. V. 2; Hebrew: *hitalalti*—i.e., "make sport," "mock."

24. Cf. v. 10. The Hebrew is somewhat difficult, yet the tone is definitely sarcastic; see also Exod. 12:32 where, following the tenth plague, Pharaoh does in fact ask for blessing.

25. Childs, *Book of Exodus*, p. 160; italics added. Notice as well the connection between this plague's thick darkness which forces people to stay put inside and the warning issued before the advent of the tenth plague—"None of you shall go outside the door of his house until morning" (Exod. 12:22).

26. See the commentary to Exod. 5:1-5, above.

VI
EXODUS 11:1–12:42; 13:17–15:27

[11:1]And the LORD said to Moses, "I will bring but one more plague upon Pharaoh and upon Egypt; after that he shall let you go from here; indeed, when he lets you go, he will drive you out of here one and all. [2]Tell the people that each man shall borrow from his neighbor, and each woman from hers, objects of silver and gold." [3]The LORD disposed the Egyptians favorably toward the people. Moreover, Moses himself was much esteemed in the land of Egypt, among Pharaoh's courtiers and among the people.

[4]Moses said, "Thus says the LORD: Toward midnight I will go forth among the Egyptians, [5]and every first-born in the land of Egypt shall die, from the first-born of Pharaoh who sits on his throne to the first-born of the slave girl who is behind the millstones; and all the first-born of the cattle. [6]And there will be a loud cry in all the land of Egypt, such as has never been or will ever be again; [7]but not a dog shall snarl[a] at any of the Israelites, at man or beast—in order that you may know that the LORD makes a distinction between Egypt and Israel. [8]Then all these courtiers of yours shall come down to me and bow low to me, saying, 'Depart, you and all the people who follow you!' After that I will depart." And he left Pharaoh's presence in hot anger.

[9]Now the LORD said to Moses, "Pharaoh will not heed you, in order that My marvels may be multiplied in the land of Egypt." [10]Moses and Aaron had performed all these marvels before Pharaoh, but the Lord had stiffened the heart of Pharaoh so that he would not let the Israelites go from his land.

[a]Others "move (or whet) his tongue"

With a series of three terse announcements, the tenth plague is heralded by God. His first declaration is directed to the

Israelites, informing them what the plague's aftermath will bring. His second pronouncement is aimed at the Egyptians, notifying them of the unparalleled horror to take place during the plague itself. But as momentous as the Lord's first two proclamations are, his last is ultimately the one of greatest consequence. For it is the message intended for the hearers of the story, apprising *us* of the reason for the plague: that God's "marvels may be multiplied."

That rationale is certainly by no means new; we have heard it repeatedly in the narrative. To be sure, the same justification given here, prior to the plagues' culmination, preceded their advent too:

> I will harden Pharaoh's heart, that I may multiply My signs and marvels in the land of Egypt. When Pharaoh does not heed . . ., I will lay My hand upon Egypt and deliver My ranks, My people the Israelites, from the land of Egypt with extraordinary chastisements. And the Egyptians shall know that I am the LORD, when I stretch out My hand over Egypt and bring out the Israelites from their midst. (Exod. 7:3-5)

By this point in the narrative, such words, while perhaps no longer novel, nevertheless bear unavoidable implications. After all the astounding and terrible things that have struck Egypt—and that *are yet to strike her*—God's words constitute far more than some purely theoretical explanation. Instead they, along with this master story as a whole, now stand as an eternal *warning* about the awesome disaster which may well await those who, like Pharaoh and his people, fail to heed the Lord.

> [12:1]The LORD said to Moses and Aaron in the land of Egypt: [2]This month shall mark for you the beginning of the months; it shall be the first of the months of the year for you. [3]Speak to the whole assembly of Israel and say that on the tenth of this month each of them shall take a lamb to a family, a lamb to a household. [4]But if the household is too small for a lamb, then let him share one with the neighbor closest to his household in the number of persons: you shall apportion the lamb according to what each person should eat. [5]Your lamb shall be without blemish, a yearling male; you may take it from the sheep or

from the goats. [6]You shall keep watch over it until the fourteenth day of this month; and all the aggregate community of the Israelites shall slaughter it at twilight. [7]They shall take some of the blood and put it on the two doorposts and the lintel of the houses in which they are to eat it. [8]They shall eat the flesh that same night; they shall eat it roasted over the fire, with unleavened bread and with bitter herbs. [9]Do not eat any of it raw, or cooked in any way with water, but roasted—head, legs, and entrails—over the fire. [10]You shall not leave any of it over until morning; whatever is left of it until morning you shall burn.

[11]This is how you shall eat it: your loins girded, your sandals on your feet, and your staff in your hand; and you shall eat it hurriedly: it is a passover offering[b] to the LORD. [12]For that night I will go hurriedly through the land of Egypt and strike down every first-born in the land of Egypt, both man and beast; and I will mete out punishments to all the gods of Egypt, I the LORD. [13]And the blood on the houses in which you dwell shall be a sign for you: when I see the blood I will pass over you, so that no plague will destroy you when I strike the land of Egypt.

[14]This day shall be to you one of remembrance: you shall celebrate it as a festival to the LORD throughout the generations; you shall celebrate it as an institution for all time. [15]Seven days you shall eat unleavened bread; on the very first day you shall remove leaven from your houses, for whoever eats leavened bread from the first day to the seventh day, that person shall be cut off from Israel.

[16]On the first day you shall hold a sacred convocation, and on the seventh day a sacred convocation; no work at all shall be done on them; only what every person is to eat, that alone may be prepared for you. [17]You shall observe the [Feast of] Unleavened Bread, for on this very day I brought your ranks out of the land of Egypt; you shall observe this day throughout the generations as an institution for all time. [18]In the first month, from the fourteenth day of the month at evening, you shall eat unleavened bread until the twenty-first day of the month at evening. [19]No leaven shall be found in your houses for seven days. For whoever eats what is leavened, that person shall be cut off from the assembly of Israel, whether he is a stranger or a citizen of the country. [20]You shall eat nothing leavened; in all your settlements you shall eat unleavened bread.

[21]Moses then summoned all the elders of Israel and said to them, "Go, pick out lambs for your families, and slaughter the

passover offering. [22]Take a bunch of hyssop, dip it in the blood that is in the basin, and apply some of the blood that is in the basin to the lintel and to the two doorposts. None of you shall go outside the door of his house until morning. [23]For when the LORD goes through to smite the Egyptians, He will see the blood on the lintel and the two doorposts, and the LORD will pass over [c] the door and not let the Destroyer enter and smite your home.

[24]You shall observe this as an institution for all time, for you and for your descendants. [25]And when you enter the land which the LORD will give you, as He has promised, you shall observe this rite. [26]And when your children ask you, 'What do you mean by this rite?' [27]You shall say, 'It is the passover sacrifice to the LORD, because He passed over the houses of the Israelites in Egypt when He smote the Egyptians, but saved our houses.'"

The people then bowed low in homage. [28]And the Israelites went and did so; just as the LORD had commanded Moses and Aaron, so they did.

[a]Or "kid." Heb. *seh* either "sheep" or "goat." Cf. v. 5
[b]Or "protective offering"; Heb. *pesa[ch]*
[c]Or "protect"; cf. v. 11 n.b.

This section, specifying rules and precepts for Israel to observe, is just the kind of passage that, despite its length, often gets short shrift from those engaged in biblical theology.[1] All too frequently, they have treated such 'legal sections' as bothersome interruptions which disrupt the flow of the narrative while detracting from the story's 'true' theological significance.

However, that kind of perspective on the present passage ignores a striking feature of these so-called 'non-narrative' portions—namely, that they do after all appear *within the framework of the larger story*. In fact, it is precisely at this stage in the Jewish master story that the people Israel receives its very first commands from God,[2] and thus, the story, besides furnishing the source for those instructions, supplies the context for their intelligibility as well. The narrative's next chapter, Exodus 13, underscores that point with even greater force. When, for instance, Israel is enjoined to redeem its firstborn males (v. 13), the story itself is invoked as the explicit basis for the practice:

Every first-born male among your children you shall redeem.
. . . Because of a strong hand the LORD brought us out from
Egypt, the house of bondage. When Pharaoh stubbornly
refused to let us go, the LORD slew every first-born in the land of
Egypt . . . Therefore I . . . redeem every first-born among my
sons. (vv. 13, 14–15)[3]

Significantly, those portrayed here as asking for a justification
of Israel's communal observances are none other than Israel's
younger generation. Likewise, for all her future generations,
Israel's story—the Jewish master story—will provide the
matrix for legitimizing and making sense of her tradition—i.e.,
Jewish tradition. If that tradition ever loses sight of the master
story which is its point of reference, it will also likely lose its
significance and warrant in a mire of obscure legalisms. Hence,
if traditional rites are not to degenerate into mere rituals, those
who would claim to be the bearers of tradition must make sure
that they are more fundamentally the bearers *of the story*. For
what is tradition in the end but a community's way of telling its
story over time?[4] As Exodus 12 and 13 remind us in depicting
the beginnings of the people Israel's traditions, tradition
properly understood enables us to tell our communal story
properly. In that respect, tradition requires us to act out our
larger master story in each of our own individual life stories
such that in the process, we become transformed. For then we
no longer simply study or recite the story; instead, we *become*
the story.[5]

Up to now, our approach to this somewhat lengthy segment
of the narrative has taken the form of a broad overview. Now,
however, our attention shall be concentrated on a few specific
verses which, though brief in comparison to the longer
passage, have far-reaching implications, for the issue such
verses raise is one of tremendous import for our lives—
namely, what is it that saves our lives?

On first impulse, of course, we might be prompted to
answer 'God'; certainly, the narrative itself would seem to
offer ample grounds for that response. Yet such a reply,
though apparently warranted by the story, is nevertheless
deficient precisely because it fails to attend to the *whole* story.

As the story tells it, God's acting to save Israel's life depends on *Israel's acting first* to take some life-saving measures of her own. Indeed, in the narrative, God himself is the one who most plainly makes that point through the instructions he gives to the Israelites telling them what they must do to escape the destruction fast approaching Egypt:

> Take some of the blood and put it on the two doorposts and the lintel of [your] houses. . . . That night I will go through the land of Egypt and strike down every first-born in the land of Egypt. . . . And the blood on the houses in which you dwell shall be a sign for you: when I see the blood I will pass over you, so that no plague will destroy you when I strike the land of Egypt. (Exod. 12: 7, 12-13)

Hitherto in the narrative, Israel has either passively borne the brunt of the plagues with everyone else in Egypt (as in the first through third plagues) or she has been spared that suffering due to the activity of God alone (as in the fourth through ninth plagues). The tenth plague, however, dramatically changes all that; it calls upon the Israelites to become active participants in the work of achieving their salvation. With the previous plagues, God was the sole source of all the signs signaling Israel's coming deliverance. But this plague is different: Israel now must send that sign herself. By being required to mark their houses, the Israelites are thereby required as well to mark themselves for either life or death. For if they fail to smear their doorposts and the plague *does* come to pass, then it will strike them that night with the same deadliness as it will strike the rest of Egypt. And alternatively, if they do mark their homes but the plague *fails* to come to pass, then they will have marked themselves as easy targets for an Egyptian reprisal next morning.[6] In other words, either Israel stakes her life on God—or she stakes it on someone else. As a result, the risk of Israel's faith inevitably involves the risk of Israel's life. Can she afford—or can she *not* afford—to proclaim her identity to the world as a people identified with God?[7] That choice ineluctably faces Israel, and yet, precisely because it is so inescapable, it is ultimately a choice that lies in Israel's hands. And in just that sense, Israel's life, survival, and salvation rest not only in the hands of God, but in her own as well.

At the story's start, Israel's act, albeit meager—a cry to God!—nonetheless proved indispensable for setting in motion all the events leading to salvation;[8] now she must take an active role again if deliverance is finally to be effected. To state the matter flatly, God can't and *won't* save Israel by himself. For salvation to come about, each needs the other; neither God nor human beings will accomplish the task alone. In light of the present narrative, that claim should hardly come as a surprise, for a theme running throughout this story of God and Israel is that virtually everything hinges on a mutually binding covenant between them. Consequently, for this Jewish master story, the joining of God *to* humankind as covenantal partner makes salvation dependent on the joint action of God *and* humankind together. And thus, the two are yoked together as co-partners in redemption.

> [29]In the middle of the night the LORD struck down all the first-born in the land of Egypt, from the first-born of Pharaoh who sat on the throne to the first-born of the captive who was in the dungeon, and all the first-born of the cattle. [30]And Pharaoh arose in the night, with all his courtiers and all the Egyptians—because there was a loud cry in Egypt; for there was no house where there was not someone dead. [31]He summoned Moses and Aaron in the night and said, "Up, depart from among my people, you and the Israelites with you! Go, worship the LORD as you said! [32]Take also your flocks and your herds, as you said, and be gone! And may you bring a blessing upon me also!"

The tenth plague at last gains Israel's release from Egypt, and its depiction forms an ironic reversal of the account of the oppression's onset. When Pharaoh first ordered the drowning of Hebrew infants, virtually every Israelite household stood to lose someone at the Egyptians' hands. When the Lord unleashes the tenth plague, however, Egypt's houses are the ones touched by death. Early on, the bondage had become so unbearable that the Israelites' only recourse was to cry out in desperation.[9] Yet as the tenth plague does its gruesome work, it is the Egyptians' cry of despair that now resounds throughout the land.

Pharaoh himself seems especially hard hit by these reversals. Following the first plague, he returned to his palace, unruffled and unconcerned. By contrast, the tenth plague quickly becomes the object of his concern, jarring the king from his bed in the middle of the night to give his full attention to issues which are quite literally matters of life and death. This is the same Pharaoh, of course, who has repeatedly resisted Israel's departure with a series of sophistic dodges and conditions: she could go serve the Lord, *but* her service had to be performed within the borders of the land; her men could go out to serve the Lord, *but* the rest of her people had to stay behind; all her people might go serve the Lord, *but* her livestock had to remain in Egypt. However, when the tenth plague strikes, Pharaoh knows he cannot dodge the real issue any longer. He must unconditionally surrender: 'All right, take all the Israelites and take all your animals, too! Just get your people away from my people! You get your wish! Go serve the Lord!' The man who once arrogantly assumed that as king and lord of Egypt he had similar dominion over life and death now finds himself humbled into acknowledging that there is indeed a power superior to his. Thus, as Moses and Aaron are about to take their leave, he pitifully implores them, "Bring a blessing upon me also!"

But what blessing—or pity—is there for Egypt? From the description of the tenth plague's magnitude, it seems none at all; the plague smites each and every firstborn in Egypt, "from the first-born of Pharaoh who sat on the throne to the first-born of the cattle." Apparently, the extent of an individual's own personal moral culpability is not the gauge by which God's punishment is meted out: how could an imprisoned captive, let alone a cow, be held morally responsible for Israel's enslavement?

Instead, the moral standard seems to be corporate in nature. We remember that from the first, this has been a story about *peoples* rather than *persons*.[10] Whole peoples, not individual persons, are portrayed as the bearers of history—and as the ones who must bear the brunt of history as well. As the tenth plague runs its course, relatively innocent Egyptians no doubt suffer alongside their plainly guilty monarch, and in exactly

102

that sense, they suffer for his wrongdoing. But for this story at least, that is the price of identifying with one community rather than another, *of being identified with* Pharaoh's people rather than with the Lord's.[11] Hence, from the standpoint of the Jewish master story, any description of human existence that denies or underestimates the full repercussions of a community's life for the life of an individual offers an account which is in the last analysis no more than a fairy tale.

> [33]The Egyptians urged the people on, to make them leave in haste, for they said, "We shall all be dead." [34]So the people took their dough before it was leavened, their kneading bowls wrapped in their cloaks upon their shoulders. [35]The Israelites had done Moses' bidding and borrowed from the Egyptians objects of silver and gold, and clothing. [36]And the LORD had disposed the Egyptians favorably toward the people, and they let them have their request; thus they stripped the Egyptians.
>
> [37]The Israelites journeyed from Raamses to Succoth, about six hundred thousand men on foot, aside from children. [38]Moreover, a mixed multitude went up with them, and very much livestock, both flocks and herds. [39]And they baked unleavened cakes of the dough that they had taken out of Egypt, for it was not leavened, since they had been driven out of Egypt and could not delay; nor had they prepared any provisions for themselves.
>
> [40]The time the Israelites remained in Egypt was four hundred and thirty years; [41]at the end of the four hundred and thirtieth year, to the very day, all the ranks of the LORD departed from the land of Egypt. [42]That was for the LORD a night of vigil to bring them out of the land of Egypt; that same night is the LORD's, one of vigil for all the children of Israel throughout the generations.

Israel's redemption from Egypt, promised and awaited over four hundred years, finally comes to pass. But like the fateful visitation of the plagues that preceded it, the redemption is an event aimed not at the isolated individual but at the people as a whole. Over the time that Israel has been held thrall, countless Israelites have both lived *and* died as slaves, and no doubt, countless more of their children have lived and died the same. For individual Israelites such as those, there will be no liberation or deliverance from Egypt. Instead, what escapes Egypt and survives Egypt and outlives Egypt is the corporate entity called

Israel. It is ultimately that aggregate body rather than the individual parts within it that God has promised in the long run to redeem.[12] Thus, the primary object of God's promised redemption is not the individual in his or her own lifetime, but the people in God's own good time; such is the bearing of the Jewish master story on Jewish hope for all time.[13]

How else does Israel's story shape Israel's expectations for the future? How else does the narrative's image of the going out from Egypt mold her self-image for her life ahead? "Leave in haste, . . . kneading bowls wrapped in . . . cloaks upon their shoulders, . . . could not delay"—she stands ready to depart at an instant's notice. "Plundered the Egyptians . . . , all the ranks of the Lord departed"—she stands equipped to move out as the victorious army of her God.[14] "[A] vigil for all the children of Israel throughout the generations"—she stands watch for the appointed time signaling her redemption. As Israel sees herself on this eventful day, so she must always see herself throughout all the days to come—i.e., as a people on the move, marching forward in its supreme commander's service, forever on the lookout for the promised triumph that may come at any moment.

13:17Now when Pharaoh let the people go, God did not lead them by way of the land of the Philistines, although it was nearer; for God said, "The people may have a change of heart when they see war, and return to Egypt." 18So God led the people roundabout, by way of the wilderness at the Sea of Reeds.

Now the Israelites went up armed[d] out of the land of Egypt. 19And Moses took with him the bones of Joseph, who had exacted an oath from the children of Israel, saying, "God will be sure to take notice of you: then you shall carry up my bones from here with you."

20They set out from Succoth and encamped at Etham, at the edge of the wilderness. 21The Lord went before them in a pillar of cloud by day, to guide them along the way, and in a pillar of fire by night, to give them light, that they might travel day and night. 22The pillar of cloud by day and the pillar of fire by night did not depart from before the people.

dMeaning of Heb. [ch]amushim uncertain

In gaining the people's release, the Lord has been faithful to Israel and his word. He had decreed that Pharaoh should "let My people go!" and sure enough, that decree has been fulfilled: "Pharaoh let the people go."[15] Just as Jacob said, God has indeed looked after Israel, and thus, along with the redemption of the people, the Lord's past promise and Israel's past trust have both been redeemed as well.

But although the Israelites have now left Egypt, they have by no means been left to their own devices. The same providence that led them out of Egypt still leads them on into the wilderness, ever watchful for dangers—e.g., hostile Philistines—that might befall them and ever cognizant of the weaknesses—i.e., faint hearts—that could beset them. Hence, at the head of Israel's column of refugees is God's column of fire and cloud, indicating that his presence has not abandoned his people, but yet guides them forward so that they might someday reach their place of promise.

14:1The Lord said to Moses: 2Tell the Israelites to turn back and encamp before Pi-hahiroth, between Migdol and the sea, before Baal-zephon; you shall encamp facing it, by the sea. 3Pharaoh will say of the Israelites, "They are astray in the land; the wilderness has closed in on them." 4Then I will stiffen Pharaoh's heart and he will pursue them, that I may *a-assert My authority against -a Pharaoh and all his host; and the Egyptians shall know that I am the Lord.

And they did so.

5When the king of Egypt was told that the people had fled, Pharaoh and his courtiers had a change of heart about the people and said, "What is this we have done, releasing Israel from our service?" 6He ordered b his chariot and took his men with him; 7he took six hundred of his picked chariots, and the rest of the chariots of Egypt, with officersc in all of them. 8The Lord stiffened the heart of Pharaoh, king of Egypt, and he gave chase to the Israelites. As the Israelites were departing boldly, d 9the Egyptians gave chase to them, and all the chariot horses of Pharaoh, his horsemen, and his warriors overtook them encamped by the sea, near Pi-hahiroth, before Baal-zephon.

a-aOr "gain glory through"
bSee on Gen. 46:29
cHeb. *shalish*; originally "third man on royal chariot"; hence "adjutant," "officer"
dLit. "with upraised hand"

Right at the story's outset, we saw that central to its evolving conflict would be the clash between Egypt's plans for Israel versus those of God.[16] But as that contest of wills reemerges here, it's abundantly clear from the narrative that it is in reality no contest at all. True, Pharaoh perceives the Israelites as aimlessly wandering in the wilderess; in truth, however, their movements are precisely in line with the aims of God—and *his* aims and objectives are the only ones that matter. Thus, even though Egypt and Israel may both have a change of heart, with the former desiring to revert to her prior policies while the latter wishes to return to her previous circumstances,[17] the Lord's heart is still firmly set on realizing his preeminent purpose: through all the awesome events affecting Egypt and Israel to establish his name throughout all the world.[18]

[10]As Pharaoh drew near, the Israelites caught sight of the Egyptians advancing upon them. Greatly frightened, the Israelites cried out to the LORD. [11]And they said to Moses, "Was it for want of graves in Egypt that you brought us out to die in the wilderness? What have you done to us, taking us out of Egypt? [12]Is this not the very thing we told you in Egypt, saying, 'Let us be, and we will serve the Egyptians, for it is better for us to serve the Egyptians than to die in the wilderness'?" [13]But Moses said to the people, "Have no fear! Stand by, and witness the deliverance which the LORD will work for you today; for the Egyptians whom you see today you will never see again. [14]The LORD will battle for you; you hold your peace!"

[15]Then the LORD said to Moses, "Why do you cry out to Me? Tell the Israelites to go forward. [16]And you lift up your rod and hold out your arm over the sea and split it, so that the Israelites may march into the sea on dry ground. [17]And I will stiffen the hearts of the Egyptians so that they go in after them; and I will assert My authority against Pharaoh and all his warriors, his chariots and his horsemen. [18]Let the Egyptians know that I am the LORD, when I assert My authority against Pharaoh, his chariots, and his horsemen."

Two sets of remarks, one modern, the other ancient, aptly catch the narrative movement here. First, Brevard Childs, always sensitive to the nuances of the text, skillfully notes the way the dramatic tension builds. On the one hand, we learn what the Egyptians and the Israelites imagine to lie ahead. Yet on the other, and of far greater significance, is what we hear concerning the forethoughts of the Lord. Thus, as Childs comments:

> The people are in despair and complain to Moses. They recognize only Pharaoh's plan as having substance and, despairing of finding any other alternative, they attack their leader. The parallel between Israel's reaction and the Egyptians when hearing of Israel's escape is striking: "What is this we have done that we have let Israel go from serving us" "What is this you have done to us . . . in bringing us out of Egypt? . . . better to serve them." The two reactions are parallel because neither reckoned with God's plan.

As Childs then continues:

> Moses replies by challenging Israel to respond to God's plan. . . . "Do not fear"—they had feared (v. 10). "Stand and see the salvation of Yahweh today"—they had seen only the Egyptians approaching. . . . "As you see the Egyptians today . . . you shall not see them ever again ever. . . ." The people had cried to Yahweh; they are to be quiet. The battle—it is not just a flight as the Egyptians thought—will be fought by Yahweh for them.[19]

Like the modern critic, the classical midrash too displays great sensitivity to the textual subtleties of the narrative, and thereby affords us substantial insight into the development of plot and theme. Noticing that the Lord's question of Moses in verse 15—"Why do you cry out to Me?"—lacks any explicit stimulus from within the text itself, the rabbinic commentary tries to provide the background for God's query and attempts as well to lay the groundwork for his subsequent charge to Moses—"Tell the Israelites to go forward":

> The Holy One, blessed be he, said to Moses, "Moses, all that Israel has to do is to go forward. . . . My children are in distress, the sea closing in and the enemy close after, and you stand here making a lengthy prayer! . . . Why do you cry out to me?"[20]

Earlier, a plaintive outburst had been enough to trigger the Lord's intervention on Israel's behalf; in total bondage and utter hopelessness, the only option open to the people was to let loose a cry to God (Exod. 2:23). Now, however, their situation is significantly different. Recent events have brought them a measure of liberation which in turn has given them a basis for acting with hope and courage for the future. Hence, a mere cry will no longer suffice to bring about deliverance. Instead, some greater action is required: Israel must move forward into the water. As the sea marks the spot where Pharaoh and his people at last are forced to acknowledge the ultimate power of the Lord, its waters set the stage for an equally meaningful acknowledgment from the Lord's own people, too.[21]

> [19]The angel of God, who had been going ahead of the Israelite army, now moved and followed behind them; and the pillar of cloud shifted from in front of them and took up a place behind them, [20]and it came between the army of the Egyptians and the army of Israel. There was the cloud with the darkness, and it cast a spell[f] upon the night, so that the one could not come near the other all through the night.
>
> [f]From root 'rr, "cast a spell" or "curse." Others "and lit up"

Darkness so thick it immobilizes people descends over the Israelite and Egyptian camps. Such darkness has appeared elsewhere in the story—right before the tenth plague's onslaught (Exod. 10:22-23). But darkness has also occurred in another biblical narrative; signifying chaos, it precedes the creative act of God: "when God began to create the heaven and the earth—the earth being unformed and void, with darkness over the surface of the deep and a wind from God sweeping over the water" (Gen. 1:1-2). Hence, darkness coming here before the crossing of the sea, a darkness reminiscent of both the culmination of the plagues and the commencement of the world, augurs an impending and momentous change: the end of life for some, the beginning of life for others.[22]

> [21]Then Moses held out his arm over the sea and the LORD drove back the sea with a strong east wind all that night, and turned the sea into dry ground. The waters were split, [22]and the Israelites went into the sea on dry ground, the waters forming a wall for them on their right and on their left. [23]The Egyptians came in pursuit after them into the sea, all of Pharaoh's horses, chariots, and horsemen. [24]At the morning watch, the LORD looked down upon the Egyptian army from a pillar of fire and

cloud, and threw the Egyptian army into panic. [25]He locked[f] the wheels of their chariots so that they moved forward with difficulty. And the Egyptians said, "Let us flee from the Israelites, for the LORD is fighting for them against Egypt."

[26]Then the LORD said to Moses, "Hold out your arm over the sea, that the waters may come back upon the Egyptians and upon their chariots and upon their horsemen." [27]Moses held out his arm over the sea, and at daybreak the sea returned to its normal state, and the Egyptians fled at its approach, and the LORD hurled the Egyptians back into the sea. [28]The waters turned back and covered the chariots and the horsemen—Pharaoh's entire army that had followed after them—into the sea; not one of them remained. [29]But the Israelites marched through the sea on dry ground, the waters forming for them a wall on their right and on their left.

[30]Thus the LORD delivered Israel that day from the Egyptians. Israel saw the Egyptians dead on the shore of the sea. [31]And when Israel saw the wondrous power which the LORD had wielded against the Egyptians, the people feared the LORD: they had faith in the LORD, and in His servant Moses.

[f]From root 'sr, with several ancient versions. Others "took off"

As God's first blow at the Egyptians was struck at the water's edge, his final stroke against them falls there too.[23] And certainly, this *is* the final stroke—and not simply because following this last catastrophe, neither Pharaoh nor any of his host remain to torment Israel further. More importantly, no further reason remains for God to continue producing these imposing feats, these *signs*, for they have at last achieved their purpose: they have won Egypt's and Israel's recognition of who is Lord! Thus, the Egyptians, faced with a pillar of fire and cloud, useless chariots, and advancing doom, have finally been made to admit the truth: "*The* LORD is fighting for [the Israelites] against Egypt." Furthermore, events have also finally overwhelmed the Israelites. As witnesses to what has happened, they too are compelled to bear truthful witness to the One who made it happen: "Israel *saw* the Egyptians dead on the shore of the sea. And *when Israel saw* the wondrous power which the LORD had yielded . . . the people . . . had faith in the LORD" (italics added). Israel's witness, her acknowledgment—her *confession*—erupts in a chorus of thanksgiving:

15:1Then Moses and the Israelites sang this song to the LORD.
They said:

I will sing to the LORD, for He has triumphed gloriously;
Horse and driver He has hurled into the sea.
2The LORD is my strength and might*a*;
He is become my salvation.
This is my God and I will enshrine*b* Him,
The God of my father and I will exalt Him.
3The LORD, the Warrior—
LORD is His name!
4Pharaoh's chariots and his army
He has cast into the sea;
And the pick of his officers
Are drowned in the Sea of Reeds.
5The deeps covered them;
They went down into the depths like a stone.
6Your right hand, O LORD, glorious in power,
Your right hand, O LORD, shatters the foe!
7In Your great triumph You break Your opponents;
You send forth Your fury, it consumes them like stubble.
8At the blast of Your nostrils the waters piled up,
The floods stood straight like a wall;
The deeps froze in the heart of the sea.
9The foe said,
"I will pursue, I will overtake,
I will divide the spoil;
My desire shall have its fill of them.
I will bare my sword; My hand shall subdue them."
10You made Your wind blow, the sea covered them;
They sank like lead in the majestic waters.

11Who is like You, O LORD, among the celestials*c*;
Who is like You, majestic in holiness,
Awesome in splendor, working wonders!
12You put out Your right hand,
The earth swallowed them.
13In Your love You lead the people You redeemed;
In Your strength you guide them to Your holy abode.
14The peoples hear, they tremble;
Agony grips the dwellers in Philistia.
15Now are the clans of Edom dismayed;
The tribes of Moab—trembling grips them;
All the dwellers in Canaan are aghast.
16Terror and dread descend upon them;

Through the might of Your arm they are still as stone—
Till Your people pass by, O LORD,
The people pass whom You have ransomed.

[17]You will bring them and plant them in Your own mountain,
The place You made Your abode, O LORD,
The sanctuary, O LORD, which Your hands established.
[18]The LORD will reign for ever and ever!

[19]For the horses of Pharaoh, with his chariots and horsemen, went into the sea; and the LORD turned back on them the waters of the sea; but the Israelites marched on dry ground in the midst of the sea.

  [20]Then Miriam the prophetess, Aaron's sister, took a timbrel in her hand, and all the women went out after her in dance with timbrels. [21]And Miriam chanted for them,
  "Sing to the LORD, for He has triumphed gloriously;
  Horse and driver He has hurled into the sea."

[a]Others "song"
[b]Others "glorify"
[c]Others "mighty"

Though originally this 'Song by the Sea' may have stood as a poetic parallel to the previous prose description of the crossing,[24] as the text now stands, it constitutes Israel's *reaction* to that event—a hymn of praise and gratitude to God. Nevertheless, it still contains its own account of what transpired that elicited such a massive, heartfelt response. To be sure, as in the case of the prose narration, the song also speaks of the Egyptians and their chariots drowned together in the sea, covered by its waters. The song, however, additionally speaks of something else: "The waters piled up, the floods stood up like a mound, the deeps congealed in the heart of the sea. . . . [The] wind [did] blow, the sea covered [the Egyptians]; they sank like lead in the mighty waters" (author's translation). While the prose version portrays Israel as marching through the sea dry-shod with walls of water flanking her on either side, such images are absent from the poetic rendering. By contrast, the song's attention centers on a phenomenon of a very different sort—namely, a violent *storm*.

We must be careful here not to make the old rationalist move embracing the so-called 'natural' events of Scripture while

111

eschewing occurrences deemed as largely supernatural. That type of distinction is simply alien to the spirit and nature of biblical narrative.[25] And more than being alien, it is in the last analysis utterly irrelevant as well. For as we have seen before,[26] the fundamental issue is not whether the event per se is to be taken as either natural or supernatural. Rather, the question is whether the event is to be taken as a *sign* that points beyond itself to the God who is actively working *through* it. Thus, even if the 'supernaturalist' prose account were totally ignored while theological attention were focused exclusively on the more 'naturalistic' poetic depiction of the crossing, the basic problem would remain the same: Does this storm point to something beyond itself? Does it serve as evidence of the hand of God? Theoretically, of course, some Israelite could have turned around to see the drowning Egyptian host and said, 'What a lucky break—a gale at a time like this!' Such a response, however, becomes less and less tenable, less and less *reasonable*, when we remember that this windstorm is no isolated event, but another in a whole train of such wondrous happenings. In that context, i.e., in the context of the master story that has recounted, chronicled, and *unfolded* such occurrences, the far more appropriate response becomes the kind uttered in the song:

> Who is like you, YHWH, among the gods!
> Who is like you, majestic in holiness,
> Awesome in splendor, working wonders! (author's translation)

In its present placement in the canon, Israel's 'Song by the Sea' reflects a profound sensitivity to the true significance of all that has taken place. For the real culmination of these events is neither the slaying of Egypt's firstborn nor the drowning of its army, but the people's climactic confession of thanks and praise to its caring, saving Lord.

Obviously, however, if *none* of these events, whether natural or supernatural, ever really happened, then all our narrative-based claims about God and everything else would simply stand unjustified. Interestingly, while the general theme of Israel's deliverance from Egypt continues to resonate throughout the rest of Scripture, the plague account tends to be played down and muted.[27] But what if even the basic story line of this redemption saga never actually happened? What if, for instance, there never was a group of people enslaved in Egypt who unexpectedly won their release and then set out on a wilderness journey in search of their own new land? The answer is plain to see: the truth of virtually all the convictions arising from the Jewish master story, no matter how deeply or sincerely held, would be fatally undermined. And all of this because whatever other criteria of truth a story may incorporate, at the very least, it must be true to itself—*it must at least be true on its own terms.*[28] In a rock-bottom way, this narrative, like all narratives, entails certain ground rules for its proper understanding and for the justification of the various convictional claims that may stem from it.[29] Hence, for the Jewish master story and its 'conviction set,' the historical facticity of particular persons, places, and events cannot justifiably be ignored.

> [22]Then Moses caused Israel to set out from the Sea of Reeds. They went on into the wilderness of Shur; they traveled three days in the wilderness and found no water. [23]They came to Marah, but they could not drink the water of Marah because it was bitter; that is why it was named Marah.[d] [24]And the people grumbled against Moses, saying, "What shall we drink?" [25]So he cried out to the LORD, and the LORD showed him a piece of wood; he threw it into the water and the water became sweet.
>
> There He made for them a fixed rule, and there He put them to the test. [26]He said, "If you will heed the LORD your God diligently, doing what is upright in His sight, giving ear to His commandments and keeping all His laws, then I will not bring upon you any of the diseases that I brought upon the Egyptians, for I the LORD am your healer."
>
> [27]And they came to Elim, where there were twelve springs of water and seventy palm trees; and they encamped there beside the water.
>
> [d]I.e., "bitter"

Now that the Egyptians have been vanquished, we might be tempted to conclude the story here with the old, familiar tagline "and all the people lived happily ever after." Yet as the incident at Marah plainly shows, the people are far from accepting of their lot. God's work is clearly far from finished, and thus the story is far from over. Although the Israelites have only recently broken forth in song praising the Lord's mighty saving power, a bit of brackish water is enough to render them panic-stricken and untrusting once again.

Consequently, though some significant progress has been made, God faces even now no small degree of unbelief and unresponsiveness. While Israel may have been delivered from Egyptian servitude, she still has yet to be delivered fully to the service of her Lord. In a larger sense, the world too still awaits its full redemption, for while the Israelites' redemption has enabled them to overcome the evil of slavery in Egypt, evil itself remains nonetheless at large on earth. Doubtless, some other Pharaoh will arise, and some other manifestation of oppressive hardheartedness will reappear in history. In short, the Exodus brings neither evil nor history to an end. It instead offers *evidence from human history* that a happy ending to that history is a live option after all.[30] And the conditions for turning that hope into a reality, that promise given into a promise kept? "If you will faithfully heed the LORD your God, doing what is right in his eyes, giving ear to His commandments, observing all his laws" (author's translation).

Such words point not only to Israel's story's distant 'grand finale,' but more imminently, to its majestic denouement. Even the tenth plague and the crossing of the sea have failed to bring the Jewish master story to its true climax, and thus, it is to that storied high point—Sinai—that the narrative, Israel, and we now move together.

Notes

1. Thus, G. E. Wright in *God Who Acts*, for example, while rightly calling attention to the importance of biblical narrative for the doing of theology, has little or nothing to say about the significance of the 'non-narrative,' 'legal' sections found in Scripture. Moreover, although there are numerous commentaries on the story-laden book of Genesis, and to a somewhat lesser extent on Exodus as well, the number of works on the 'law books' of Leviticus and Numbers pales in comparison.

2. The classical Jewish commentators were quick to notice this point. Cf., for example, Rashi on Gen. 1:1 and Ibn Ezra and Ramban on Exod. 12:1-2.

3. Somone might wish to argue here that the 'real' basis of the injunction on Israel to redeem its firstborn males (rather than sacrifice them) was the desire to prohibit among Israelites the kind of practice found among their pagan neighbors. But even if that assertion were to prove *historically* valid, *theologically* its force would be minimal. For even if one were to be correct in pointing out such differentness, one would still be left with the task of explaining *the point* of Israel's being different. In other words, if Israel conceives of itself as being a different kind of community, wherein lies the significance of and the justification for that conception? For our part, we would claim that Israel's communal story is what provides the surest groundwork for understanding and interpreting Israel's communal self-image. Thus, while historical criticism offers an important tool for helping to construct—or reconstruct—the theological edifice, in the last analysis, it is not that edifice itself. Or as Childs has judiciously summed up the issue: "It is a source of frustration common to most readers of commentaries that so much energy is spent on the analysis of the pre-history of a text as to leave little for a treatment of the passage in its final form. The complaint is certainly justified. Ultimately the use of source and form criticism is exegetically deficient if these tools do not illuminate the canonical text" (*Book of Exodus*, p. 149). Ultimately, to overlook or ignore a community's canonical text and the role that final text plays in terms of the community's canonical practices is to lapse into the genetic fallacy in a most egregious way. For other instructive examples in the present section of the narrative connecting Israel's practices to Israel's story, see Exod. 12:39; 13:7-8; and 13:9.

4. Importantly, Exod. 13:8 gives a storied mode of explanation as the basis for Israel's observances; it specifically charges those entrusted with passing such observances on to the next generation, *v'higadata l'vincha*—literally, "And you shall *narrate* it to your child." Of course, it is the *haggada*—the narration of Israel's going out from

Egypt—that constitutes the basis of the traditional Jewish celebration of the Passover seder.

5. Thus, Stanley Hauerwas writes: "Any story that fails to provide institutional forms is powerless, for it is not enough merely to offer the story. One must know how to tell it in such a way that persons can become the story" (*Truthfulness and Tragedy*, p.97).

6. A medieval Jewish commentator cogently captures this idea when he notes: "The Israelites themselves were responsible in part for . . . their own redemption. . . . If they were willing to place their lives in danger in order to carry out the wishes of the Almighty, that would be a true token of their love of God. Consequently, God commanded them to slay the [lamb] under conditions of the widest publicity . . ., [slaughtering] it family by family, in groups and finally [sprinkling] its blood on the doorposts for every Egyptian passer-by to see, [thus] braving the vengeance of their former persecutors. Their fulfillment of every detail of this rite would be a proof of their complete faith in God" (*Ha-ketav Veha-kabbalah*, cited in Leibowitz, *Studies in Shemot*, p. 198).

7. Obviously, putting the blood on the doorposts is not the only way the Israelites are now to identify themselves as people who are the faithful followers of the Lord. All of the other practices prescribed here by God, e.g., eating unleavened bread and partaking of the Passover meal, also constitute ways that Israel distinctively marks itself as a people marked off to God. In precisely that sense, Jewish observance might best be viewed as the practice of various sign-acts *signifying* for what and Whom the Jewish people stands.

8. See again Exod. 2:23-25 and the commentary *ad loc.*

9. Ibid.

10. Cf. comments to Exod. 1:1-5.

11. The narrative seems clearly to imply that Egyptians who were willing to mark the doorposts of their houses could have found, along with the faithful Israelites, protection from "the Destroyer."

12. Cf., e.g., Gen. 15:13-14; Exod. 3:7-8; and Exod. 7:4. Typically, collective nouns are used.

13. This point has enormous theological import for the Holocaust—a time during which great numbers of individual Jews perished, but at the end of which the Jewish people, though severely weakened, nevertheless still lived on. Hence, from the vantage point of Exodus at least, the Holocaust raises no significant challenge to the working of God's providence; such providence can still be found operative as always at the corporate, communal level.

14. For other references in Exodus to Israel as God's "armies," cf. 13:18; 7:4; and 12:41. Furthermore, leaving aside the putative moral problem of Israel's despoiling the Egyptians (12:36), the image rendered within the context of the narrative is plainly one of a triumphant army carrying off the spoils of war. Author's translation.

15. The same Hebrew root *shlch*—"send forth"—is used in each case. See also Exod. 12:23 where the root word appears again in describing how the whole Egyptian people presses Israel to get going. The point of such texts is unmistakable. Whereas previously Egypt had repeatedly refused to obey the Lord's command to let his people go, now they can hardly comply fast enough! As God had earlier predicted in Exod. 11:1 (and 6:1 as well), the Egyptians don't simply 'release' the Israelites—they virtually *drive them out!*

16. See commentary to Exod. 1:8-12.

17. Cf. Exod. 13:17, above.

18. As the narrative now stands, the tenth plague, though culminating in Israel's release from Egypt, has not culminated in either Israel's *or* Egypt's full recognition or acknowledgment of the Lord. It appears, therefore, that they both need another lesson, i.e., another mighty act striking the Egyptians while simultaneously saving the Israelites.

Such an act, however, would seem to have all the earmarks of another plague; consequently, the tenth plague, instead of being the last in a series, becomes the penultimate in the chain. Contemporary biblical scholarship explains this 'transformation' by ascribing the killing of the first-born to J while attributing the drowning of the Egyptian host to P, for whom the plagues serve not simply or primarily to gain Israel's liberation, but more significantly, to make known God's power and sovereignty to all who witness or hear of these awesome acts. And indeed, the present canonical redaction of these various sources into one overarching narrative squarely puts the portrayal and meaning of the people Israel's release from bondage into the framework of a larger story of all peoples coming to know the Lord.

19. Childs, *Book of Exodus*, pp. 225-26.

20. *Mechilta d'Rabbi Ishmael*, Beshallach, chap. 4.

21. As before with the onset of the Egyptians' attempt at genocide and the beginning of the plagues, the appearance of water marks a major turning point in the narrative.

22. Notice as well that below, in v. 21, a strong wind from God precedes the crossing of the sea; a similar wind also preceded the creation of the world. Moreover, both the world's creation and the sea's crossing are predicated on a division of the waters; cf. Gen. 1:6-10 and Exod. 14:21.

23. Compare 14:21 with 7:19.

24. See Childs, *Book of Exodus*, pp. 243-48.

25. As Childs rightly states: "The elements of the wonderful and the ordinary are constitutive to the greatest of Old Testament events.

There never was a time when the event was only understood as ordinary, nor was there a time when the supernatural absorbed the natural. But Israel saw the mighty hand of God at work in both the ordinary and the wonderful, and never sought to fragment the one great act of redemption into parts" (ibid., p. 238).

26. Cf. the commentary to Exod. 7:10-13 and n. 2 *ad loc.*

27. See Childs, *Book of Exodus*, p. 169, and see as well his comments on p. 143 where he notes how out of keeping the plague account seems to be with the rest of the Exodus narrative due to its "stereotyped, inflexible framework [which gives it] a flavor of historical unreality."

28. See my specific remarks on Exod. 1:11, above.

29. Cf. the author's *Theology and Narrative*, pp. 214-26.

30. For a fine summary statement of this point, see Irving Greenberg's "Judaism and History: Historical Events and Religious Change," in *Perspectives in Jewish Learning* 1:44-45.

VII
EXODUS 19:1–20:14; 24:3-8

19:1On the third new moon after the Israelites had gone forth from the land of Egypt, on that very day, they entered the wilderness of Sinai. 2Having journeyed from Rephidim, they entered the wilderness of Sinai and encamped in the wilderness. Israel encamped there in front of the mountain, 3and Moses went up to God. The LORD called to him from the mountain, saying, "Thus shall you say to the house of Jacob and declare to the children of Israel:4 'You have seen what I did to the Egyptians, how I bore you on eagles' wings and brought you to Me. 5Now then, if you will obey Me faithfully and keep My covenant, you shall be My treasured possession among all the peoples. Indeed, all the earth is Mine, 6but you shall be to Me a kingdom of priests and a holy nation.' These are the words that you shall speak to the children of Israel."

The story has come full circle. Moses first encountered God in the middle of the wilderness where he responded to a call. Now he—and Israel—meet the Lord there again and are asked to respond to such a call once more. From the beginning, even at the burning bush, the story pointed forward to this moment: "And when you have brought the people from Egypt, you shall serve God at this mountain" (Exod. 3:12). Later, back in Egypt, in virtually all the confrontations with Pharaoh, one goal was repeatedly articulated with single-minded purpose: to let the people go out to the wilderness so that they might serve the Lord.1 The present gathering at the mountain is thus

119

no chance encounter, but a prearranged rendezvous, where both the narrative and God's plan will meet their culmination. Somehow, Israel's destiny lies at this destination; the fulfillment, the *meaning*, of her exodus is tied to Sinai and God's service. As long as the Israelites were in Egypt, they were bound to Pharaoh's service; now, at Sinai, they are finally free for the service of the Lord.

But what kind of service might that be? "You shall be to Me a kingdom of priests and a holy nation." As priests' service has two sides, so Israel's service shall be twofold as well. For the priestly service is not simply ministering to the deity; it is more basically ministering to the deity by ministering to those who would draw near to him. Such is the model for the sacred service that Israel is now called upon to do: she is to serve the Lord by enabling others to serve him also. The Lord's mighty saving acts in the Exodus have firmly secured his reputation; there is indeed none like him in all the earth.[2] If Israel now accepts the call to enter into his service—which is simultaneously the service of humanity—she will be consecrated as God's own priestly people, and thus become, like him, distinctively known throughout all the world as unique, special, *holy*. And in the process of performing such mutual service to God *and* world, this lowly band of former Egyptian slaves shall be transformed, assuming a majesty among the nations.

But as enticing as the Lord's words may sound, why should Israel place her trust in them? Why should she stake her life on them and thus act as though they might come true? The answer is not hard to find: because of what has come true already. As God reminds the people, "You have seen what I did to the Egyptians, and how I bore you on eagles' wings and brought you to Me." The people's warrant for believing that God can redeem his promise here is that he has redeemed their lives heretofore. Hence, by faithfully binding their lives to God at Sinai now, they will be binding their future to a provenly faithful, life-sustaining Lord.[3]

[7]Moses came and summoned the elders of the people and put before them all the words that the LORD had commanded him. [8]All the people answered as one saying, "All that the LORD has

spoken we will do!" And Moses brought back the people's words to the LORD. [9]And the LORD said to Moses, "I will come to you in a thick cloud, in order that the people may hear when I speak with you and so trust you thereafter." Then Moses reported the people's words to the LORD, [10]and the LORD said to Moses, "Go to the people and warn them to stay pure[a] today and tomorrow. Let them wash their clothes. [11]Let them be ready for the third day; for on the third day the LORD will come down, in the sight of all the people, on Mount Sinai. [12]You shall set bounds for the people round about, saying, 'Beware of going up the mountain or touching the border of it. Whoever touches the mountain shall be put to death: [13]no hand shall touch him, but he shall be either stoned or pierced through; beast or man, he shall not live.' When the ram's horn [b]sounds a long blast,[b] they shall come up unto the mountain."

[14]Moses came down from the mountain to the people and warned the people to stay pure, and they washed their clothes. [15]And he said to the people, "Be ready for the third day: do not go near a woman."

[16]On the third day, as morning dawned, there was thunder, and lightning, and a dense cloud upon the mountain, and a very loud blast of the horn; and all the people who were in the camp trembled. [17]Moses led the people out of the camp toward God, and they took their places at the foot of the mountain.

[18]Now Mount Sinai was all in smoke, for the LORD had come down upon it in fire; the smoke rose like the smoke of a kiln, and the whole mountain[c] trembled violently. [19]The blare of the horn grew louder and louder. As Moses spoke, God answered him in thunder. [20]The LORD came down upon Mount Sinai, on the top of the mountain, and the LORD called Moses to the top of the mountain and Moses went up. [21]The LORD said to Moses, "Go down, warn the people not to break through to the LORD to gaze, lest many of them perish. [22]The priests also, who come near the LORD, must purify themselves, lest the LORD break out against them." [23]But Moses said to the LORD, "The people cannot come up to Mount Sinai, for You warned us saying, 'Set bounds about the mountain and sanctify it.'" [24]So the LORD said to him, "Go down, and come back together with Aaron; but let not the priests or the people break through to come up to the LORD, lest He break out against them." [25]And Moses went down to the people and spoke to them.

[a]Cf. v. 15
[b-b]Meaning of Heb. uncertain
[c]Some Hebrew manuscripts and the Greek, "all the people"; cf. v. 16

The story line here seems somewhat tangled and so becomes increasingly hard to follow. As one commentator has observed, "Moses is pictured as ascending and descending Mount Sinai at least three times without any apparent purpose."[4]

Nevertheless, what brackets Moses' trips up and down the mountain makes one thing very clear: some sort of negotiating process appears to be taking place between God and Israel, with Moses serving as a kind of 'covenantal middleman.' For his part, the Lord has held out to Israel some rather bright prospects for the future. And yet, at this point in the story, what God has put forward still remains only a proposal, an *offer*, awaiting the people's reply: "Now then, *if* you will obey Me faithfully and keep My covenant. . . ." Just as Israel's release from serving Pharaoh has left her free to begin to serve the Lord, it has to that same extent also left her free to reject his overture. Indeed, were she now to find herself in the position of being forced or pressed into his service, what would the exodus have in the end accomplished? The Israelites would have merely gone from serving one Pharaoh back in Egypt to serving another Pharaoh in the wilderness, perhaps the greatest Pharaoh in the world! For the narrative to make sense, the Lord must be a significantly different kind of king, a significantly different kind of *character*, than the king of Egypt. And surely, after all that has transpired to this point, how could the one depicted previously as Israel's caring, gracious savior possibly be pictured now as just another autocratic tyrant? As call-and-response has consistently marked the previous relationship between God and human beings, here again the divine call has been sent out in search of a human response, freely given.

What will the people's reaction be: one of acceptance—or rejection? The talks get under way as Moses informs the people of God's general offer (v. 7); he subsequently reports back to God their initially favorable response (v. 8). Apparently, the time has come to hear the specifics of the deal. However, before the Lord can go into the details of the proposed new pact, some further *ground*work needs be done.

For Israel to be allied with God, reflecting his holiness to the world, her character must be like his, and consequently, the people must take some steps even now to prepare themselves for the Lord and for his service. Bounds must be set and precautions must be taken to ensure Israel's purity and sanctity as well as God's (Exod. 19:10, 12, 14, 21-24). Hence, Moses is once again enlisted as a go-between; he ascends and descends Sinai, relaying messages between the parties at the mountain's base and summit (Exod. 19:9, 14, 19-20, 25).

Finally, everything is in order. While a covenant has been proposed, and while the people have so far eagerly responded, the covenant's conditions—and implications—have yet to be revealed. At last, the moment has arrived for God to begin laying out the particulars of the compact—those obligations to which Israel shall be asked to commit her life:

20:1God spoke all these words,ª saying:

²I the LORD am your God who brought you out of the land of Egypt, the house of bondage: ³You shall have no other gods beside Me.

⁴You shall not make for yourself a sculptured image, or any likeness of what is in the heavens above, or on the earth below, or in the waters under the earth. ⁵You shall not bow down to them or serve them. For I the LORD your God am an impassioned God, visiting the guilt of the fathers upon the children, upon the third and upon the fourth generations of those who reject Me, ⁶but showing kindness to the thousandth generation of those who love Me and keep My commandments.

⁷You shall not ᵇswear falsely byᵇ the name of the LORD your God; for the LORD will not clear one who swears falsely by His name.

⁸Remember the sabbath day and keep it holy. ⁹Six days you shall labor and do all your work, ¹⁰but the seventh day is a sabbath of the LORD your God: you shall not do any work—you, your son or daughter, your male or female slave, or your cattle, or the stranger who is within your settlements. ¹¹For in six days the LORD made heaven and earth and sea, and all that is in them, and He rested on the seventh day; therefore the LORD blessed the sabbath day and hallowed it.

¹²Honor your father and your mother, that you may long endure on the land which the LORD your God is giving you.

¹³You shall not murder.

You shall not commit adultery.

You shall not steal.

You shall not bear false witness against your neighbor.

¹⁴You shall not covet your neighbor's house: you shall not covet your neighbor's wife, or his male or female slave, or his ox or his ass, or anything that is your neighbor's.

ᵃTradition varies as to the division of the Commandments in vv. 2-14, and as to the numbering of the verses from 13 on
ᵇ⁻ᵇOthers "take in vain"

At the burning bush, God's revelation of his plans for Israel was accompanied by the revelation of his name. Now, at Sinai, those plans are about to reach their fulfillment with Israel's entry into the covenant. Strikingly, at the covenant's introduction is the reintroduction of the Name, thereby making manifest to all that God is most rightly recognized as Lord when his purposes are properly recognized as well: "I am YHWH, your God,[5] who brought you out of the land of Egypt, out of the house of bondage: You shall have no other gods beside Me." The redeemer God and the God of the covenant are in the end the same God. He is the one to whom Israel ought genuinely to be obliged, because he is the one to whom Israel truly owes her life.[6]

The Lord starts specifying the covenant's conditions. Importantly, the first terms presented—i.e., the Ten Commandments—do not form the full disclosure of the pact, but only its initial clauses. After all, at this juncture of the story, Israel has taken but her first steps toward following the Lord. In order to keep on following him, not only must she still take a long journey across the wilderness, but along the way she must undertake several more such covenantal obligations.[7] What the Decalogue therefore represents in the building of God's pact-bound people is its *cornerstone* rather than its *capstone*.

Thus, these inaugural commandments aim at inaugurating a community of which God himself shall be a member.[8] They mean to lay the groundwork for what this covenant community will need if it is to progress from here, i.e., the

same thing it has required to come this far: firm and basic *trust.*
To remain allied with Israel, the Lord, for his part, must be able
to trust that the people will remain allied with him; that they
will not enter into the service of other gods; that they will not
resort to graven images and magical formulae to overturn the
covenantal relationship in order to have him do *their* bidding;[9]
that they will not lay claim to that which belongs to him and
him alone.[10] For their part, the people must be able to trust that
the Lord will stand as the covenant's (and thus the
community's) ultimate guardian and guarantor—the one who
will not stand for such acts of treachery and betrayal as theft,
adultery, and murder.[11] Significantly, through such trust in
God, the people can come to trust one another, facing the
future together without anyone's having to fear that while he
is looking the other way, a fellow Israelite will snatch away his
property, spouse, or life. Hence, by being committed to the
Lord, the people in the process will become committed to one
another; in the bargain, this ragtag band of outcasts will
become a community—*a people*—in the profoundest sense.
Earlier, in Israel's making her preparations to enter God's holy
presence, bounds had to be set around the mountain. Now, for
Israel to enter the Lord's holy service, covenantal bounds must
be set to mark the outer limits of the community-to-be. As
Childs has summed it up: "One who breaks these commands
sets himself outside the established life of God's people. To
transgress is not to commit a misdemeanor but to break the
very fibre of which the divine-human relation consists."[12] For a
cohesive community to be formed, a compact must be made at
whose heart stand these primary obligations. For this
particular community to be founded, such *covenantal duties*
must rest at its foundation.[13]

> [24:3]Moses went and repeated to the people all the commands of
> the Lord and all the norms; and all the people answered with
> one voice, saying, "All the things that the Lord has commanded
> we will do!" [4]Moses then wrote down all the commands of the
> Lord.
>   Early in the morning, he set up an altar at the foot of the

mountain, with twelve pillars for the twelve tribes of Israel. ⁵He delegated young men among the Israelites, and they offered burnt offerings and sacrificed bulls as offerings of well-being to the Lᴏʀᴅ. ⁶Moses took one part of the blood and put it in basins, and the other part of the blood he dashed against the altar. ⁷Then he took the record of the covenant and read it aloud to the people. And they said, "All that the Lord has spoken ᵃwe will faithfully do!"ᵃ ⁸Moses took the blood and dashed it on the people and said, "This is the blood of the covenant which the Lᴏʀᴅ now makes with you concerning all these commands."

ᵃ⁻ᵃLit. "we will do and obey"

Following God's disclosure of the first commandments in Exodus 20:1-14, the flow of the story's action—and dialogue—becomes once more problematic.[14] Yet as before, certain other elements in the narrative remain sharply well defined. Moses and the people learn (in chaps. 21–24) that their obligations shall include several more than just the initial ten; these precepts too are to be counted as part of the covenant at Sinai. Furthermore, when Moses had previously put God's general proposal before the people, they had enthusiastically responded. Now that they have heard the covenant's specifics, their enthusiasm seems in no way diminished. Not once, but twice, the people fervently voice their affirmation, "All that the Lᴏʀᴅ has spoken we will faithfully do!" All that remains is for the pact to be formally signed and sealed.

"Then Moses took the blood and dashed it on the people." Previously, Moses has taken blood and splashed it at the altar, i.e., 'in the direction' of the Lord. In other words, this is a covenant signed in blood, a mutually binding pact sealed with life itself. For this contract to take effect, it must take hold in Israel's communal life while God in turn takes care to keep that community alive—a community that is now *his* community as well. From here on, at the center of the story of Israel and her Lord will stand the chronicle of their covenantal relationship, its ups and downs, its observances and breaches. Of course, all through this Jewish master story of the Exodus, we have repeatedly found inklings of that kind of relationship. Yet as the story has awaited Sinai for the narrative to reach its climax, the covenant has likewise awaited Sinai for the bond between God and Israel to find its articulation. Thus, Sinai represents more than the rendezvous point in the Jewish master story where the Lord and the children of Israel are reunited; it is the turning point in Jewish history where God and the Jewish people are firmly united as allies trying to unite the world. But while the Jews may be the first to be enlisted in God's service, they are by no means to be the last. For as we saw above, the people Israel's task—its *sacred* task—is to enable other peoples also to draw near to God and in so doing, to draw near to each other too. If Israel's oppression in Egypt reflected a breakdown in creation, with some creatures setting up false barriers against others on the basis of false claims of who is truly the Creator,[15] then the Exodus stands as a beginning toward restoring the world to its proper order—and to its rightful Lord.

However, precisely because it is but a beginning, the real fulfillment of the Exodus must lie *beyond* the scope of the Exodus master story itself. As we concluded earlier,[16] the Exodus does not bring history to an end as though to work out all of history in advance. But what the Exodus does do in fact is bring some proof from history, namely, the evidence of Jewish history, that there is some reason to believe that history may yet work out *if* God and humankind will work together. Or to put it another way: God and humankind can keep their hope in the world, providing *both* parties are willing to keep their commitments to each other. Consequently, the Exodus as a master story serves as a model, a guide, for suggesting how we are to go on from here. It thus not only relates some past events in the life of one particular people, but simultaneously holds out a vision of how the life of all peoples may be sustained—and even transformed!—in the future. Hence, in the last analysis, the Exodus master story is quite literally one of *promise,* speaking of our duties and obligations as well as of the world's hopes and dreams.

Notes

1. Cf. Exod. 7:16, 26; 8:16; 9:1, 13; 10:3; cf. as well Lev. 25:55.
2. Cf. Exod. 9:14.
3. Importantly, God's covenantal proposal here contains no threat of sanctions. Whatever compelling force there is behind the offer comes from its reminder of the past benefits that Israel has received from being allied with the Lord and of the gracious boon yet to be realized if she will continue that alliance—she shall be God's own "treasured possession among all the peoples."

This aspect of the narrative's portrayal of Israel's entry into the covenant has a significant consequence. It distinguishes her pact with God from the 'Hittite Suzerainty Treaty,' which some scholars have too quickly identified as the model for the covenant at Sinai. In such treaties, the liege lord typically concludes his compact with his (conquered) vassals by threatening them with severe sanctions should they break the agreement. Thus, the Hittite sovereign undergirds his alliance with oaths vowing what he will do *to* his people for their noncompliance. In the Sinai account, by contrast, Israel's King underwrites his covenant with promises pledging what he shall do *for* his people in return for their steadfastness.

Moreover, the master story here preceding the enunciation of the concrete terms of the covenant—i.e., the commandments—keenly undercuts the theological constructs of various sorts of 'orthodoxy' which would claim that regarding the performance of these commandments which are none other than 'manifestations of God's will,' human reason is of little consequence at best and of great impediment at worst. Besides the shadow cast on that claim by the biblical account, the philosopher Alasdair MacIntyre also has some pertinent things to say which similarly call in question these purportedly orthodox beliefs. First, in his book, *A Short History of Ethics* (New York: Macmillan, 1966), MacIntyre points out the traditional biblical rationale underlying the commandments: "God is our father. God commands us to obey him. We ought to obey God because he knows what is best for us, and what is best for us is to obey him. We fail to obey him and so become estranged from him. We therefore need to learn how to be reconciled to God so that we can once more live in a familial relationship with him. These themes are of course susceptible of doctrinal development in a number of quite different directions" (p. 111). In a later work, *Against the Self-Images of the Age* (New York: Schocken Books, 1971), MacIntyre goes on to describe what subsequently happened to that traditional biblical rationale: "The Protestant Reformation changes [all] this. First, because human beings are totally corrupt, their nature cannot be a foundation for [judging what is good]. And next, because men cannot

128

judge God, we obey God's commandments not because God is good, but simply because He is God. So the . . . law is a collection of arbitrary fiats unconnected with anything we may want or desire" (pp. 123-24).

But such an understanding, divorced from any notion of 'the good,' let alone from any story-based idea of God's character, makes the performance of the commandments quite literally irrational! While some may pride themselves on such irrational obedience, from the vantage point of the master story of the Exodus, that is certainly *not* what the people Israel glories in. Rather, her pride and glory is in her having been previously redeemed by God. It is from just that reason, that fact, that *debt*, of the Lord's having saved her life before—and of his promising to do so again in the future—that Israel owes him her covenantal faithfulness, and that she ought thus to keep the commandments that delineate the details for maintaining that relationship between herself and God.

4. Childs, *Book of Exodus*, p. 344. Childs suggests that part of the difficulty lies in the fact that two different sources, J and E, have apparently been fused together in the final redacted version; see pp. 350-55.

5. Even though NJPS has "I the Lord am your God" (a syntactical possibility followed by exegetes like Ibn Ezra), nevertheless, in light of both recent studies *and* the present narrative context, the preferred translation here seems to me to be, "I am the Lord your God."

6. Cf. Childs, *Book of Exodus*, p. 401. Cf. also n. 3, above.

7. See, for example, the subsequent commandments given in the so-called 'Book of the Covenant' immediately following the present chapter; not until after these additional commandments have been given is the whole of the Sinaitic covenant presented to the people (in chap. 24) for their ratification. See the commentary to 24:3-8, below.

8. I am indebted to Professor James McClendon for this insight.

9. In the ancient Near East, idols representing the deity and various invocations of his name in spells and incantations were typically used in pagan rites of sympathetic magic. Through such rites, the cult's adherents tried to manipulate the deity such that his will conformed to theirs and so that his power was thus in actuality a manifestation of their own.

From the perspective of the second and third commandments, however, the dynamic of the relationship between the Lord and his followers flows the other way. In order to be the Lord's adherents, the service Israel carries out must be one in which her will conforms to his, such that to whatever degree she finds herself empowered by and through that service, the Lord himself nevertheless clearly stands as the sole and ultimate source of all her strength. Hence, in these first few commandments—the covenant's first 'clauses'—Israel is asked to act in a way commensurate with the belief that her Lord is indeed the holy God, that is, the One who though involved with the world, nonetheless stands unequivocally 'above' and 'beyond' all else in it—including all the magic in the world as well. The people's willingness to act out that conviction will serve as credible testimony to the claim that the Lord can be trusted to come to their aid without their first having to resort to various (and ultimately useless) attempts at coercing or manipulating him. More than that, however, Israel's willingness to live by such faith in God shall provide the staunchest evidence that she can in turn be trusted to be God's true and faithful people.

10. The commandment enjoining observance of the sabbath is more than merely a reminder of the world's creation: it is, more basically, a reminder of the world's *Creator*. Consequently, if the people will cease from all creation on that day and thus let the rest of creation—humans and animals alike (Exod. 20:10)—have its caesura also, their action—or rather, their *inaction*—will display a fundamental truth about the world: it does not *belong* to them (mere creatures among others!) to control, use, or dispose of as they wish. Instead, the earth's true lord and master is someone else—the same One, it turns out, who is Israel's lord and master, too. Cf. Deut. 5:12-15 for another expression of the same idea.

11. Originally, the point of the fifth commandment was that parents should be able to trust their children not to betray them when they had become old by abandoning them to die. A notion of trust similarly lies at the heart of the prohibition against coveting. The biblical term *chamad* signifies something more than mere wishful thinking; it connotes an active scheming, plotting, or *intrigue* meant to get one's hands on that which at present is someone else's.

12. Childs, *Book of Exodus*, p. 398.

13. Obviously, on the interpretation presented here, the Decalogue does not stand as the distillate of 'universal reason' or as the manifestation of 'natural law.' Though the precepts contained in Exod. 20:2-14 may have some resemblance and even application to the basic regulations concerning other communal ways of life, nevertheless, these Ten Commandments in general—and the first four in particular—gain their greatest significance in the context of regulating the way of life of a community called Israel—a community called to be *God's own special people*.

Moreover, these covenantal bonds between God and Israel are fundamentally misunderstood if they are seen as the mutually, reasonably agreed upon conditions of some formative social contract à la Rousseau or Hobbes. They are, after all, termed *mitsvot*—i.e., "*commandments*." Thus, while the rationale for Hobbes' society's underpinnings may have its source in some primal myth about the state of nature, the roots of Israel's self-understanding go back to her master story of the Exodus from Egypt.

From the standpoint of *that* narrative, it seems that a more appropriate and fruitful model for understanding the kind of communal bonds formed between God and Israel is *not* that of a group of equal strangers meeting in the state of nature, but that of a band of potential recruits called on to enlist in the great cause of a proven military leader. To be sure, under his direction, the members of that band have already personally experienced a taste of the final promised triumph over the powers arrayed against him. But to gain that ultimate victory, he needs their help, for without troops, he cannot wage the battle. Even more fundamentally, if he has no *followers*, he cannot truly be said to be a *leader*. Hence, if these first few will now enlist in his service, they will occupy a special place, comprising his prime, hand-picked troops. However, if they *do* sign up—and the decision is freely theirs—they do so 'for the duration' and with the understanding that *he* is their supreme and sole commander whose commands to them are from this point forward forever binding upon them all.

For additional remarks concerning Israel as God's 'troops,' see the commentary and notes to Exod. 12:41, above.

14. Modern critics have tended to explain the problem as the result of the 'grafting' of one narrative sequence onto another. They have suggested that the 'original' sequence was 19:1-19; 20:18-21; 20:1-17; 24:3ff. Onto this basic framework, they conclude, chaps. 19:20-25; 20:15-18; and 24:1ff. were later added. Cf. Childs, *Book of Exodus*, pp. 453-56.

15. See the commentary to Exod. 1 in general and to vv. 8-12 in particular.

16. See my previous comments on Exod. 15:22-27.

THE CHRISTIAN
MASTER STORY

VIII
MATTHEW 1

¹The book of the genealogy of Jesus Christ, the son of David, the son of Abraham.

In its very first sentence, this Christian master story tells us something absolutely essential for understanding all that is to follow. First and foremost, *this* story is related to another that starts with Abraham and runs through David; that, of course, is none other than the story of the Jews. From beginning to end, this narrative presupposes that one—and a thorough knowledge of it. Hence, the appearance of the Greek word *genesis* in the beginning of Matthew is more than mere circumstance. It calls to mind Israel's ancient tale of the world's genesis and thus hints to us that it too may just speak of events that mark the dawn of a new creation.[1]

In one respect, however, there is a crucial difference between the opening lines of the Christian and Jewish master stories. The initial verse of Exodus introduces the people Israel as the focal point of the story's action and development. But Matthew introduces us to someone else as the story's prime 'lead' and bearer. The focus for Matthew's story is not an entire people, but instead a single person: Jesus Christ.

And so we are not at all sure what to make of Matthew. So far, he has informed us that his story is tied to that other narrative originating with creation and continuing to Abraham and David. But he has yet to explain exactly how that tie is made. Is the present story just one more episode in Israel's long, ongoing story? Or does this narrative about Jesus Christ—about Jesus *Messiah*—constitute instead the climactic chapter in Israel's story, thus bringing it to its long-awaited end? How then does Matthew's story about the savior Jesus fit in with that prior Jewish story about salvation, Exodus?

At best, Matthew's initial verse sheds only a little light on issues such as these. For the most part, we are still completely in the dark. We have no choice, therefore, but to turn to the rest of the story to look for the answers to our questions. Of course, that is precisely how it should be for any story worth the telling.

[2]Abraham was the father of Isaac and Isaac the father of Jacob, and Jacob the father of Judah and his brothers, [3]and Judah the father of Perez* and Zerah by Tamar, and Perez the father of Hezron, and Hezron the father of Ram,[a] [4]and Ram the father of Amminadab, and Amminadab the father of Nahshon, and Nahshon the father of Salmon, [5]and Salmon the father of Boaz by Rahab, and Boaz the father of Obed by Ruth, and Obed, the father of Jesse, [6]and Jesse the father of David the king.

And David was the father of Solomon by the wife of Uriah, [7]and Solomon the father of Rehoboam, and Rehoboam the father of Abijah, and Abijah the father of Asa,[b] [8]and Asa the father of Jehoshaphat, and Jehoshaphat the father of Joram, and Joram the father of Uzziah, [9]and Uzziah the father of Jotham, and Jotham the father of Ahaz, and Ahaz the father of Hezekiah, [10]and Hezekiah the father of Manasseh, and Manasseh the father of Amos,[c] and Amos the father of Josiah, [11]and Josiah the father of Jechoniah and his brothers, at the time of the deportation to Babylon.

[12]And after the deportation to Babylon: Jechoniah was the father of Shealtiel,[d] and Shealtiel the father of Zerubbabel, [13]and Zerubbabel the father of Abiud, and Abiud the father of Eliakim, and Eliakim the father of Azor, [14]and Azor the father of Zadok, and Zadok the father of Achim, and Achim the father of Eliud, [15]and Eliud the father of Eleazar, and Eleazar the father of Matthan, and Matthan the father of Jacob, [16]and Jacob the father of Joseph the husband of Mary, of whom Jesus was born, who is called Christ.

[17]So all the generations from Abraham to David were fourteen generations, and from David to the deportation to

Babylon fourteen generations, and from the deportation to
Babylon to the Christ fourteen generations.

*I have omitted the RSV's diacritical marks.
ᵃGreek *Aram*
ᵇGreek *Asaph*
ᶜOther authorities read *Amon*
ᵈGreek *Salathiel*

In the first verse, we have heard that the present narrative is
somehow tied to the story of Israel; the verses that follow now
help to show where the connection lies. While verse 1 may have
reminded us of the world's beginnings, verses 2 through 17
draw our attention to more specific beginnings—those of Jesus.
And as we look at Jesus' line, we notice something quite
remarkable about it. It is none other than the story line of Israel!
Jesus stands in line with a story that begins with Abraham,
ascends to David "the king," plummets with the Babylonian
exile, and now finally converges on him "who is called Christ."

But what exactly does that mean? What does it mean to say
that Israel's story 'comes together' in Jesus Christ? As his
genealogy plainly shows us, understanding the relationship of
Jesus to Israel's larger narrative hinges on our understanding
first his relationship to Israel's storied ancestors.

Not surprisingly, the first of Jesus' family ties is made with
Abraham, progenitor of both Israel and her story. Still, why
forge the first link here? Why not instead trace Jesus all the way
back to Adam—progenitor of all humankind? After all, if we
are seeking a narrative that really is a *master story*, we must find
one whose significance extends beyond Israel herself.

And yet, what is Israel's story but just that? At its most
fundamental level, what that narrative has to say about one
particular people carries a universal promise for all peoples. As
that story tells it, Abraham was the first person to receive that
story's promise—a promise guaranteed by God:

> I will make of you a great nation,
> And I will bless you;
> I will make your name great,
> And you shall be a blessing:

I will bless those who bless you
And curse him that curses you;
All the families of the earth
Shall bless themselves by you. (Gen. 12:2-3)

Hence, as Abraham's descendant, Jesus now stands as both the heir to that promise and the bearer of that blessing made not only to Abraham and Israel, but indeed to all the world.

We look again at Jesus' genealogy and see that his pedigree reaches back to another of Israel's cherished ancestors—King David. In being so linked with David, Jesus' line thus becomes a royal one, and moreover, the royal line in Israel *par excellence*. Although others may from time to time lay claim to kingship over Israel, nevertheless in the end they all remain mere pretenders to the throne. That seat of rightful authority over Israel belongs to David's house alone, for as we recall, David too has been the object of God's promise and God's blessing: "Your house and your kingship shall ever be secure before you; your throne shall be established forever" (II Sam. 7:16).

But Jesus shares more with David than an eternally legitimate claim as Israel's king. More importantly, he shares in common the title of *Messiah*—"the anointed one of God." In her history, Israel has seen others (such as Saul and Cyrus) temporarily designated as God's anointed. Through it all, though, David's claim still stands firm. He remains Israel's paradigmatic messiah, forever appointed by Israel's God, "who grants wondrous victories to his king and deals graciously with his anointed [*limshicho*], with David, and with his offspring evermore."[2] And now that titled claim is borne by Jesus Christ. Now *he* is God's anointed, the one appointed throughout history to bring God's people victory and salvation.

With the coming of Jesus Christ, therefore, history itself has come to a critical turning point—perhaps to *the* critical turning point: "So all the generations from Abraham to David were fourteen generations, and from David to the deportation to Babylon fourteen generations, and from the deportation to Babylon to the Christ fourteen generations." With Jesus, the Christ, a new and critical epoch in history has begun.[3] On the one hand, Jesus' epoch follows an earlier period that had witnessed a sharp rise in Israel's fortunes; David's kingdom seemed to be an actual fulfillment of God's promised blessing to Abraham. On the other hand, however, Jesus' epoch more immediately follows another era—the Babylonian exile—that saw Israel's historical fortunes in steep decline; even her subsequent restoration to the land under Zerubbabel had been a disappointment, falling far short of the glory days of David. Consequently, God's promise—the promise of history itself— that once seemed so firmly established, now appears to be very much in question, resting on extremely shaky ground. Hence, if Jesus truly is the one appointed by God to bring victory and salvation, his arrival at this time may signify God's answer to Israel's question for all time: Can God's promise be vindicated, and can human history thus be saved?

But at any rate, Jesus' credentials seem to be very much in order, giving him roots that go deep in Israel's story. And yet, if we look at Jesus' lineage a little more closely, we notice something that seems a bit odd and out of place. While Jesus' origins may derive from such 'kosher' ancestors as Abraham and David, they also go back to such 'sullied' stock as Tamar, Rahab, Ruth, and Bathsheba. In the kind of biblical genealogy typically reserved for the names of men alone, finding women's names would be unusual enough. But finding women such as these included in a genealogy meant to show 'the purity of the line' is simply inconceivable! After all, who are Tamar, Rahab, and Ruth but women who originate among the gentile nations with whom Israel is forbidden to intermarry? Even worse, Tamar, Rahab, and Bathsheba are women who have been 'tainted' by scandals involving prostitution and adultery. Something strange is indeed going on. With all the stress laid on Jesus' unbroken ties to Abraham, father of Israel, and David, king of Israel, what possible purpose can it serve to tie Israel's Messiah to those outside of Israel, and especially, to those whose relationships with Israel have been up to now prohibited?

One thing more about Jesus' descent seems peculiar too. All through the account of generations leading up to Jesus, we have heard (monotonously) repeated, "So-and-so was the father of Such-and-such and Such-and-such was the father of . . ." Yet when we come to Jesus himself, we hear something altogether different: "and Jacob the father of Joseph *the husband* of Mary, *of whom Jesus was born*" (italics added). What a pall of suspicion has suddenly been cast over Jesus' origins—and Jesus' standing in Israel and her story! For if Joseph is not his father, then who is?

A little while ago, everything seemed so clear; with bloodlines going all the way back to Abraham and David, Jesus' status in Israel could hardly be more exalted. Now, however, everything seems muddled and confused; we aren't even clear about who Jesus' own father is. And so our doubts begin to surface. Here is Jesus, a person of dubious origins. His immediate origins in Israel are unknown, and some of his ancestral origins are known to lie outside Israel, suspect and forbidden. Can this Jesus, then, still be the one promised in Israel's story generation after generation?

> [18]Now the birth of Jesus Christ[f] took place in this way. When his mother Mary had been betrothed to Joseph, before they came together she was found to be with child of the Holy Spirit; [19]and her husband Joseph, being a just man and unwilling to put her to shame, resolved to divorce her quietly. [20]But as he considered this, behold, an angel of the Lord appeared to him in a dream, saying, "Joseph, son of David, do not fear to make Mary your wife, for that which is conceived in her is of the Holy Spirit; [21]she will bear a son, and you shall call his name Jesus, for he will save his people from their sins." [22]All of this took place to fulfill what the Lord had spoken by the prophet:
> [23]"Behold, a virgin shall conceive and bear a son,
>   and his name shall be called Emmanuel"
> (which means, God with us). [24]When Joseph awoke from sleep, he did as the angel of the Lord commanded him; he took his wife, [25]but knew her not until she had borne a son; and he called his name Jesus.
>
> [f]Other ancient authorities read *of the Christ*

Until now, the story has been about Jesus' origins in the broadest sense, tracing his line back to forefathers of the distant past. But now, the focus shifts to Jesus' own origin and father. In verse 18, we find once more the word *genesis*; it is the same word we saw in verse 1 meaning "origin," "birth," "beginning." More significantly, however, as we read on in this passage, we discover another form of that word used in a totally unexpected way. Just as the form *gennaō* had previously appeared in verse 16 ascribing Jesus' birth to Mary, the form *gennēthen* now likewise appears in verse 20 to ascribe his genesis to the Holy Spirit of God![4] Even if the narrative failed earlier to reveal all the details of Jesus' origins, it is certainly clear enough now about the specific source of his origination: the creative power of God. Thus born of Mary and born of God, Jesus is accordingly both *of* the fully human and *of* the fully godly—and consequently, the full embodiment of each. He is rightly therefore called "Emmanuel," for it is precisely in the person of this one human being, Jesus, that the rest of us human beings truly find *God-with-us* and hence, through Jesus' story, we shall hear the story of God present and alive at work among us.

How fitting, then, that Israel's new anointed should be named "God is salvation,"[5] for he is the one *in whose very person God himself* will be actively working to deliver and save. After what seems like a very long absence, Israel's ultimate messianic savior—God himself—has come back upon the scene to rescue his people once more. Better yet, his timely entry into the story here is significantly different from his 'grand entrances' before. We remember that previously, at the beginning of the Exodus narrative, God had stayed outside the story, as though waiting to come to Israel's rescue until she called out to him and thus reminded him of his covenantal obligations and the demands of justice.[6] By contrast, nothing holds God back from entering this story. He comes to save his people here out of his own accord, i.e., *graciously*. He comes here simply because he wants to and *cares to*. Things do indeed seem to be looking up for Israel. If all appears to be going right with the world, it's because God's not only in his heaven—he's actually here in the world with us as well. Salvation is quite literally at hand.

Yet for all that seems so right, other things appear quite wrong. We have been told that the new messiah's name means "God is salvation," and we felt that name appropriate, for in the past, Israel's messiahs have always been those appointed by

God to save her from various foreign adversaries—Egyptians, Philistines, and the like. But we are also told something else about the significance of the messiah's name. It is something unanticipated, and it leaves us feeling astounded and uneasy. This new messiah will be called Jesus, not because he will save Israel from her enemies roundabout, but because he will save her from her sins—*because he will save her from herself!* Thus, this new messiah, long awaited but totally unexpected, gives Israel's story a twist no one could have guessed. Simultaneously, this messiah gives us questions whose answers now elude our grasp. For example, we know that in the past God's saving power has spelled life for Israel and death for Israel's enemies. But now, *if Israel herself is her own worst enemy,* what salvation can God bring her without also destroying her? Is this to be the end of Israel's story, or can her story live on? And if so, how?

The first chapter of the Christian master story only intensifies such questions, for as the narrative up to now has been telling us all along, the events surrounding Jesus' birth make it most perplexing, to say the least. For instance, we have already seen that Jesus' family tree includes four women of somewhat dubious repute. But our suspicions about their 'virtue' pale when compared to our doubts about the character of the fifth woman on the list—Jesus' own mother. Earlier, we noted that Jesus' links to Abraham and David seemingly legitimize his claim as heir to Israel's promise and Israel's throne. But the circumstances surrounding his conception make everything about him seem illegitimate indeed.

Perhaps there is only one who can make all of it legitimate and so set it right—the same One who sets things right for Joseph when he reveals to him the truth about Jesus' special entry and purpose in the world. And might that not be the aim of this whole narrative? Perhaps this story's purpose is to get all of us to see the truth about how God, despite all appearances to the contrary, can still be counted on to save his world and thus set things right for his creation. At this point, though, we can only speculate how—and if—the story will work out. Consequently, our only choice is to go through with the rest of the story, and then look back to see whether the story has gone through us as well.

Notes

1. The phrase, "book of the genealogy"—Greek: *biblos geneseos*—may also call to mind Gen. 2:4*a* and 5:1; see Raymond E. Brown, *The Birth of the Messiah* (Garden City, N.Y.: Doubleday & Co., 1977), pp. 66-67. For different views, however, regarding the specific reference of these opening words in Matthew, see Jack Dean Kingsbury, *Matthew* (Philadelphia: Fortress Press, 1977), p. 25; J. C. Fenton, *Saint Matthew* (Harmondsworth, Middlesex: Pelican Books Ltd., 1963), p. 36; and Stendahl, "Matthew" s. 674*a*.

2. II Sam. 22:51; cf. also Ps. 18:51 for a parallel citation.

3. Brown notes that from Matthew's standpoint, part of the significance of the number fourteen may have derived from the fact that "in the ancient Hebrew orthography the numerical value of David's name was fourteen" (*Birth of the Messiah*, p. 80). Consequently, Jesus' messianic mission—and God's messianic plan—are both neatly underscored by Matthew's patterned division of Jesus' genealogy.

4. There may well be an allusion here to the same divine spirit that was at work in the birth of the world; cf. Gen. 1:2. If so, Jesus' birth then signifies a new creation of cosmic consequence. In any case, see Brown, *Birth of the Messiah*, pp. 61-64, 123-25, 133-43, 160-61, and Kingsbury, *Matthew*, pp. 25-29.

5. From Hebrew: *Yehoshua* or more simply, *Yeshua*.

6. Cf. Exod. 2:23-25 and my comments *ad loc.*

IX

MATTHEW 2

¹Now when Jesus was born in Bethlehem of Judea in the days of Herod the king, behold, wise men from the East came to Jerusalem, saying, ²"Where is he who has been born king of the Jews? For we have seen his star in the East, and have come to worship him." ³When Herod the king heard this, he was troubled, and all Jerusalem with him; ⁴and assembling all of the chief priests and scribes of the people, he inquired of them where the Christ was to be born. ⁵They told him, "In Bethlehem of Judea; for it is written by the prophet:

⁶"And you, O Bethlehem, in the land of Judah,
are by no means least among the rulers of Judah;
for from you shall come a ruler
who will govern my people Israel.'"

⁷Then Herod summoned the wise men secretly and ascertained from them what time the star appeared; ⁸and he sent them to Bethlehem, saying, "Go and search diligently for the child, and when you have found him bring me word, that I too may come and worship him." ⁹When they had heard the king they went their way; and lo, the star which they had seen in the East went before them, till it came to rest over the place where the child was. ¹⁰When they saw the star, they rejoiced exceedingly with great joy; ¹¹and going into the house they saw the child with Mary his mother, and they fell down and worshiped him. Then, opening their treasures, they offered him gifts, gold and frankincense and myrrh. ¹²And being warned in a dream not to return to Herod, they departed to their own country by another way.

The portrayal of the beginnings of the Christian master story that was presented us in the first chapter is unique in the

Gospels to Jewish-rooted Matthew; so too is that given in the second. However, while the first chapter sought to lay the groundwork for showing Jesus' story as a new and surprising development in the older story of Israel, the second chapter aims at something significantly different. Its concern is not so much with the novel implications of Jesus' story for the future; instead, its primary focus is on the past. This chapter pointedly hearkens back to the Exodus from Egypt—the original redemption narrative that first held out a redemptive promise for the world. If Jesus' story is truly to be the fulfillment of that promise, then it must firmly establish its credentials as the true successor to that earlier narrative—the story of the Jews.

And what better way for one narrative to do that with another than by displaying *literary* parallels with it, e.g., parallel motifs, characters, and actions? Thus, we find that just as the life of Moses, Israel's first deliverer, was threatened during infancy by a tyrant, the life of Israel's new savior is likewise threatened. We might also recall that in Exodus, when Pharaoh desired to thwart God's covenant promising Abraham numerous offspring, he enlisted his people's aid to help him "deal shrewdly" with the matter. Similarly, we now see that Herod too enlists the wise counsel of his people— "all the chief priests and scribes"—to frustrate another divine promise, namely, God's covenant pledging *Davidic* rulership of Israel for all time.

Furthermore, in addition to these parallels between the two stories, there are others that are just as striking. In Exodus, the 'wise' Pharaoh was rather easily outwitted by the midwives whose disobedience saved the baby's life. Here in Matthew, the supposedly cunning Herod is rather handily foiled by the Magi. Instead of following orders and reporting back to him the baby's whereabouts, they simply pick up and go home. Again, a future redeemer's life is saved. Importantly, *in both stories,* the Jewish baby is spared due to the intervention of non-Jews. Clearly, the heroic role of non-Jews in the Exodus has not been lost on Matthew, and throughout the account he has to give, he will make sure that it will not be lost on us either.

The figures of the non-Jewish Magi offer an instructive case in point. In the narrative, they are the first to bow down and worship Jesus. That is, they are the first to acknowledge the meaning of Jesus' birth for what it really is: the appearance of Israel's king. Likewise, in the Exodus story, the Egyptian (i.e., Gentile) magicians were the first to acknowledge the plagues' significance for what *it* really is: "This is the finger of God!"[1] Admittedly, this last parallel may seem so subtle as to make it of almost marginal concern. But to repeat: for Matthew and the master story he has to tell, the role of non-Jews in the story is anything but marginal. Hence, any parallels, however slight, that he can find between the Exodus account and his own involving the actions of Gentiles will be for him anything but insignificant.

[13]Now when they departed, behold, an angel of the Lord appeared to Joseph in a dream and said, "Rise, take the child and his mother and flee to Egypt, and remain there till I tell you; for Herod is about to search for the child, to destroy him." [14]And he rose and took the child and his mother by night, and departed to Egypt, [15]and remained there until the death of Herod. This was to fulfill what the Lord had spoken by the prophet, "Out of Egypt have I called my son."

[16]Then Herod, when he saw that he had been tricked by the wise men, was in a furious rage, and he sent and killed all the male children in Bethlehem and in all that region who were two years old or under according to the time which he had ascertained from the wise men. [17]Then was fulfilled what was spoken by the prophet Jeremiah:
[18]"A voice was heard in Ramah,
wailing and loud lamentation,
Rachel weeping for her children;
she refused to be consoled,
because they were no more."

[19]But when Herod died, behold, an angel of the Lord appeared in a dream to Joseph in Egypt, saying, [20]"Rise, take the child and his mother, and go to the land of Israel, for those who sought the child's life are dead." [21]And he rose and took the child and his mother and went to the land of Israel. [22]But when he heard that Archelaus reigned over Judea in place of his father Herod, he was afraid to go there, and being warned in a dream he withdrew to the district of Galilee. [23]And he went and

dwelt in a city called Nazareth, that what was spoken by the prophets might be fulfilled, "He shall be called a Nazarene."

The parallels between this narrative and that of Exodus continue to be drawn. Like Pharaoh before him, Herod, having been frustrated in his original efforts, now seeks to achieve his objectives by implementing a program of infanticide. As a result, here—as in Exodus—rescuing the hero's life from the clutches of the evil king necessitates a sudden flight to another country. And finally, in perhaps the most vivid parallel of all, the present narrative uses virtually the same words of the earlier one to provide the information that the coast is clear for the hero's safe return: here, in Matthew 2:20, "go [back] . . . for those who sought the child's life are dead"; there, in Exodus 4:19, "go back . . . for all the men who sought your life are dead."[2]

However, despite all the parallels between the two narratives, the redemption story of Jesus is, after all, more than a mere retelling of the Exodus redemption story, for as Matthew's opening chapter showed us, Jesus' story contains from the very first some surprises for which the Exodus left us totally unprepared: ". . . for he will save his people from their sins." In this narrative, unlike Exodus, the Jewish people are not God's instrument through which he works salvation. Instead, Israel appears here as the greatest obstacle to the work of deliverance that God is trying to perform. To be sure, there were certain moments at the beginning of the Exodus account when the people also resisted the efforts made to save them.[3] But in the last analysis, there was never really any doubt in that story that the Egyptians stood as the chief impediment to God's plan. For Matthew's narrative, however, things are decidedly different. As the second chapter tells it, and as we will be told repeatedly in the chapters to follow, the real heart of opposition to God in this story lies within Israel itself. In the perceptive words of one commentator contrasting the two narratives' central themes and motifs at this point:

In Exodus, the king of Egypt is the enemy of Israel; here, a king of Jerusalem is the enemy. In Exodus, Moses flees for safety out of Egypt and then returns; here, Jesus is taken into Egypt for safety and then returns. In the Old Testament, Egypt and Pharaoh are the symbols for disbelief and hardness of heart; in the New Testament, Jerusalem and Herod fulfill this role.[4]

Now it may be one thing to give a story an unexpected twist. But what we have here seems to be a reversal to end all reversals! What seemed to start out as a continuation and parallel of Israel's story now appears to be almost another story entirely!

However, just when we might be tempted to dismiss this story of Jesus as a profound perversion of Israel's previous story, the narrative itself calls on us not to act so hastily. For when we read in this narrative a verse such as Matt. 2:15—"Out of Egypt have I called my son"—we cannot help but be reminded of some key verses in that other story: "Israel is My first-born son, . . . Let My son go that he may serve Me" (Exod. 4:22-23). The interplay between such verses, instead of resolving our dilemma, only deepens it. Who then *is* God's firstborn? Who is the one, *who as firstborn,* stands first in line both as heir to his Father's testament and as the son devoted to his God's service?[5] Is it this single person Jesus or the Jewish people as a whole? And what about all the other verses here that tell us that the events depicted in Matthew's narrative come so that certain words—i.e., certain *prophetic promises*—spoken in the older story "might be fulfilled"?[6] Hence, there is no way of our avoiding the issue; there is no way of our evading what has been the point at issue between Jews and Christians for twenty centuries: Is the story of Jesus right on course with the Jewish people's prior saga—or is it instead totally off track?

That is, to be sure, no small question. For in the end, how we read the Jewish and Christian master stories may well decide how we come to read the world and our own lives in it.

Notes

1. Exod. 8:15. Richmond Lattimore notes in his translation of Matthew that in classical Greek *magoi* may denote "a priest or seer, within the Medo-Persian empire" (*The Four Gospels and the Revelation* [New York: Pocket Books, 1979], p. 268).

Also of particular interest is the parallel between the non-Jewish magi who come to Jesus having seen 'his' star and that other Gentile magus, Balaam, who foresaw a star coming forth from Jacob (see Num. 24:17). For Matthew, therefore, Jesus' prophesied messiahship is once more unmistakable. See Brown, *Birth of the Messiah*, p. 188-96.

2. Besides all these explicit parallels, there may be another, more subtly implied one as well. As Childs suggests (*Book of Exodus*, p. 25), Matt. 2:18 may be intimating that just as the Israelite mothers in Egypt most likely wept over their infants slain by Pharaoh, so too Rachel—one of Israel's ancestral, paradigmatic mothers—now weeps over her children slaughtered by Herod.

3. Cf., e.g. Exod. 2:13-15 and 5:20-23.

4. Fenton, *Saint Matthew*, p. 50.

5. In Israel, as in most of the ancient Near East, the firstborn stood as both his father's primary heir and as *the child consecrated from birth as belonging to the deity*. Originally, that status probably meant that all firstborn Israelites were specially designated as the ones to perform the Lord's cultic service throughout their lives. Later, however, this role was transferred to the tribe of Levi as a whole and to the clan of Aaron in particular; see Num. 18:15-16. Interestingly, Matt. 2:23, which describes Jesus as a "Nazarene," may appeal to much the same idea. That is, it may be alluding to the concept of the *Nazirite*, one who was likewise dedicated to God's service from birth.

But see Brown as well, *Birth of the Messiah*, pp. 209-19. He takes Matt. 2:23 as an allusion to Isa. 11:1— "A shoot shall grow out of the stump of Jesse, a branch (Hebrew: *netzer*) shall sprout from his stock"—and consequently, as yet another Matthean stress on Jesus' Davidic/messianic mission.

6. Among the Gospels, Matthew's repeated use of these formulaic citations of earlier biblical prophecies is quite distinctive. The point of such citation was not merely to accentuate incidental agreements between Jesus and Jewish scripture; more importantly, Matthew used these prophetic quotations "because they fit his general theology of the oneness of God's plan" (Brown, *Birth of the Messiah*, p. 104).

X
MATTHEW 3:1-2, 13-17; 4:1–5:2

^{3:1}In those days came John the Baptist, preaching in the wilderness of Judea, ²"Repent, for the kingdom of heaven is at hand." . . .

¹³Then Jesus came from Galilee to the Jordan to John, to be baptized by him. ¹⁴John would have prevented him, saying, "I need to be baptized by you, and do you come to me?" ¹⁵But Jesus answered him, "Let it be so now, for thus it is fitting for us to fulfill all righteousness." Then he consented. ¹⁶And when Jesus was baptized, he went up immediately from the water, . . . and he saw the Spirit of God descending like a dove, and alighting on him; ¹⁷and lo, a voice from heaven, saying, "This is my beloved Son, *h* with whom I am well pleased."

*h*Or *my Son, my* (or *the*) *Beloved*

The preceding chapter describing Jesus' infancy and early childhood portrayed his story as bearing certain similarities to Moses' story, and as the next few chapters continue relating Jesus' saga, they likewise continue emphasizing such similarities. In the Exodus narrative, Moses was initially prepared for his subsequent work of deliverance through a journey out into the wilderness where he received divine authorization for his future mission, learning there that one of his first acts in God's service would involve the water of a river.[1] So, too, in Matthew's version of the Christian master story, these selfsame elements surround the preparations for Jesus' mission of salvation: he goes out into the wilderness of Judea, is baptized in the waters of the Jordan, and is greeted by a heavenly voice affirming him as God's own.

Yet despite all the resemblances between the events surrounding Moses' call and Jesus', there are nonetheless clear and crucial differences between the two story lines. At the burning bush, for instance, Moses repeatedly resisted doing God's bidding.[2] But not so Jesus at the Jordan. Although John offers some resistance to Jesus' baptism, Jesus himself single-mindedly insists that he undergo immersion, not because, e.g., he needs to cleanse himself of sin, but because "it is fitting . . . to fulfil all righteousness"—i.e., because submitting humbly and completely to God's will is the one fully right thing to do. And what is God's response to such unqualified obedience by Jesus but an equally unqualified avowal of him: "This is my beloved Son, with whom I am well pleased." At the time of Moses' call, the Lord had designated the whole people Israel as his "first-born son."[3] But now, he has apparently named another to carry on his name and work—this one man, Jesus. Through his baptism, Jesus has revealed himself worthy of such favor, because unlike inconstant Israel, he has shown himself to be the Father's truly faithful and devoted offspring. Thus, this one Jew, Jesus—and not the Jewish people as a whole—will henceforth be the prime heir and bearer of whatever blessing the Father shall bestow.[4]

4:1Then Jesus was led up by the Spirit into the wilderness to be tempted by the devil. 2And he fasted forty days and forty nights, and afterward he was hungry. 3And the tempter came and said to him, "If you are the Son of God, command these stones to become loaves of bread." 4But he answered, "It is written,

'Man shall not live by bread alone,
but by every word that proceeds from the mouth of God.'"

5Then the devil took him to the holy city, and set him on the pinnacle of the temple, 6and said to him, "If you are the Son of God, throw yourself down; for it is written,

'He will give his angels charge of you,'
and
'On their hands will they bear you up,

lest you strike your foot against a stone.'"
[7]Jesus said to him, "Again it is written, 'You shall not tempt the Lord your God.'" [8]Again, the devil took him to a very high mountain, and showed him all the kingdoms of the world and the glory of them; [9]and he said to him, "All these will I give you, if you will fall down and worship me." [10]Then Jesus said to him, "Begone, Satan! for it is written,

'You shall worship the Lord your God
and him only shall you serve.'"

[11]Then the devil left him, and behold, angels came and ministered to him.

In the Jewish master story, even after Moses had reluctantly acceded to God's behest, his commitment nevertheless wavered the first time it was tested.[5] But in this Christian master story, the character of Jesus' devotion to God's will is markedly different, for his fidelity to the Lord remains firm despite repeated attempts to shake it. At his baptism, Jesus had spoken of the unconditional necessity of following God's wishes in their entirety. On trial now, however, is his capacity not merely *to speak* but *to act* with such thoroughgoing obedience.

Once more, Matthew draws on the parallels between the Jewish and Christian master stories. Hence, as Jesus embarks on his fateful undertaking, like Moses before him, he fasts for "forty days and forty nights."[6] However, the congruity ends there. For Jesus passes all his wilderness tests—unlike Israel, who failed virtually all hers. Through the various scriptural citations in this passage, Matthew reminds us that Israel, when tried, repeatedly abandoned her faith in God's ability to save: e.g., in the wilderness of Sin (Exod. 16:1-8), by the rock of Massah (Exod. 17:1-7), at the golden calf (Exod. 32:1-8). In sharp contrast, Jesus never succumbs to the temptation to turn his back on God while turning instead to someone else for succor—even should that someone be himself, or even should that someone promise him the world. Consequently, though the tempter taunts him to use his vaunted powers to save himself miraculously from starvation and/or destruction ("If you *are* the Son of God . . ."), Jesus nevertheless refuses to act so *self-servingly*. Rather, he quotes the devil Scripture—and not just any Scripture, but the very words citing Israel's previous defections from the Lord while at the same time stressing the crucialness of keeping His charge faithfully.[7] Still undeterred, Temptation has one final trial in store for Jesus to test his loyalty to God. If Jesus will but betray the Lord by acknowledging another in His place, he himself can be lord of all the world. But showing the same resolve with which he withstood the previous two tests, Jesus rejects the kind of majesty offered by the devil, and instead, *with a majesty all his own*, he *commandingly* responds, "Begone, Satan! . . . 'Worship the Lord your God . . . him only shall you serve.'"

Thus, Jesus' utter obedience to God has unfailingly survived all these tests. Indeed, precisely for that reason, Jesus has himself survived; he has been saved through nothing more or less than his sheer fidelity to God. Earlier, when he had come to John to be baptized, Jesus had manifested exactly that kind of humble submission, and a heavenly voice had affirmed him as God's beloved. Now, following his latest display of that same sort of *subservience to the Lord*, a heavenly host of angels similarly confirms Jesus by *ministering to him*. Put another way, Jesus' profound self-effacement *before God* has resulted in his equally profound exaltation *by God*.

> [12]Now when he heard that John had been arrested, he withdrew to Galilee; [13]and leaving Nazareth he went and dwelt in Capernaum by the sea, in the territory of Zebulun and Naphtali, [14]that what was spoken by the prophet Isaiah might be fulfilled:
> [15]"The land of Zebulun and the land of Naphtali,
> toward the sea, across the Jordan,
> Galilee of the Gentiles—
> [16]the people who sat in darkness
> have seen a great light,
> and for those who sat in the region and shadow of death
> light has dawned."

After Moses had received God's wilderness call to deliver the Israelites, he had straightaway returned to them to carry out his charge. By contrast, Jesus, subsequent to his divine commission, sets off in a direction just the opposite from Israel, that is, toward "Galilee of the Gentiles." We recall that as an infant, Jesus had also had to flee from Israel—and for much the same reason: potential threats to his life from those whom he has come to save.

Nevertheless, even in Galilee among a large non-Jewish population, neither Jesus' mission nor God's goal is wholly thwarted. Remembering that Jesus Messiah is the seed of Abraham, we remember as well that he is by that very token the current bearer of God's ancient promise to Abraham, namely, that through Abraham and his family all the families on earth shall eventually be blessed (Gen. 12:3). Hence, through Jesus' present sojourn in a region where there are both Jews *and* Gentiles, that age-old pledge has started to reach fulfillment by bringing, in the prophet's words, the dawning of a "great light" to those who formerly "sat in darkness."

[17]From that time Jesus began to preach, saying, "Repent, for the kingdom of heaven is at hand."

[18]As he walked by the Sea of Galilee, he saw two brothers, Simon who is called Peter and Andrew his brother, casting a net into the sea; for they were fishermen.

[19]And he said to them, "Follow me, and I will make you fishers of men."

[20]Immediately they left their nets and followed him. [21]And going on from there he saw two other brothers, James the son of Zebedee and John his brother, in the boat with Zebedee their father, mending their nets, and he called to them.

[22]Immediately they left the boat and their father, and followed him.

Upon returning to Egypt following his wilderness initiation, Moses' communique to Pharaoh on the Lord's behalf had been simple and to the point: "Let my people go!" Throughout the Jewish master story, that one demand was constantly reiterated to the Egyptian king—and quite fittingly too, for clearly, if Pharaoh stood as the continuing source of Israel's afflictions, who needed to hear God's ultimatum more than he?

However, in the Christian master story, the content and target of Jesus' message are altogether different: "Repent, for the kingdom of heaven is at hand!" It is a divine proclamation no longer directed at some alien oppressor, but aimed instead at a homegrown cause of Israel's troubles—Israel herself! Significantly, that insistent cry not only identifies Israel as the author of her own predicament, but as importantly, it simultaneously identifies Jesus as one to lead her out of it. Therefore, in just that sense, his name—"Jesus"—seems well suited, for he does indeed appear to be someone whose task is to "save his people from their sins" (Matt. 1:21). As Moses had met Pharaoh with a stark and pressing summons to turn from his misguided policies, Jesus now confronts his errant people with a call every bit as urgent.[8]

To be sure, some in Egypt—e.g., Pharaoh—at first dismissed Moses' proclamation out of hand (Exod. 5:2), and others—i.e., the Hebrew slaves—welcomed it only to doubt it later.[9] Nevertheless, it did receive immediate and sure acceptance from at least one quarter—Aaron, Moses' brother.[10] Jesus' proclamation now finds similar 'fraternal' pockets of responsiveness among the brothers Peter and Andrew, James and John, and the narrative underscores the point that the brothers' following Jesus' call is firmly rooted in the readiness with which they "*immediately . . . followed him.*" Without any hesitation whatsoever, both pairs of brothers leave their work and homes to set off after Jesus. Apparently, the timely message that Jesus brings demands no less, and in helping him to carry it to others, these newfound followers of his will in turn find themselves newly formed as well, for though they have left their old occupations and families behind, they will now gain in their stead a new vocation and kinship—in sum, a brand new life.

> [23]And he went about all Galilee, teaching in their synagogues and preaching the gospel of the kingdom and healing every disease and every infirmity among the people. [24]So his fame spread throughout all Syria, and they brought him all the sick, those afflicted with various diseases and pains, demoniacs, epileptics, and paralytics, and he healed them. [25]And great crowds followed him from Galilee and Decapolis and Jerusalem and Judea and from beyond the Jordan.

Jesus continues on his mission—teaching, preaching, and healing as he goes. The extreme exigency of that mission requires that it be a *roving* ministry as Jesus spreads the word throughout Galilee—and as word of him spreads beyond. Yet how ought people to view Jesus' words? In Egypt, Moses' dispatches from God foretokened impending disaster for Pharaoh and his subjects. Do Jesus' tidings now presage similar dire events?

No—for the proclamation Jesus brings is deemed a *gospel*: literally, "good news." And indeed, Jesus' activities, comprised not only of effective teaching and preaching, but of *effective healing* too, *bear out* just how good is the news *he bears*. If disease is an indication that something has gone wrong, then Jesus' ability to heal indicates his capacity to put things right again, and thus, Jesus' drawing near to people in ways that are truly *salvic* seems somehow intimately connected with the kingdom's drawing close. Moreover, something else also apparently corroborates Jesus' message even while substantiating his own relationship to it. For Jesus has called on the masses to repent, and now we learn that in response to his summons to turn to God,[11] "great crowds followed him." Hence, in the plan of salvation unfolding in this Christian master story, following God and following Jesus are increasingly becoming synonymous with each other.

> [5:1]Seeing the crowds, he went up on the mountain, and when he sat down his disciples came to him. [2]And he opened his mouth and taught them.

As we hear now that Jesus goes up a mountain to teach the assembled throngs, we might think again of the Exodus narrative when Moses ascended Sinai. However, despite all the comparisons in these most recent chapters of Matthew's narrative between Jesus on the one hand and Moses on the other, we need to keep in mind quite clearly something that happened at the story's inception: Jesus was named "Emmanuel"—literally "God-with-us." If Jesus really *is* God present among us human beings, then he speaks with an authority like *that of God himself*, and as a result, all analogies between Jesus and Moses are radically undermined. As messengers of God, as teachers in Israel, *as authoritative representatives of God's will*, the two differ not merely in degree, but more significantly, in kind. Consequently, as Jesus ascends the mountain to teach the crowds assembled below, he does so to deliver instruction for the world whose import is unmatched even by Sinai's. Thus, as he takes his place to begin his unique, momentous teaching, Israel's story—which is the world's story—takes an unparalleled new turn.

Notes

1. See Exod. 3. See also Exod. 4:9, where Moses is instructed to perform some of his initial signs with waters from the Nile. The river, of course, is the site of the first plague; cf. Exod. 7:20.

2. Cf. Exod. 3:11, 13; 4:1, 10, 13.

3. Cf. Exod. 4:22 and my comments at that point.

4. In addition to the above-mentioned Exod. 4:22, see as well Ps. 2:7 and Isa. 42:1 which likewise bear on the theme of 'sonship.'

5. Cf. Exod. 5:22-23 relating Moses' reaction after Pharaoh and the Israelites rebuff his first efforts at deliverance.

6. Cf. Exod. 34:28 and Deut. 9:9, 18.

7. Deut. 8:3; 6:16 (see also 6:17). Robert H. Gundry, in his book *Matthew: A Commentary on His Literary and Theological Art* (Grand Rapids: Wm. B. Eerdmans Publishing Co., 1982), aptly notes that Matthew's citation of these verses together with his previous portrayal of Jesus' insistence on fulfilling 'all righteousness' is all intended to show us in no uncertain terms that "[Jesus] was no antinomian" (p. 56). Hence, for the Jewish-rooted Matthew, whatever conflicts his narrative may involve, they are not to be construed as clashes between Jesus and Torah, i.e., between 'Gospel' and 'Law.' See Matt. 28:16-20 and the commentary *ad loc.*

8. Even though Jesus is currently residing in "Galilee of the Gentiles," the primary objects of his preaching here are nevertheless the Jews—as shown by the fact that his first calls for disciples apparently goes out to them alone.

9. Cf. Exod. 4:31 and 5:20-21.

10. Cf. Exod. 4:14-16, 27-30.

11. As Stendahl points out ("Matthew," 677i), "The Gr. word translated 'repent' (*metanoeite*, lit. 'change your mind') is in NT times and especially in eschatalogical literature equivalent not to 'grieve for one's sins' . . . but to 'turn around, return.' . . ."

XI
MATTHEW 13:1-3, 24-36

13:1That same day Jesus went out of the house and sat beside the sea. 2And great crowds gathered about him, so that he got into a boat and sat there; and the whole crowd stood on the beach. 3And he told them many things in parables.

When we last left Jesus, he was sitting atop a mountain, beginning his teachings to the ostensibly receptive crowds below. Yet we remember hearing earlier that his initial reception among his people—who are purportedly *God's* people—was anything but enthusiastic; far from welcoming him, some even acted to drive him away.[1] Sadly, in the intervening period between Jesus' opening discourse on the mountain and his most recent pronouncements here by the sea, relations between himself and Israel have not gotten appreciably any better. They have in fact grown worse, for as the narrative has unfolded, the hostility toward Jesus has extended well past Herod, additionally encompassing others among the people's representatives, as, for example, the Pharisees.[2] Despite Jesus'—despite God's!—repeated efforts to reach the people through preaching, teaching, and healing,[3] Israel, for her part, has remained virtually unresponsive. Consequently, a change in tactics and strategies seems very much in order.

Such a change is exactly what Matthew 13 signals. In the words of one commentator, it stands as "the great 'turning-

159

point' in [Matthew's] Gospel."[4] Just as the Jews have apparently turned away from Jesus' teaching, Jesus will now in kind turn from teaching them. Or rather, he will turn from teaching them about God's rule—and fidelity to it—in clear and straightforward proclamation and henceforth only speak to them about such matters indirectly and enigmatically: *in parables*.[5] While there are several different views on the nature and function of parables,[6] on this much, at least, there seems to be agreement: a parable is a story whose power stems from its capacity to metaphorically reveal something not only about the world, but about the story's hearers too.[7]

What then will Jesus' parables disclose about *their* audience—and their audience's world? With the Jewish crowds standing before him, the seated Jesus[8] tells his stories, which, though somewhat cryptic, may prove singularly eye-opening nonetheless:

[24] . . . The kingdom of heaven may be compared to a man who sowed good seed in his field; [25]but while men were sleeping, his enemy came and sowed weeds among the wheat, and went away. [26]So when the plants came up and bore grain, then the weeds appeared also. [27]And the servants^j of the householder came and said to him, "Sir, did you not sow good seed in your field? How then has it weeds?" [28]He said to them, "An enemy has done this." The servants^j said to him, "Then do you want us to go and gather them?" [29]But he said, "No; lest in gathering the weeds you root up the wheat along with them. [30]Let both grow together until the harvest; and at harvest time I will tell the reapers, Gather the weeds first and bind them in bundles to be burned, but gather the wheat into my barn."

^jOr *slaves*

From the start, the focus of Jesus' preaching has been the fast-approaching arrival of "the kingdom of heaven."[9] For Matthew, that phrase is of the utmost significance. In all the Gospels, it is unique to his, appearing in connection with no fewer than eleven different parables. Synonymous for Jews with the expression "the kingdom of God," it denotes God's sovereignty, his kingly rule.[10] To be sure, the Jewish master story of the Exodus has previously portrayed God, in his struggle with the king of Egypt, to be the lord whose dominion ultimately holds sway. Accordingly, for those who have taken up that Exodus narrative, the essential *fact* of God's status as king of the world is beyond all doubt; all that remains in doubt is when *the world* will come to acknowledge that fact in the future. Or to put it another way: When will the kingdom of heaven be *realized* on earth? Although the precise moment may be virtually impossible to gauge, nevertheless, from Israel's experience in the Exodus, the basic scenario of its arrival seems fairly well defined. The full realization of God's lordship will occur when God decisively breaks into history again to reveal himself once more through 'signs and wonders' that will awesomely vanquish his people's adversaries and thereby compellingly elicit from them a recognition of his true and ultimate supremacy.

But if everything is so readily apparent, why then the need for Matthew—and Jesus—to tell these parables of the kingdom? Why not simply retell the old Exodus story one more time? Presumably, therefore, this Christian master story envisages God's kingdom coming in a way different from that previously imagined, one which calls for a correspondingly different response from those who would be the Lord's faithful subjects. How, then, are Jesus' parables meant to (re)shape the prior vision of the advent of God's kingdom—and the appropriate human response to it? In short, what will the kingdom—God's rule!—be like?[11]

With the parable of the weeds, Jesus offers part of the answer. In the first place, the kingdom's actual arrival will not be made manifest, Exodus-like, through a series of marvelous, mighty acts which are plain for all to see. Instead, its spread and growth will be ambiguous such that events can easily be misread as if to reflect a lack of care and attention on God's part: "Sir, did you not sow good seed in your field? How then has it weeds?"

In the second place, moreover, the Exodus story's distinction between friend and enemy will not be so clear-cut either. Hence, in the parable of the weeds, the Greek word *zizania* signifies a type of vegetation "botanically related to wheat and all but indistinguishable from it until the individual plants begin to mature."[12] Such is exactly the outcropping that has seemingly taken root in God's own chosen field of labor, the people Israel. For a long time, Israel may have looked as though it would one day flower with human beings who might fittingly be called God's "treasured possession."[13] In the end, however, it has burgeoned with worthless impostors. Far from being the Lord's own handiwork, much of what has sprouted in Israel appears to be work opposed to God's.

Consequently, in the last place, but of first-rank importance, is the need to sort things out. But how? In the parable of the weeds, human beings are portrayed as being somehow unqualified for that role. As the parable tells it, the task of putting things right belongs to God and God alone. By contrast, in the Exodus narrative, God's acts of rectifying the situation were again and again dependent on—and in some sense limited by—corresponding human action.[14] Yet in the parable of the weeds, the householder's servants are specifically told *not* to act, as though their activity would constitute a fundamental usurpation of the authority which is rightfully their master's, and even worse, botch the job to boot! No, their proper role is simply to *stand by and wait* until, in their lord's own good time—i.e., at his sole discretion and direction—everything will finally be sorted out once and for all.

And yet for all the stress it lays on the future, the parable of the weeds nevertheless places a crucial emphasis on the present too, for it tells us how that even now the seeds of the kingdom have already been planted, and despite all appearances to the contrary, the kingdom's fruit is already being yielded. Thus, we can expect to hear further word of the kingdom's growth, and indeed, that is just what Jesus proceeds to tell:

[31]Another parable he put before them, saying, "The kingdom of heaven is like a grain of mustard seed which a man took and sowed in his field; [32]it is the smallest of all seeds, but when it has grown it is the greatest of shrubs and becomes a tree, so that the birds of the air come and make nests in its branches."

[33]He told them another parable. "The kingdom of heaven is like leaven which a woman took and hid in three measures of flour, till it was all leavened."

[34]All this Jesus said to the crowds in parables; indeed he said nothing to them without a parable. [35]This was to fulfill what was spoken by the prophet:[k]

"I will open my mouth in parables,
I will utter what has been hidden since the foundation of the world."

[36]Then he left the crowds and went into the house.

[k]Other ancient authorities read *the prophet Isaiah*

The parables of the mustard seed and the leaven are prime examples of the ways that stories develop their ideas and concepts—not linearly, through the strict parameters of syllogisms inexorably moving to a conclusion, but spirally, through an ever-widening web of associations progressively expanding various motifs and themes. Hence, the motifs of implantation and yield previously found in the parable of the weeds are taken up once more by the mustard seed and leaven parables: the kingdom's beginnings are even now set in place, and moreover, they are beginnings that will eventually, *inevitably*, lead to a fruition of enormous proportions. These two new parables, however, expand these themes by introducing additional elements vital to a fuller understanding of the kingdom. We thus come to learn that the onset of God's rule will not be marked by public displays of lordly grandeur, but by common happenings of seeming insignificance. No burning bush, but a tiny mustard seed;[15] no terrifying plagues, but the ordinary baking of bread.[16]

In sum, God's arrival as the world's sovereign will not occur in a flourish of gloriously awesome majesty, but in the guise of the humbly ordinary and everyday. And in this master story as a whole, what better, more concrete instance of that humble way of being in and with the world can we find than this lowly vagabond called Jesus? In this sense, not only Jesus' words, but *Jesus' life*, give voice to the inauguration of the kingdom. Seen from this perspective, Jesus is no longer merely a teller of

parables of God, but is instead *the parable of God* himself; he is
the transcendent touching the worldly in and through
ordinary life.[17] Understanding Jesus' story therefore becomes
the key for interpreting 'God's story' as well as all these
parabolic stories of God's kingdom, for as reflected in and
through Jesus' life, that kingdom is one in which full
citizenship depends on nothing more or less than total fidelity
to its sovereign—the very kind of utter constancy shown by
the kingdom's sovereign to all his would-be subjects.
Consequently, at a fundamental level, the Christian master
story asks us to envisage life itself as one great parable in which
the new and the extraordinary may break in—indeed may
have *already* broken in—upon our world through the familiar
and the commonplace, such that in the process our life in the
world may be transformed.[18]

For those whose expectations of the inauguration of
God's reign have been formed in the light of the Exodus, the
kind of advent of which Jesus speaks is something totally
unanticipated—and virtually *unrecognizable.* No wonder then
that the Jews are blind to it—and blind to the parables that tell
of it as well. Importantly, Jesus' speaking in parables to the
Jews does not *make* the people blind to what he has to say.
Rather, the parables function as a vivid indication of just how
hopelessly blind they are, or, more precisely, of just how
totally deaf to the word of God they are.[19] For Matthew's
Gospel, therefore, we have reached the turning point not only
of its present chapter, but also of its larger master story: "Then
[Jesus] left the crowds and went into the house. And his
disciples came to him." From now on, the disciples, his own
faithful followers, will be the select audience for the message
that he bears. There is no longer any reason for Jesus to speak
to the Jewish masses, whether in dark parables or in lucid
proclamation.

Even more significantly, however, there is thus no longer
any reason for anyone else to pay particular attention to the
Jews, either. During the time of the Exodus, as plague upon
plague rained down upon the Egyptians while sparing the
Hebrews, the people Israel increasingly took on the role of

God's clearest manifestation of his activity in the world;[20] in a sense, the body of the Jewish people profoundly *embodied* the presence of the Lord on earth. But this Christian master story heralds an acute revision of all that. *Now*, the Lord's true embodiment is Jesus, and it is *his* activity that shall provide the surest sign of what and how God works among us. Hence, the master story of the Exodus has been succeeded—*superseded*—by another: that of Jesus Christ.

Thus, as the preeminence of the corporate history of Israel gives way to that individual life story, a theme sounded throughout Matthew's narrative from the beginning resounds again with even greater clarity and force: following Jesus' saga is indispensable for properly following the ongoing saga of God's dealings with the world.

Notes

1. See the comments to Matt. 2:13-23.
2. Cf. in particular chaps. 11 and 12 of Matthew.
3. Cf. Jack Dean Kingsbury, *Jesus Christ in Matthew, Mark, and Luke* (Philadelphia: Fortress Press, 1981), pp. 77-83. Cf. also, e.g., Matt. 5; 9:35; and 12:24-29.
4. J. D. Kingsbury, *The Parables of Jesus in Matthew 13* (London: SPCK, 1969), pp. 31, 130.
5. Ibid.
6. Thus, see, for instance, the following writers' views on the subject: John Dominic Crossan, *In Parables* (New York: Harper & Row, 1973); Dan Otto Via, Jr., *The Parables* (Philadelphia: Fortress Press, 1967); Sallie McFague, *Speaking in Parables* (Philadelphia: Fortress Press, 1975); Amos N. Wilder, *Early Christian Rhetoric* (Cambridge: Harvard University Press, 1971), and *Jesus' Parables and the War of Myths* (Philadelphia: Fortress Press, 1982).
7. That is, a parable typically depicts a situation which is in some ways analogous to the hearer's own, but which in other ways is strikingly dissimilar. Thus, it presents its hearer with both a new way to envision his or her situation and consequently a challenge to respond appropriately on the basis of that transformed vision. Hence, even though a parable generally relates a fictional event, its power derives from its ability to 'ring true' to life, such that while portraying ordinary, real-life situations that are usually set in the past, it nevertheless holds out present real-life options for the future. See Crossan, *In Parables*, pp. 15-16; Via, *The Parables*, pp. 11-12, 52; McFague, *Speaking in Parables*, pp. 13, 78-79; and Wilder, *Early Christian Rhetoric*, pp. 60, 74.
8. Kingsbury makes a pair of noteworthy points in reference to v. 2. In the first place, "crowds" here signifies the Jews *en masse* (*Parables*, p. 25). And in the second, the portrayal of the crowds standing in contrast to Jesus sitting is an allusion to Jesus' implicit authority. On the one hand, it points to the figure of the seated rabbinic master whose listeners stood out of respect, and on the other, it draws on the traditional image of the throne of God. As Kingsbury observes (p. 23), "It would seem [therefore] that Matthew's intention in v. 2 is to fashion a setting that will in itself attribute honour to Jesus and underline, not merely a Rabbinic, but even a divine dignity." Cf. also Matt. 5:2.
9. See Matt. 4:17.
10. Kingsbury, *Parables*, pp. 17-20.
11. As Wilder has pointed out (*Early Christian Rhetoric*, p. 72, n. 2), "It is generally recognized today that such introductory phrases [i.e.,

'the kingdom of heaven is like . . . '] . . . mean: the following story bears upon some aspect of the kingdom."

12. Kingsbury, *Parables*, p. 71; see as well as his larger treatment of this parable, pp. 63-76.

13. Cf. Exod. 19:5.

14. Thus, see, for example, Exod. 2:23-25; 3:1–4:17; 12:21-27, together with my comments on these various passages.

15. "Proverbial among the Jews as the most minute of quantities" (Kingsbury, *Parables*, p. 79).

16. Normally 'woman's work' in Palestine—just as it was typically the task of men to do the sowing; cf. ibid., p. 85.

17. See Frederick H. Borsch's book *God's Parable* (Philadelphia: The Westminster Press, 1976) and McFague, *Speaking in Parables*, pp. 3 and 82.

18. Cf. Via, *The Parables*, p. 104, and McFague, *Speaking in Parables*, p. 3. For a particularly valuable account of Jesus' life as initiating and displaying the kingdom, see Stanley Hauerwas, *The Peaceable Kingdom* (Notre Dame, Ind.: University of Notre Dame Press, 1983). In an attempt to stick close to the narrative's overall story line and its decisive story segments, I have not given as much attention to some of its other narrative portions, such as those in Matt. 8, or for that matter, some of its non-narrative passages, such as the Sermon on the Mount. Yet I clearly recognize that these parts, too, play a role in depicting the nature of the kingdom, and thus, I would urge that after having studied our work here—especially that dealing with Christ's passion and resurrection—the reader go back and reread these other episodes in the light of those storied events which this commentary both reflects and reflects upon.

19. Cf. Kingsbury, *Parables*, on Matt. 13:13 and the contrast with Mark 4:10-12.

20. See my comments to Exod. 9:1-7.

XII
MATTHEW 26

²⁶:¹When Jesus had finished all these sayings, he said to his disciples, ²"You know that after two days the Passover is coming, and the Son of man will be delivered up to be crucified."

³Then the chief priests and the elders of the people gathered in the palace of the high priest, who was called Caiaphas, ⁴and took counsel together in order to arrest Jesus by stealth and kill him. ⁵But they said, "Not during the feast, lest there be a tumult among the people."

All along, the Christian master story has been riddled with perplexing ambiguities. First, it began with mixed news: the glorious announcement of the arrival of Israel's long-awaited Messiah—combined with disturbing reports about both his legitimacy and Israel's receptiveness to him. Later, at the story's center, were enigmatic parables which told of the fast-approaching reign of Israel's Lord—even as they foretold that most of Israel would be unready for its coming. Now, near the narrative's conclusion, where we would at last expect for everything to be straightened out, we nonetheless again receive cross signals: word of the Passover commemorating Israel's deliverance—yet also word of Jesus' being delivered over to crucifixion through the agency of Israel!

Matthew cast the opening chapters of Jesus' story in the light of Israel's earlier saga of the Exodus. But if the present narrative is indeed like that older one, i.e., a story of deliverance and redemption, then whatever saving meaning it contains had better be made evident—and soon. Two days' time to the Passover; two days' time to Jesus' being handed over to death. One way or another, the narrative is moving toward its denouement. In short, as this master story unfolds its climactic final episodes, it must unfold as well the plain and unmistakable significance of all that has taken place.

However, while *we* may still be in the dark, Jesus, as he has throughout, seems to understand full well everything that will transpire. Just as he knows that the time for the Passover is coming, he knows that his own time is coming too. And if his time is anything like that eventful occasion of the Exodus, when it finally does arrive, God's purposes will be revealed, His powers displayed, and His promises fulfilled. How then best for us to follow all that is so rapidly occurring? By following from here on what happens to Jesus—the one who has been at the story's center from its beginning.

> 6Now when Jesus was at Bethany in the house of Simon the leper, 7a woman came up to him with an alabaster flask of very expensive ointment, and she poured it on his head, as he sat at table. 8But when the disciples saw it, they were indignant, saying, "Why this waste? 9For this ointment might have been sold for a large sum, and given to the poor." 10But Jesus, aware of this, said to them, "Why do you trouble the woman? For she has done a beautiful thing to me. 11For you always have the poor with you, but you will not always have me. 12In pouring this ointment on my body she has done it to prepare me for burial. 13Truly, I say to you, wherever this gospel is preached in the whole world, what she has done will be told in memory of her."

Again, at Bethany, ambiguity permeates events, making any simple understanding of their import utterly impossible. On the one hand, the woman's act of kindness toward Jesus seems to be a morally praiseworthy deed. But on the other, the disciples' objections to that act, expressing a broader concern for the needs of the poor, also appear to carry moral weight. And then, as if the woman and the disciples had not already created enough of a moral quandary, Jesus' words only seem to confuse issues even further, by apparently expressing a gross indifference to any ethical considerations whatsoever: Isn't there something callously cavalier in his sweeping claim that there will always be poor? Is he only worried about himself? Isn't *he* concerned about the poor at all?

And what about the pouring of the oil itself? While the woman probably sees it as an act of generous hospitality, and while the disciples obviously see it as an act of wasteful extravagance, those two perspectives do not exhaust all the possibilities. "She poured it on his head." Just so had oil in ancient days been poured over the heads of those thereby designated as Israel's king, God's anointed: i.e., the *Messiah*.[1] Jesus, however, takes the pouring of the oil to signify something altogether different: "In pouring this ointment on my *body* she has done it to prepare me for *burial*" (italics added); in Israel, the pouring of oil not only prepared kings for coronation, but also *corpses* for interment. And as the ambiguities mount here, they raise up the most vexing question of all: How can a dead king save us?

Nevertheless, despite all the vagaries, Jesus' reply to the disciples expressing his attitude toward the woman's act would seem to make one thing absolutely certain: what might happen later is not as important as what is happening *now*. For whatever the woman may or may not have done, the fact remains that in responding to Jesus, she has responded to the immediate, the concrete—and the urgent. *Two days* to the deliverance celebrated at the Passover; *two days* to Jesus' being delivered to death. Not much time remains to worry about the future: the challenge of the present is all too close at hand. Thus, anyone who, like the woman at Bethany, responds to such momentous—and momentary—events has in some way met the challenge of the hour. But what then of the future? That will be the time for commemorating actions like the woman's, for whenever this story is told—"wherever this gospel is preached"—such a one will be remembered as having properly responded to what Jesus' very presence calls for at this very moment.

[14]Then one of the twelve, who was called Judas Iscariot, went to the chief priests [15]and said, "What will you give me if I deliver

him to you?" And they paid him thirty pieces of silver. [16]And from that moment he sought an opportunity to betray him.

In stark contrast to the act of kindness performed by the woman, the narrative quickly shifts ("*then*")[2] to Judas' act of treachery.[3] Certainly the chapter's first few verses have already alluded to such treachery by depicting the chief priests and elders busily conspiring to do away with Jesus. Perhaps someone might wish to 'explain' such reprehensible behavior on the part of the people's religious leadership by attributing it, for example, to the sort of jealousy and envy typically expressed by an institutionalized establishment when confronted with a new, charismatic figure like Jesus. Even so, the priests' actions still remain quite shocking. Nevertheless, they are nothing compared to Judas' doings, which are totally astounding. After all, *he* is supposed to be one of Jesus' inner circle, part of a new brotherhood in Israel ("the twelve"), and whereas Caiaphas and his colleagues may be motivated by some kind of political consideration however base, Judas is moved by the basest reason of all: raw greed.[4]

If the woman at Bethany has tried to make the most of the opportunity afforded by the present moment, so too apparently has Judas: "And from that moment he sought an opportunity to betray him." Of course, only time—and the narrative—will tell which of them has really seized the opportunity presented and truly realized the moment for what it is.

> [17]Now on the first day of Unleavened Bread the disciples came to Jesus, saying, "Where will you have us prepare for you to eat the passover?" [18]He said, "Go into the city to a certain one, and say to him, 'The Teacher says, My time is at hand: I will keep the passover at your house with my disciples.'" [19]And the disciples did as Jesus had directed them, and they prepared for passover.

Though Judas and the high priest Caiaphas no doubt believe that they plan in secret, Jesus leaves as little doubt that he is well aware of the upshot of their scheme: "My time is at hand."

Yet for someone who seems so conscious of the swirl of conspiracies surrounding him, Jesus also seems surprisingly serene about it all, thereby giving the impression that *he*, rather than Judas or Caiaphas, is the one genuinely in control. Indeed, with a kind of regal bearing, he orders his disciples to make preparations for the only thing he does appear concerned about—the keeping of the Passover. Quite fittingly, the disciples proceed to carry out his charge without an instant's hesitation.

All this seems somehow familiar. Through the Exodus narrative, we have heard how once before the Lord directed his followers to make ready for the Passover soon to come, and furthermore, we have heard that then, as now, those loyal to God immediately complied with his instructions. Such orders had to be carried out in haste, for prior to that first Passover, there was not a second left to spare; then, as now, being prepared when the appointed time arrived was literally a matter involving life and death.[5]

Little wonder then that Jesus seems practically obsessed with the short time left to put all in readiness for the arrival—and observance—of such a historic, fateful moment.

> [20]When it was evening, he sat at table with the twelve disciples;[e] and as they were eating, he said, [21]"Truly, I say to you, one of you will betray me." [22]And they were very sorrowful, and began to say to him one after another, "Is it I, Lord?" [23]He answered, "He who has dipped his hand in the dish with me, will betray me. [24]The Son of man goes as it is written of him, but woe to that man by whom the Son of man is betrayed! It would have been better for that man if he had not been born." [25]Judas, who betrayed him, said, "Is it I, Master?"[f] He said to him, "You have said so."

[e]Other authorities omit *disciples*
[f]Or *Rabbi*

As the celebration of the Passover meal begins, the narrative continues its emphasis on Jesus' uncanny ability to remain virtually impassive albeit completely in command while the turbulence around him builds. Thus, his almost casual remark about one of the disciples' treachery sets off a tumultuous chain reaction among them all: "one after another, 'Surely not I, Lord?'"[6] Yet his reply to them shows the same imperturbability as before, as he merely restates what he has said to them before. Nevertheless, even *that* response manages to cause further agitation, prompting Judas to blurt out: 'Who, *me*, Rabbi?' But even then, in the face of such a blatant, maddeningly perverse feigning of innocence, Jesus stays strangely distant, seemingly confirming Judas' guilt, although, to be sure, in a most ironic way: "You have said it."[7]

Now someone might demur here, claiming the reason Jesus can remain so composed in the face of both imminent treachery and death is that for him, there really are no surprises. As the narrative has made extremely plain on several occasions, Jesus knows only too well what awaits him. Therefore (our hypothetical dissenter might continue), the *real* object of our sympathy ought not to be Jesus, but *Judas*, who apparently has no choice at all in the part he will play triggering the tragic chain of events, but who will evidently pay heavily for his actions nonetheless: "Woe to that man . . . !" If so—concludes our objector—the narrative has led us to an impasse: divine foreknowledge and predestination on the one hand versus human freedom and responsibility on the other.

Obviously, arriving at such an impasse remains a distinct possibility on one reading of the story. However, on a *Matthean reading* of events, that particular theological problem may not be the central issue meriting our attention. Throughout the narrative, we have repeatedly come upon the phrase, "as it is written"; we come across it here again in verse 24. For Matthew, such allusions to Israel's long-standing prophecies reflect the core conviction that the God portrayed in Jewish Scripture is one who *inevitably* brings his promises to fruition despite all the barriers erected in his way. In fact, whatever drama there is in the story at this juncture depends heavily on that very notion, because while God's assurances to the world have certainly been made clear by now, what still remains entirely unclear is how—and indeed, *if*—God can fulfill his word given the world's profound contrariness. And just as the

Christian master story continually poses that rather troubling question, so too Jesus' presence—the presence of God-with-us—proves equally troubling to all who encounter it: the Jewish authorities, Judas, the disciples—and even the story's hearers.

> [26]Now as they were eating, Jesus took bread, and blessed, and broke it, and gave it to the disciples and said, "Take, eat; this is my body." [27]And he took a cup, and when he had given thanks he gave it to them, saying, "Drink of it, all of you; [28]for this is my blood of the[g] covenant, which is poured out for many for the forgiveness of sins. [29]I tell you I shall not drink again of this fruit of the vine until that day when I drink it new with you in my Father's kingdom."

[g]Other ancient authorities insert *new*

In a variety of ways, Matthew shows us Jesus observing the traditional Jewish rites surrounding the time-honored Passover meal of the seder: he reclines at the table,[8] dips as is the custom,[9] recites the required blessings over the unleavened bread and wine, and concludes by singing[10] the prescribed hymns of praise to God.[11]

Nevertheless, there is something strangely different in the way that Jesus goes about his seder. The unleavened bread (i.e., the matzah) he identifies with his body; the wine he calls "my blood of the covenant." While the basic symbols of the seder have remained the same, Jesus has transformed their significance, and in the process, he has also changed the significance of what the Passover celebrates. Heretofore, the matzah, "the bread of affliction" (Deut. 16:3), has commemorated Israel's harrowing flight from Egypt, the act terminating her sojourn there; now, however, the matzah's broken pieces will call to mind Jesus' body broken in the harrowing event ending his sojourn on earth. For Jews at their seder, wine symbolizes the sweetness of God's past deliverance of his people from their Egyptian masters. But for the disciples at *their* seder, the wine stands as a sanguine—and sanguinary—token of Jesus' coming act of delivering all people from the mastery of sin. Hence, Jesus' words point not merely to the transformation of the seder, but ultimately to the

✓transformation of the covenant itself. We might remember that that old pact at Sinai, establishing the original bond between God and Israel, was concluded with a sacrifice which thereby sealed it with "the blood of the covenant" (Exod. 24:8). So too shall be the case for this new covenant binding the Lord and all mankind; as Jesus tells us, it likewise shall be sealed with a blood-sacrifice—*his*.

Of course, the sacrifice that is the center of attention at Passover is the paschal offering. Celebrating Israel's redemption from Egypt, it recalls how at that time, a slain lamb's blood on the Israelites' doorposts provided life-giving protection from the forces of death without, even as its flesh offered sustenance to those who partook of it within. So shall it be with Jesus now. In ways not yet fully clear, his sacrificial death shall somehow ward off death while bringing life for those who, like the disciples, eat up, drink in—i.e., *digest and internalize*—what he offers to share with them. In a sense, the sharing of that first Passover meal called a new community into being; now, this meal with Jesus shall do the same. Hence, for Jesus' disciples, this present seder meal, though apparently their last supper with their lord, is in reality only a foretaste of the grand banquet soon to come, celebrating the inauguration of God's redemptive reign when all will feast together once again.

> [30]And when they had sung a hymn, they went out to the Mount of Olives. [31]Then Jesus said to them, "You will all fall away because of me this night; for it is written, 'I will strike the shepherd, and the sheep of the flock will be scattered.' [32]But after I am raised up, I will go before you to Galilee." [33]Peter declared to him, "Though they all fall away because of you, I will never fall away." [34]Jesus said to him, "Truly, I say to you, this very night, before the cock crows, you will deny me three times." [35]Peter said to him, "Even if I must die with you, I will not deny you." And so said all the disciples.

By Jesus' own account, the disciples still have failed to follow the thrust of his previous teaching, and as a result, they will similarly fail to follow *him*. Indeed, Peter's very words seem to confirm Jesus' own assessment, "Even if I must die with you . . ." *Even*? Such an utterance plainly ignores one of the starkest implications of Jesus' prior distribution among the disciples of the bread and wine signifying his body and his blood. For whatever else his act betokened then, at the very least it indicated that those who would share in the life he offers must *necessarily* share in his death as well.

Hence, Jesus' situation has an increasingly poignant quality about it. Rejected by the people's leaders, betrayed by Judas, and misunderstood by his disciples, as he nears what seems his end, Jesus appears to be more and more alone, and the words of dialogue here between himself and Peter only serve to emphasize his isolation even more: "scattered," "fall away," "deny." If Jesus really is the only one who clearly sees the truth to which everyone else is blind, how can it be said that Peter and the others are in any sense the *followers* whom he *leads*?

Yet say it Jesus does: "After I am raised up, I will go before you." Even if the disciples desert him, he will not abandon them. How the bond between them will be maintained has yet to be revealed. But in any case, despite the sense of inevitable tragedy inherent in Jesus' current circumstances, inherent in them also is an inescapable element of hope.

[36]Then Jesus went with them to a place called Gethsemane, and he said to his disciples, "Sit here, while I go yonder and pray." [37]And taking with him Peter and the two sons of Zebedee, he began to be sorrowful and troubled. [38]Then he said to them, "My soul is very sorrowful, even to death; remain here, and watch[h] with me." [39]And going a little farther he fell on his face and prayed, "My Father, if it be possible, let this cup pass from me; nevertheless, not as I will, but as thou wilt." [40]And he came to the disciples and found them sleeping; and he said to Peter, "So could you not watch[h] with me one hour? [41]Watch[h] and pray that you may not enter into temptation; the spirit indeed is willing, but the flesh is weak." [42]Again, for the second time, he went away and prayed, "My Father, if this cannot pass unless I drink it, thy will be done." [43]And again he came and found them sleeping, for their eyes were heavy. [44]So, leaving them again, he went away and prayed for the third time, saying the same words. [45]Then he came to the disciples and said to them, "Are you still sleeping and taking your rest? Behold, the hour is

at hand, and the Son of man is betrayed into the hands of sinners. [46]Rise, let us be going; see, my betrayer is at hand."

[h]Or *keep awake*

At the seder, the disciples had readily shared Jesus' wine cup of celebration. But now, at Gethsemane, they are altogether unprepared to share his bitter cup of destiny. To be sure, Jesus himself, despite his previous rather stoic attitude toward the future, now looks as though he would prefer not to have to drink it either. With the disciples at the seder, Jesus too had taken up the *Passover* goblet wholeheartedly; yet in the garden, he prays three times to let this other cup "*pass by.*" [12] Nevertheless, in the end, Jesus' own wishes yield to those of God, and in the last analysis, that is what makes him stand out as so markedly different from everyone else around him.

The scene in the garden vividly captures that difference. For there, Jesus speaks not only to God, but also to the disciples whom he implores to remain awake with him on watch for the arrival of the fated time. Once before, there had been another such momentous nightwatch—in preparation for God's climactic, redemptive act on behalf of Israel in Egypt (Exod. 12:42). In that hour, the people obeyed the charge to stay alert and were delivered as a result. But in Jesus' last hours, the charge—the *plea*—falls instead on the deaf ears of those sound asleep.

And notice: the disciples fail to respond to Jesus, not because, for example, they are too full of themselves to care about anybody else, but because they are simply too full of wine and consequently too deep in slumber even to *hear* him, much less heed or help him. Unlike the Jewish leaders, who turn on Jesus out of envy, and unlike Judas, who deserts him out of greed, the disciples abandon Jesus in a way far more disconcerting: apparently, they just *cannot help not helping* him. That is, they let him down, not because they are intentionally mean or uncaring or evil beings, but because they are merely *human* beings—i.e., beings whose essential makeup, *despite* their best intentions, imposes limits on their abilities and strengths: "The spirit indeed is willing, but the flesh is weak." And beings so limited by nature may to that extent find themselves equally limited in their own capacities to come fully to *anybody's* aid, be it Jesus' or others'—be it *God's or even theirs*.

Here then is Jesus standing all alone in the garden—all alone, that is, save one: God. In fact, Jesus' standing here as one with God—and with what God wants—is precisely what makes him stand out so strikingly from all the rest. Paradoxically, his yielding to God's will and power appears to be the very thing giving him the virtually superhuman willpower to overcome his genuine human fear, keep his lonely vigil, and face the travails that presently await him.

"See, my betrayer is at hand." The hour of betrayal has finally struck, and in but a few instants more, Jesus will be separated from his disciples as he is given over "into the hands of sinners." As the disciples have failed to attend to his words, they have likewise failed to attend to what is called for by the moment, by Jesus—in short, *by God himself*. And the result is separation, estrangement, and tragedy besides. Thus far, at least, Jesus' only real support has appeared to come from God, and hence, whatever chances this narrative may hold for a happy ending would seem to lie in hands other than human ones.

But in this story of faithlessness, treachery, and betrayal, can even God be counted on? For what kind of father is it that lets his only son be treated—or rather, *mis*treated—in such a manner?

[47]While he was still speaking, Judas came, one of the twelve, and with him a great crowd with swords and clubs, from the chief priests and elders of the people. [48]Now the betrayer had given them a sign, saying, "The one I shall kiss is the man; seize him." [49]And he came up to Jesus at once and said, "Hail, Master!"[i] And he kissed him. [50]Jesus said to him, "Friend, why are you here?"[j] Then they came up and laid hands on Jesus and seized him. [51]And behold, one of those who were with Jesus stretched out his hand and drew his sword, and struck the slave of the high priest, and cut off his ear. [52]Then Jesus said to him, "Put your sword back into its place; for all who take the sword

will perish by the sword. [53]Do you think that I cannot appeal to my Father, and he will at once send me more than twelve legions of angels? [54]But how then should the scriptures be fulfilled, that it must be so?" [55]At that hour Jesus said to the crowds, "Have you come out as against a robber, with swords and clubs to capture me? Day after day I sat in the temple teaching, and you did not seize me. [56]But all this has taken place, that the scriptures of the prophets might be fulfilled." Then all the disciples forsook him and fled.

ⁱOr *Rabbi*
^jOr *do that for which you have come*

The ironies accompanying Jesus' arrest are almost too much to bear; were they not so bitter, they would be practically comical. Jesus, though knowing full well what each one intends to do, nevertheless lets them all go through their antics. Thus, he lets Judas play out the charade of acting as though he is still one of Jesus' faithful disciples. But Judas' kiss, normally a friend's token of devotion, is instead the traitor's mark of death. Later, Jesus lets the chief priests and elders have their way in arresting him; after all, they are supposedly the authorities who legitimately represent the Law. Yet even as they take him away, Jesus calls attention to how odd it seems that though they could have seized him any *day* while he sat teaching *publicly* at the temple, they have nonetheless chosen to come in the middle of the *night* and carry him off by *stealth*. And finally, when one of the disciples at last rises to Jesus' defense in what is doubtless meant as a courageous show of loyalty, his sword stroke falls ludicrously wide of the mark: instead of hitting the appropriate target of his moral outrage, i.e., the high priest, he hits the high priest's slave, an innocent bystander who just happens to be in the wrong place at the wrong time.

Yet however much the whole situation might seem better suited to bathos than pathos, the scene depicted is after all a somber one, and one aspect of it that Jesus himself takes with unequivocal seriousness is the disciples' attempted resort to swordplay. He makes a point of telling them that had he wanted that kind of 'help,' he could have gotten far more of it than their puny minions could provide. But he has rejected that option for two reasons. First, all such violence does is beget more of the same—whether executed by the crowds who have come to get him with their "swords and clubs" or by the God who would come to save him with his own "legions of angels." To be saved that way is ultimately no salvation at all, for while perhaps bringing life to some, it invariably brings death to others. Thus second, and more important, were Jesus' own salvation to come through such deadly means, then how could the prophecy of Scripture—God's promise of life to all the world—ever come about?

For those witnessing Jesus' acts and words as he is betrayed by Judas, arrested by the authorities, and abandoned by the disciples, his behavior is bewildering to say the least. What kind of man *is* this? And even more than that, what kind of *messianic savior* is this? For he at once appears both strangely passive and impotent while yet eerily majestic and powerful. How then are *we* to see him—as a naïve weakling loose in the world? Or as the bearer of a mysterious power soon to be let loose, but as yet unknown to the world?

[57]Then those who had seized Jesus led him to Caiaphas the high priest, where the scribes and the elders had gathered. [58]But Peter followed him at a distance, as far as the courtyard of the high priest, and going inside he sat with the guards to see the end. [59]Now the chief priests and the whole council sought false testimony against Jesus that they might put him to death, [60]but they found none, though many false witnesses came forward. At last two came forward [61]and said, "This fellow said 'I am able to destroy the temple of God and to build it in three days.'" [62]And the high priest stood up and said, "Have you no answer to make? What is it that these men testify against you?" [63]But Jesus was silent. And the high priest said to him, "I adjure you by the living God, tell us if you are the Christ, the Son of God." [64]Jesus said to him, "You have said so. But I tell you, hereafter you will see the Son of man seated at the right hand of Power, and coming on the clouds of heaven." [65]Then the high priest tore his robes, and said, "He has uttered blasphemy. Why do we still need witnesses? You have now heard his blasphemy. [66]What is your judgment?" They answered, "He deserves death." [67]Then they spat in his face and struck him;

and some slapped him, [68]saying, "Prophesy to us, you Christ! Who is it that struck you?"

The inquiry before the council of the chief priests, scribes, and elders seems not so much to put Jesus on trial as to put the truth itself on trial, for the Jewish court's display of perverted justice displays an equally perverted vision of reality. Although the tribunal seeks to give the impression of being just and upright through its compliance with the Torah's requirement that *two* witnesses must testify that So-and-so deserves the death penalty (Deut. 19:15), the witnesses it actually seeks out are ones it definitely knows to be lying. Finally, two come forward who fit the bill. Ironically, however, their declaration—'He says he can destroy and rebuild the temple in three days'—only further indicates how topsy-turvy human conceptions of truth and falsehood have become, because their testimony, though perjured, nevertheless ends up corroborating the true state of affairs. For in a sense, Jesus *has* continually been speaking of dismantling the old locus of God's service and of reconstructing a new setting for devotion in its stead—and all to be effected in a very short time. When Caiaphas then goes on with his pretense of legal rectitude by asking Jesus if he has anything to say in his own defense, Jesus' response is silence—as though bespeaking a certain majesty and authority—which suggests that while the others present are completely blind to what is really proper and improper, just and unjust, good and evil, Jesus—and Jesus alone—nonetheless sees everything for what it truly is.

Yet Caiaphas remains undeterred from continuing the sham. He instead presses Jesus again with a supposedly trumped-up charge: 'Tell us, by God, are you the Messiah, the Son of God?' Jesus' reply once more underscores the unsettling way that human value judgments about what is true or false have become horribly inverted. While Caiaphas undoubtedly believes his allegation to be the farthest thing from the truth, Jesus' answer—'As you say'—implies that on the contrary, the high priest has hit the nail squarely on the head, and moreover, Caiaphas and all his cohorts shall most assuredly come to see how matters truly stand when Jesus one day sits enthroned, exalted by the power of heaven. And what is the high priest's perception of Jesus' faithful witness to God's unfolding plan? "Blasphemy!" With that, the other members of the court spit on Jesus and strike and taunt him. In other words, in perhaps the greatest inversion of all, they *mock* Jesus, simply because *he has told the truth*. Hence, in the end, it appears that it is not the accused Jesus, but rather, his accusers, that these proceedings have shown to be in the wrong. The trial, it seems, has been theirs, not his, and the verdict handed down in their case is clearly, 'Guilty!'

Meanwhile, through it all, Peter has "sat with the guards to see the end." Forgetting—or ignoring—Jesus' words that he will be "raised up" (v. 32), Peter believes that the trial does indeed spell the beginning of the end for Jesus; he cannot imagine that it might instead signal the beginning *of the beginning*.

> [69]Now Peter was sitting outside in the courtyard. And a maid came up to him, and said, "You also were with Jesus the Galilean." [70]But he denied it before them all, saying, "I do not know what you mean." [71]And when he went out to the porch, another maid saw him, and she said to the bystanders, "This man was with Jesus of Nazareth." [72]And again he denied it with an oath, "I do not know the man." [73]After a little while the bystanders came up and said to Peter, "Certainly you are also one of them, for your accent betrays you." [74]Then he began to invoke a curse on himself and to swear, "I do not know the man." And immediately the cock crowed. [75]And Peter remembered the saying of Jesus, "Before the cock crows, you will deny me three times." And he went out and wept bitterly.

From the sad news of Jesus' trial, the narrative shifts to the even sadder news of Peter's denial of him. Despite all Peter's earlier protestations of fidelity (v. 33), he has nevertheless abandoned Jesus—just as Jesus predicted he would. As if to accentuate such sad tidings even further, the chapter's final words depict Peter's shame and remorse over his act(s) of faithlessness: "And he went out and wept bitterly."

Yet despite its current bad news, the account being related is after all still called a *gospel*—"good news." Thus, there simply *must* be some good news in it somewhere. But where? When will all our troubling uncertainties about the Christian master story finally be cleared up so that we might at last see its vision of human life rightly? As the chapter began with ambiguous news, so too such ambiguities are present at its conclusion. Perhaps therefore at this point in the narrative, the only unequivocally good news we have is that the story is not yet over—either for Jesus or for us.

Notes

1. See, for instance, II Kings 9:6 where the prophet, following the instructions of the Lord, anoints Yehu with oil, thus setting him over Israel. The English derivative of the Hebrew word used there—*meshachti*—is none other than *messiah*.

2. Stendahl, "Matthew," 693e.

3. Fenton, *Saint Matthew*, p. 413.

4. Judas' betrayal of Jesus here in exchange for pieces of silver is interpreted by many commentators to be an allusion to Zech. 11:12, which occurs in the context of the prophet's describing God's annulling of his previous covenant with Israel. However, one wonders whether there might not also be an allusion to Gen. 37:26-28, in which Joseph's brothers betray him by selling him into slavery for silver at the specific urging of *Judah*. And in that case, for the present narrative involving *Judas*, might there be not only such an implied connection with Judah, but also with all of Judah's 'descendants'—i.e., the *Jews*?

5. Cf. Exod. 12.

6. Fenton, *Saint Matthew*, p. 416.

7. See as well 26:64 and 27:11, where Jesus gives this same response. While from the context of the narrative it is evident that Jesus' answer is meant to be taken as an affirmative, nevertheless, it seems equally clear that there is something strikingly and ironically significant in the fact of the truth's having been uttered by the very people who are portrayed as Jesus' adversaries, as if to suggest that even *they* cannot help but acknowledge the reality of God's power manifested before them in the person of Jesus.

8. The literal sense of v. 20. Reclining imitated the customary practice of the guests at Greco-Roman symposia; at a seder, it signified that those in attendance at *that* time were also free-men, worthy of respect, dignity, and honor.

9. Cf. v. 23. Although Jesus uses the expression "dipped his hand"—and certainly the ritual washing of the hands prior to the meal was a distinctive (and normative) Pharisaic practice—nevertheless, the reference may be instead to the dipping of some sort of green vegetable at the seder's beginning which was once more an imitation of the customary procedures at symposia. Typically, the symposia, too, started with a similar kind of 'dip' meant as an *hors d'oeuvre;* hence once again, engaging in the symposium-based practice signified for the participant at the seder his or her own freedom.

10. See 26:30.
11. I.e., part of the 'Hallel'; namely, Pss. 115–118.
12. See Fenton, *Saint Matthew*, p. 422.

XIII
MATTHEW 27

^{27:1}When morning came, all the chief priests and the elders of the people took counsel against Jesus to put him to death; ²and they bound him and led him away and delivered him to Pilate the governor.

Thematically as well as chronologically, the present chapter is a continuation of the preceding one. Earlier, Matthew 26 had commenced with scenes of the Jewish leaders 'taking counsel' to do away with Jesus and with Jesus himself foretelling that he would shortly be "delivered" over for execution (Matt. 26:1-4). Now, as though to reiterate and confirm Jesus' own words, the opening two verses of chapter 27 repeat those selfsame phrases: "the chief priests and elders . . . *took counsel* . . . to put [Jesus] to death . . . and *delivered* him to Pilate the governor." The predicted events are clearly coming to pass; moreover, they are coming to pass quite quickly. The conspirators have arrested Jesus the previous night, and as morning dawns, they straightaway hand him over to the Romans—and presumably his end.

Nevertheless, the current chapter's talk about 'delivery time' also calls to mind the last chapter's repeated references to another such occasion: the Passover—i.e., the *time for deliverance*. Thus, from the outset, Matthew 27 dramatically intensifies the quandary posed continually by its predecessor: Which time is it really? Time for being delivered over to death?

Or time for being delivered up to life?

> [3]When Judas, his betrayer, saw that he was condemned, he repented and brought back the thirty pieces of silver to the chief priests and the elders, [4]saying, "I have sinned in betraying innocent blood." They said, "What is it to us? See to it yourself." [5]And throwing down the pieces of silver in the temple, he departed; and he went and hanged himself. [6]But the chief priests, taking the pieces of silver, said, "It is not lawful to put them into the treasury, since they are blood money." [7]So they took counsel, and bought with them the potter's field, to bury strangers in. [8]Therefore that field has been called the Field of Blood to this day. [9]Then was fulfilled what had been spoken by the prophet Jeremiah, saying, "And they took the thirty pieces of silver, the price of him on whom a price had been set by some of the sons of Israel, [10]and they gave them for the potter's field, as the Lord directed me."

Before the narrative moves on to Jesus' arraignment in front of Pilate, it takes one brief backward look at Judas, who, having had some 'second thoughts'[1] about his actions, is frantically trying to extricate—and exculpate—himself from the conspiracy's web. First, he attempts to return his blood money to the priests and elders. Next, following their refusal to take it, he hurls it into the temple. Finally, in one last effort to rid himself of guilt, Judas casts away his life.

For their part, the chief priests, though likewise fully implicated, similarly do not want to be stained either by the money or by the guilt associated with it. 'On religious grounds,' they cannot accept such funds for the temple treasury, and yet they cannot simply leave the silver pieces lying where they are. Consequently, they decide to take the money and buy a plot of land in which to bury strangers. Ironically, these officials who have only recently played a major role in the death of one man—Judas—and who are about to play that part again in the death of another—Jesus—proceed to use the tainted money in ways connected with death yet again. With alarming perversity, they do all this for the sake of keeping up *the appearance of being righteous*—just as they have been concerned with keeping up such appearances all along. Crucially, however, neither Judas nor the Jewish leaders perform the one act necessary for truly putting matters right: righting things with Jesus. And by dooming him, they doom themselves as well.

Yet despite the warped behavior of Judas and the council members, God's plan remains straight on course—as Matthew's citation of biblical prophecy is plainly meant to show.[2] For without their even realizing it, and regardless of their own intent, both Judas and the priests have nevertheless acted to bring God's purposes to fruition.

> [11]Now Jesus stood before the governor; and the governor asked him, "Are you the King of the Jews?" Jesus said, "You have said so." [12]But when he was accused by the chief priests and elders, he made no answer. [13]Then Pilate said to him, "Do you not hear how many things they testify against you?" [14]But he gave him no answer, not even to a single charge; so that the governor wondered greatly.

As the story shifts back to Pilate's interrogation of Jesus, it unsettlingly calls to mind Jesus' prior questioning by the Jewish court. There, when Jesus had been ordered to answer the allegations made against him, he had responded either by having the charges tellingly recoil on those who uttered them—'You have said it'—or by remaining totally silent. Here as well, Jesus takes the same approach in responding to the Roman's queries, and the net result is virtually identical: Jesus' apparent indifference to being on trial for his life makes him appear eerie—*unearthly*. He seems like anything *but* someone completely dependent on this court's power, mercy, and sense of justice. At the earlier proceedings before the Jewish council, Jesus' disinterested demeanor had given him a certain majesty. At his hearing now with Pilate, his manner displays much the same kind of regal bearing as though affirmatively answering the procurator's question: "Are you the King of the Jews?" Hence, Jesus has a strange effect once more on those confronting him—and on those whom he confronts in turn: "The governor wondered greatly."

> [15]Now at the feast the governor was accustomed to release for the crowd any one prisoner whom they wanted. [16]And they had then a notorious prisoner, called Barabbas.[k] [17]So when they

had gathered, Pilate said to them, "Whom do you want me to release for you, Barabbas[k] or Jesus who is called Christ?" [18]For he knew that it was out of envy that they had delivered him up. [19]Besides, while he was sitting on the judgment seat, his wife sent word to him, "Have nothing to do with that righteous man, for I have suffered much over him today in a dream." [20]Now the chief priests and the elders persuaded the people to ask for Barabbas and destroy Jesus. [21]The governor again said to them, "Which of the two do you want me to release for you?" And they said, "Barabbas." [22]Pilate said to them, "Then what shall I do with Jesus who is called Christ?" They all said, "Let him be crucified." [23]And he said, "Why, what evil has he done?" But they shouted all the more, "Let him be crucified."

[k]Other ancient authorities read *Jesus Barabbas*

Yet again, a scene in this chapter is hauntingly reminiscent of another from the preceding one. Like the priests and elders previously, Pilate knows full well that Jesus has been bound over on false charges. The Roman governor has even guessed the reason the Jewish leadership has indicted Jesus—"out of envy"—and furthermore, his wife has sent him word that she has had dreams concerning the prisoner's innocence, thereby confirming Pilate's original assumption—albeit in a way that is literally 'out of this world.'[3]

But the resemblance between Jesus' two court appearances runs still deeper. In the prior trial before the Jews, truth had been stood on its head, and in the current inquiry before the Romans, reality is turned upside down again. For when Pilate tries to get Jesus—and himself—off the hook by giving the crowd its choice of having him release the accused yet innocent Jesus, or another prisoner, the "notorious" Barabbas, the crowd picks—who else?—Barabbas. However, the extent of the crowd's distorted judgment is far worse than its 'mere' decision to spare the guilty while condemning the innocent. For notice what the Aramaic name "Barabbas" means: "son of the father." In essence, therefore, the throng has been asked to decide which man is the *real* Son of the Father—Barabbas or "Jesus who is called Christ"?[4] And in answering that, of course, the assembled masses also answer whom they accept as being truly the issue of the Father and whom they reject outright as impostor. Significantly—and tragically—the crowd has got the answer just plain wrong. Even when Pilate gives the crowd a second chance, the response remains unchanged: 'Let Barabbas go, and as for Jesus, "let him be crucified."'

Hence, Jesus' trial before the Romans has produced the same verdict as his trial before the Jews—death—and as importantly, it has produced the same nagging question as before: When will human beings stop being so blind to the truth facing them in the person of this man Jesus?

> [24]So when Pilate saw that he was gaining nothing, but rather that a riot was beginning, he took water and washed his hands before the crowd, saying, "I am innocent of this man's blood;[j] see to it yourselves." [25]And all the people answered, "His blood be on us and on our children!" [26]Then he released for them Barabbas, and having scourged Jesus, delivered him to be crucified.

> [j]Other authorities read *this righteous blood* or *this righteous man's blood*

Jesus' last hope would seem to be Pilate. Surely if anyone has the power to save him, it ought to be the governor who is backed by the might of imperial Rome. But up to now, other sources of human strength—whether close friendship or religious authority or popular appeal—have consistently failed to save; the disciples, the Jewish leaders, and the masses have failed in turn to deliver Jesus the succor needed. So too, the kind of dominion manifested by human government now proves equally powerless to rescue him from death. Pilate, though he has all of Rome behind him and though he knows Jesus to be guiltless, nevertheless fears a riot brewing and thus, to keep the peace, determines that Jesus' life is expendable. Washing his hands of the whole affair, the procurator tells the crowd, "See to it yourselves"—the same instructions the priests and elders had earlier given Judas when, as people in similar positions of power and authority, they too had turned their backs on the spilling of "innocent blood."[5] In the end, Pilate completely capitulates to the crowd's wishes. He complies with their verdict in the case of

Jesus-called-Christ, agreeing to "*let* him be crucified."

And what is the crowd's reaction? "And all *the people* answered, 'His blood be on us and on our children!'" Not only are the people—*God's people*[6]—enthusiastic about taking responsibility for putting someone to death, but the someone they so fervently want to have put to death is not just anyone, but their own Messiah, *the embodiment of God himself*. What could serve as a more striking instance of their profound failure to see the truth? Worse yet, what could serve as a more blatant indication of Israel's sinfulness, of her *estrangement* from her Lord? For by seeking to have Jesus killed, she has rejected God—and his covenant—in perhaps the most basic way of all.

The covenant's fulfillment was to have depended in part on the people's single-minded devotion to keeping its end of the agreement. However, the people's response to Pilate suggests that there is now in fact only one thing to which it wholeheartedly agrees: to have Jesus "delivered . . . to be crucified." But if Israel has so totally turned her back on covental promises—and turned her back as well on the promise of salvation inherent in the covenant itself—then how can Israel be saved? And even more distressing, if Israel's actions have so plainly demonstrated her to be unfit as the bearer of God's saving promise to all humanity, what then has become of human hope for the redemption of the world?

> [27]Then the soldiers of the governor took Jesus into the praetorium, and they gathered the whole battalion before him. [28]And they stripped him and put a scarlet robe upon him, [29]and plaiting a crown of thorns they put it on his head, and put a reed in his right hand. And kneeling before him they mocked him, saying, "Hail, King of the Jews!" [30]And they spat upon him, and took the reed and struck him on the head. [31]And when they had mocked him, they stripped him of the robe, and put his own clothes on him, and led him away to crucify him.

Apparently, the Jews are not the only ones bent on Jesus' destruction; according to the narrative, the Romans—i.e., *non-Jews*—are also eager participants in bringing about his downfall. Just like the Jewish leaders before them,[7] the Roman soldiers take their turn at taunting Jesus for being what in truth he is: King of the Jews. Thus, they garb him in a scarlet robe, put a crown of thorns around his head, and place a reed in his right hand while kneeling before him in mock reverence.

Consider, however, the image depicted. Shown here is the ruler the Jews are to serve: one robed in a mantle of humiliation, crowned by a halo of suffering, invested with a scepter of vulnerability—and before whom even Gentiles bow in homage. This is a strange king indeed, for his power to command the recognition that is rightly due him comes not from his apparent strength, but rather from his seeming weakness, a weakness further underscored by the narrative's portrayal of what immediately follows Jesus' ridicule at the praetorium: "[The Romans] *stripped him* and *mocked him*, . . . and *led him away* to crucify him."

Despite Pilate's previous disclaimer of responsibility, the non-Jews, it seems, are nevertheless extremely willing to lend the Jews a hand in doing away with Jesus.[8] The irony, of course, is that Jesus, the one named at birth "God-with-us" (Matt. 1:23), is not simply the King of the Jews, but the King of the World, and hence, the Romans' own true King as well.

> [32]As they went out, they came upon a man of Cyrene, Simon by name; this man they compelled to carry his cross. [33]And when they came to a place called Golgotha (which means the place of a skull), [34]they offered him wine to drink, mingled with gall; but when he tasted it, he would not drink it. [35]And when they had crucified him, they divided his garments among them by casting lots; [36]then they sat down and kept watch over him there. [37]And over his head they put the charge against him, which read, "This is Jesus the King of the Jews." [38]Then two robbers were crucified with him, one on the right and one on the left. [39]And those who passed by derided him, wagging their heads [40]and saying, "You who would destroy the temple and build it in three days, save yourself! If you are the Son of God, come down from the cross." [41]So also the chief priests, with the scribes and elders, mocked him, saying, [42]"He saved others; he cannot save himself. He is the King of Israel; let him come down now from the cross, and we will believe in him. [43]He trusts in God; let God deliver him now, if he desires him; for he said, 'I

am the Son of God.'" [44]And the robbers who were crucified with him also reviled him in the same way.

Jesus' time has at last arrived: he *has* been delivered over; he *is* crucified. With unremitting irony, all the maddening ambiguities and exasperating misperceptions present in the Christian master story throughout its telling finally come to focus on a common point—the cross.

For the cross confronts us with two possible visions of reality. From one perspective, there is nothing but an endless litany of suffering and humiliation: the Romans ignominiously pressing Simon of Cyrene into service to carry the condemned man's cross; the spectators sitting like vultures who watch and wait for death to come; even the very manner of Jesus' execution apparently mocking him as he hangs beneath the charge "King of the Jews," while nonetheless suspended between two common criminals. And through it all, the unceasing jeers and gibes—from Romans, from Jews, from passersby, even from the robbers dying next to him: 'If you are Israel's king, messiah, son of God, one so powerful to save, then let's see you save yourself!'

Yet from another viewpoint, the scene depicted yields an entirely different understanding. Simon's taking up Jesus' cross is not a disgraceful act at all, but a praiseworthy one, signifying devotion and fidelity.[9] Moreover, the spectators' vigil may be no deathwatch after all, but rather a watch for a totally different kind of outcome altogether.[10] And as for all the mocking, it might prove instead to be an unwitting admission of the truth—that Jesus really is God's appointed one whose presence, even on the cross, spells an imminent salvation that even *death* cannot hold back.[11]

But how? In the Exodus, salvation was wrought by the Lord's mighty acts of justice done on behalf of Israel in fulfillment of God's promises to Israel's fathers. Yet in the present situation, justice has seemingly miscarried, for the one absolutely innocent is being executed while those undeniably responsible and hence *unabsolvably guilty* are getting off scot-free. Indeed, why *doesn't* Jesus come down off that cross and let God put up there in his place those *who truly deserve to die*: Jews, Romans—in sum, *all humanity* which has in one way or another taken part in committing such a heinous crime? Where, then, is God's *sure justice* in what is happening?

> [45]Now from the sixth hour there was darkness over all the land[m] until the ninth hour. [46]And about the ninth hour Jesus cried with a loud voice, "Eli, Eli, lama sabachtani?" that is, "My God, my God, why hast thou forsaken me?" [47]And some of the bystanders hearing it said, "This man is calling Elijah." [48]And one of them at once ran and took a sponge, filled it with vinegar, and put it on a reed, and gave it to him to drink. [49]But the others said, "Wait, let us see whether Elijah will come to save him."[n] [50]And Jesus cried again with a loud voice and yielded up his spirit.
>
> [m]Or *earth*
> [n]Other ancient authorities insert *And another took a spear and pierced his side, and out came water and blood*

If possible, Jesus' final moments on the cross are more wrenching than his first ones. More jeering from the bystanders, more misperceptions of what is taking place before their very eyes—and all juxtaposed against Jesus' mounting suffering. In his death throes, he experiences not only the excruciating pain of crucifixion, but even worse perhaps, the unendurable *agony* of a human being hanging heckled and alone, as though abandoned by everyone—even God: "My God, my God, why have you forsaken me?" Indeed, how *can* God let this happen? Where, then, is his mercy, his compassion—his *fatherly love* in this?

For just see how pathetic Jesus appears to all who cast their gaze on him. Pinioned with legs fastened together and arms spread wide, the human being displayed before us is quite literally *open and vulnerable*; totally immobilized, he is virtually *unable to do anything for himself*. On the cross, all Jesus can really do is what he has done from the beginning—submit his will to God's. Thus, despite his growing pain, Jesus does not fight the suffering; on the contrary, he seems to accept it, for even at the last, he offers no resistance to what is taking place. He does not yield to the bystanders' tempting challenge to invoke God's power to save him from the cross, nor for that matter does he yield to the equally tempting prospect of using his last gasp to summon God's righteous judgment to condemn those who have condemned him. Instead, at the end, Jesus simply *yields*, giving up to God his last breath of life. Hence, one more question cries out to be answered in light of the image forged by Jesus' passion on the cross: Where is God's *saving power* manifested here?

However, while the cross stands at the forefront of our attention, there is something in the background also worth our notice: "There was darkness over all the land." Such darkness had descended once before—in Egypt, when the ninth plague had spread "thick darkness throughout . . . the land."[12] Back then, it preceded plague ten whose climactic arrival carried in its wake both death *and* life. But whereas in Egypt the darkness lasted three days, on Golgotha its duration is considerably shorter: three hours. Thus, like so many times before, the Christian master story rushes forward as though driven by an overwhelming sense of urgency, signaling that whatever is transpiring, it is taking place—indeed, it *must* be taking place—at a faster clip than anyone had hitherto expected.

> [51]And behold, the curtain of the temple was torn in two, from top to bottom; and the earth shook, and the rocks were split; [52]the tombs also were opened, and many bodies of the saints who had fallen asleep were raised, [53]and coming out of the tombs after his resurrection they went into the holy city and appeared to many. [54]When the centurion and those who were with him, keeping watch over Jesus, saw the earthquake and what took place, they were filled with awe, and said, "Truly this was the Son[x] of God!"
>
> [x]Or *a son*

Something surely is happening, and just as surely, it is happening very rapidly. Fissures are occurring everywhere: in the earth, in the temple, in rocks, in tombs. It is as though the old understanding of reality itself were rupturing as a new vision suddenly breaks in upon it. "The curtain of the temple was torn in two . . . ; and . . . the tombs also were opened."

Just as death seems to be losing its former hold over the world, so Israel seems to be losing its prior claim to God's presence. From now on, for the whereabouts of the dead as well as for the activity of the Lord, we must look elsewhere.

Being on the lookout for God's activity had been critical during that first Passover night leading up to Israel's deliverance from Egypt. However, in the present narrative relating the momentous events of another Passover eve, Jesus' disciples have previously failed at Gethsemane to maintain the kind of vigilance that might have offered even a minimum of aid. But now we hear of another posted vigil—here at the foot of the cross: "the centurion and those . . . with him, keeping watch over Jesus." As the soldiers keep an eye on Jesus, they simultaneously stand wide-eyed watching all the fantastic goings-on before them. At last, awestruck and overcome *by what they see*, the Romans make a confession which in turn makes these *Gentiles* the first in the Christian master story *to come to see* what has been the story's truth from start to finish: 'This was indeed God's Son.'

In the Exodus narrative, so much went right for Israel because she performed various crucial acts, such as crying out from under her bondage, smearing lamb's blood on her doorposts, and taking her first steps forward through the Sea of Reeds. But in this story, most of what has gone wrong has essentially been due to a continual failure to perform one act above all others, and that is simply this: *to see truly*. Thus, God's anointed has been profoundly misidentified, his plan has been radically misinterpreted, and his promise of salvation has been utterly misunderstood. Therefore, from the vantage point of the Christian master story, unless we first come to see such matters clearly, we will never come to live our lives rightly. Consequently, we must become like the soldiers at the foot of the cross, such that as our vision is transformed, we ourselves become somehow changed in the process also.

[55]There were also many women there, looking on from afar, who had followed Jesus from Galilee, ministering to him; [56]among whom were Mary Magdalene, and Mary the mother of James and Joseph, and the mother of the sons of Zebedee.

[57] When it was evening, there came a rich man from Arimathea, named Joseph, who also was a disciple of Jesus. [58] He went to Pilate and asked for the body of Jesus. Then Pilate ordered it to be given to him. [59] And Joseph took the body, and wrapped it in a clean linen shroud, [60] and laid it in his own new tomb, which he had hewn in the rock; and he rolled a great stone to the door of the tomb, and departed. [61] Mary Magdalene and the other Mary were there, sitting opposite the sepulchre.

[62] Next day, that is, after the day of Preparation, the chief priests and the Pharisees gathered before Pilate [63] and said, "Sir, we remember how that impostor said, while he was still alive, 'After three days I will rise again.' [64] Therefore order the sepulchre to be made secure until the third day, lest his disciples go and steal him away, and tell the people, 'He has risen from the dead,' and the last fraud will be worse than the first." [65] Pilate said to them, "You have a guard[o] of soldiers; go, make it as secure as you can."[p] [66] So they went and made the sepulchre secure by sealing the stone and setting a guard.

[o] Or *Take a guard*
[p] Greek *know*

The watching continues—first with many women witnessing Jesus' crucifixion, later with the two Marys "sitting opposite [his] sepulchre," and finally with the soldiers guarding his tomb. In its own way, each group is poised waiting to see what will happen next.

And certainly, for those of us like Matthew, that is, for those whose expectations are 'Exodus-shaped,' the singular importance of watching and waiting at this juncture of the narrative is readily understandable.[13] For during the night of the first Passover, although the tenth plague had ravaged Egypt bringing death to every Egyptian household, it had *not yet* delivered any Israelite from Egyptian bondage. At best, in sparing Israel's lives while taking Egypt's, the plague had functioned as a harbinger of the larger salvation still anxiously awaited.

The situation is quite analogous at this point in Jesus' story. There has been death, and in its aftermath, there has been a bit of wondrous news—'The tombs are open!'—but still no ultimate salvation. Hence, there are good grounds to wait and see what will transpire. There are, however, equally good reasons for doubting whether anything at all will happen, because not only has Jesus been killed, but, moreover, he has been laid to rest in a sealed tomb with a guard posted to make sure he *stays* there. Little wonder then that all concerned—i.e., the women, the Romans, the Jews, the *story's hearers*—are so concerned with what is consequently the most pressing question for this or *any* story: What happens *next*?

Yet as insistent as that question is, we remember that there are three others also requiring answers. They are questions we posed not in regard to what happens next, but in relation to what happened before while Jesus was on the cross: Where was God's justice then? Where his love? Where his power?

Strangely though, what happens next may well provide the key for understanding everything that happened earlier—and not only in terms of unlocking the enigmas surrounding the crucifixion, but also the perplexities attending the entire Christian master story. And in unscrambling those puzzles, what happens next may just lay bare the greatest mysteries of all: the character of God, the world, and humankind.

Notes

1. When v. 3 says that Judas "repented," it may only mean to suggest that he changed his mind and 'got cold feet'—and not necessarily that he was filled with remorse. See Fenton, *Saint Matthew*, p. 432.

2. Although Matthew cites the prophecy as Jeremiah's, most scholars agree that in actuality, the reference is to Zech. 11:13. For suggestions regarding the reasons behind Matthew's apparent 'confusion,' see Fenton, *Saint Matthew*, pp. 431-32, and K. Stendahl, *The School of St. Matthew* (Philadelphia: Fortress Press, 1969), pp. 120-27.

3. Cf. Matthew, chaps. 1 and 2, where Joseph, too, receives divine confirmation through dreams.

4. This choice is made even clearer in some of the ancient manuscripts which give the criminal's name as *"Jesus* Barabbas." Thus, the crowd must judge which of the two Jesuses before them is the one who is truly the Son of *the* Father.

5. Cf. v. 4.

6. See Fenton, *Saint Matthew*, p. 436.

7. See Matt. 26:67-68 and the commentary at that point.

8. Many writers have commented that given the politically vulnerable situation of the fledgling Christian community of his time, Matthew may have been trying to exonerate the Romans for killing Jesus while putting the blame squarely on the Jews. Nevertheless, from a *literary* perspective, the Romans are portrayed as being deeply implicated, and furthermore, from a *theological* perspective, they *must* be so implicated. First, as we have seen repeatedly thus far, Jesus' treatment at the hands of the Roman tribunal in chap. 27 parallels, literarily speaking, his treatment by the Jewish court in chap. 26. Second and more important, however, Matthew's theological point of Jesus' coming to save all humanity will succeed only if Matthew's story first succeeds in showing that in some way or other all humanity—represented by the Jews (i.e., God's paradigmatic people) and the Romans (i.e., the paradigmatic Gentile people)—has had a hand in initially rejecting Jesus' coming, and thus God's presence and sovereignty in the world.

9. Cf. Matt. 16:24.

10. Cf. vv. 54, 62-66, below. And naturally, cf. also Exod. 12:42-43, a passage which speaks of an earlier eventful act of keeping watch.

11. Notice, too, how the Matthean depiction of the crucifixion relies heavily on scriptural elements such as those present in Ps. 22. Thus, Matt. 27:35 alludes to Ps. 22:18, Matt. 27:39 to Ps. 22:7, and Matt. 27:43 to Ps. 22:8. Of course, best known perhaps of all these allusions is Matt. 27:46 which is a direct citation of Ps. 22:1: "My God,

my God, why have you forsaken me?" In any event, though, Matthew's references to these texts and others like them (e.g., those from Ps. 69) make his attitude here extremely clear. Despite all present appearances which make it seem as though everything is quickly coming apart, on the contrary, God's plan is still firmly set and its pieces are rapidly coming together.

12. As Fenton germanely notes (*Saint Matthew*, p. 442), Matthew has changed Mark's wording from "darkness over the whole *earth*" (Mark 15:33) to "over all the *land*"—thereby recalling Exod. 10:22; see my comments *ad loc*.

13. Stendahl's observation ("Matthew," 695b) is quite relevant here: "It is a consistent trait in Mt. that there is a constant watch over what happens: [v.] 36 (the soldiers), [vv.] 55 and 61 (the women . . .), [v.] 66 (the guard); and 28:1-15."

XIV

MATTHEW 28

---

¹Now after the sabbath, toward the dawn of the first day of the week, Mary Magdalene and the other Mary went to see the sepulchre. ²And behold, there was a great earthquake; for an angel of the Lord descended from heaven and came and rolled back the stone, and sat upon it. ³His appearance was like lightning, and his raiment white as snow. ⁴And for fear of him the guards trembled and became like dead men. ⁵But the angel said to the women, "Do not be afraid; for I know that you seek Jesus who was crucified. ⁶He is not here, for he has risen as he said. Come, see the place where he*q* lay. ⁷Then go quickly and tell his disciples that he has risen from the dead, and behold, he is going before you to Galilee; there you will see him. Lo, I have told you." ⁸So they departed quickly from the tomb with fear and great joy, and ran to tell his disciples.

*q*Other ancient authorities read *the Lord*

The sabbath has ended, and events have moved forward "toward the dawn of the first day of the week" with the two Marys coming to visit Jesus' tomb.[1] As the Jewish sabbath observance had witnessed a cessation of all work in commemoration of God's consummating his initial work of creation, the day following the sabbath sees the recommencement of activity, thus giving similar testimony to the conviction that just as God had resumed his ongoing work of creation following that original sabbath, so too, following this latest one, he still actively continues bringing forth *new life*.

For what do the Marys find upon their return but dazzling manifestations of God's liveliness and life-giving power? Not only do they encounter an earthquake, but more significantly, they come upon a radiant angel who rolls away the stone blocking the sepulchre, indicating to them that the once-dead Jesus is imprisoned in this place of death no longer, but instead is again alive, just waiting to be reunited with them and the disciples in Galilee! Hence, the Marys' long night of waiting is over. The Israelite vigil in Egypt during the death-filled night of the first Passover had ended with the dawning of a new day filled with prospects for new life, great joy, and *imminent salvation*. So it is as *this* new day breaks forth. Armed with such good news, the women instantly embark to proclaim it, departing "quickly . . . with . . . great joy . . . to tell [the] disciples."[2]

> [9]And behold, Jesus met them and said, "Hail!" And they came up and took hold of his feet and worshiped him. [10]Then Jesus said to them, "Do not be afraid; go and tell my brethren to go to Galilee, and there they will see me."

As they rush off to Galilee to fulfill their mission—"Behold!" —the Marys come face-to-face with the risen Jesus, and like the centurions at the cross,[3] their *seeing him and recognizing him for who he is* have a singularly telling effect: "And they came up and took hold of his feet and worshiped him." The women's reaction here is reminiscent of a scene at the story's outset, when the sight of Jesus had a corresponding impact on the magi, who upon seeing him in the midst of a similarly foreordained journey, likewise "fell down and worshiped him" (Matt. 2:11). Importantly, therefore, despite the complex and often disheartening twists and turns in between, the narrative's conclusion seems nonetheless right on line with the auspicious promise of its beginning.

And current events appear to be bearing out past promises in another way as well. For ironically, the fact of the women *worshiping* at Jesus' feet serves as confirmation of the claims previously made by Jesus' would-be detractors—claims which, significantly, Jesus himself never denied: namely, that he could "destroy the temple of God, and [re]build it in three days" (Matt. 26:61). Three days earlier during the crucifixion, the curtain of the temple, the seat of God's presence, was torn wide open. Now, three days later, Jesus' sepulchre has been opened wide, and consequently at present, the place where there is worship of the Lord is not back in Jerusalem at the temple, but on the way to Galilee with the risen Christ. Bluntly stated, the Temple of God is now the Son of God.[4]

> [11]While they were going, behold, some of the guard went into the city and told the chief priests all that had taken place. [12]And when they had assembled with the elders and taken counsel, they gave a sum of money to the soldiers [13]and said, "Tell people, 'His disciples came by night and stole him away while we were asleep.' [14]And if this comes to the governor's ears, we will satisfy him and keep you out of trouble." [15]So they took the money and did as they were directed; and this story has been spread among the Jews to this day.

While the women hasten to Galilee to make their report to the disciples of all the wondrous happenings, the Roman guards for their part race back to Jerusalem to give the chief priests their own account of "all that had taken place." Although the two groups of messengers bear similar tidings—earthquake, angel, open sepulchre, empty tomb!—the guards, in contrast to the women, are probably far from overjoyed about the information they must relay. After all, they have utterly failed in their assignment: to make sure that the tomb stayed shut—and that Jesus' body stayed put.

For the Jewish leadership, however, the guards' news presents no problem; they simply deal with it the way they have dealt with other such 'difficulties' in the past. Once more, they 'take counsel' to plot their course of action, and the course they decide upon is by now a quite familiar one. Money has previously served them well both in obtaining Judas' cooperation to betray Jesus and in purchasing the potter's field to hush up their own part in that scandalous act. Therefore, why not use such means again to buy the soldiers' cooperation, thereby hushing up the guards—and the truth about Jesus? Hence, "they gave a sum of money to the soldiers and said . . . '[If] this comes to the governor's ears, we will satisfy him and keep you out of trouble.'" The guards, if asked what happened to Jesus' body, are simply to say that while they were dozing, the disciples came and spirited it away.

Crucially, however, in Matthew's telling of the story, though Jesus' followers and the Jewish leaders' minions may disagree about what happened to the body in the sepulchre, there is nevertheless one thing about which all parties implicitly agree: there was *no-body* in the tomb.[5] As a result, the *real* dispute between the two sides hinges on their answer to the question, 'Where is Jesus now?'

> [16]Now the eleven disciples went to Galilee, to the mountain to which Jesus had directed them. [17]And when they saw him they worshiped him; but some doubted. [18]And Jesus came and said to them, "All authority in heaven and on earth has been given to me. [19]Go therefore and make disciples of all nations, baptizing them in the name of the Father and of the Son and of the Holy Spirit, [20]teaching them to observe all that I have commanded you; and lo, I am with you always, to the close of the age."

The climactic episode in Matthew's rendering of the Christian master story dramatically parallels the denouement of the Exodus narrative: both accounts reach their 'high point' at a mountain rendezvous where a new relationship with God is offered. Those accepting that new offer are to be bound faithfully to God by being bound devotedly to his directives, which they are to carry out even as they journey forward— escorted by their Lord—to their promised destination.

Nevertheless, for all the remarkable resemblances between the rendezvous at Sinai and the one in Galilee, the dissimilarities between them are equally distinctive. For in Galilee, the legitimate representative of God is not Moses but Jesus, the total range of whose sanctioned warrant is manifestly different, precisely because the range of Jesus' authority *is* total, encompassing "all authority in heaven and on earth." Unlike Moses, therefore, Jesus does not simply speak *for* God, but speaks *as God himself*, such that those who would bind themselves to "the Father" cannot be so allied unless they simultaneously devote themselves to "the Son and . . . the Holy Spirit"—i.e., to the one whom we have met before as the earthly Jesus and whom we now meet again as the risen Christ.[6] In the Exodus, the Israelites became followers of the Lord by following his charges from Sinai as imparted through Moses. However, those who would now follow God from Galilee must be, like the disciples, ready to follow *Jesus* and *his* teachings—or in Jesus' own words, "all that *I* have commanded you."[7]

And where does Jesus bid *his* people go? Not, as in Exodus, to *a* land pledged long ago to Abraham's descendants, but rather to "all nations," that is, to *all* the lands on earth. Thus, an equally ancient promise to Abraham starts to reach fulfillment, namely, that through Abraham's descendants— descendants like Jesus and the disciples—all the world's peoples one day would be blessed.[8] Hence, the conclusion of Matthew's narrative recalls once more its opening proclamation, declaring it to be the story of Jesus Savior, Abraham's offshoot, whose full genealogy encompassed even Gentiles— just as non-Jews are fully included here in Jesus' closing instructions to the faithful to "make disciples of *all* nations."[9] In anticipation of its departure on that mission, Jesus solemnly assures his little band, "I will be with you always."[10] Thus, from Matthew's viewpoint, Jesus' assurance is in the end only a reassurance of what was vouchsafed from the outset: Jesus is indeed "Emmanuel . . . *God with us*" (Matt. 1:23); *his very presence* testifies to God's abiding commitment to remain with human beings, come what may. In sum, the risen Jesus, back alive from the dead, is proof positive the divine promise is still alive.

If all these concluding circumstances sound familiar, the reason may be due to our having heard such occurrences described before in the various 'kingdom parables' of Matthew 13. Parables such as the sower, the mustard seed, the leaven, and treasures old and new essentially all spoke of what has subsequently taken place through Jesus' crucifixion and resurrection: God's kingdom, although coming in an apparently insignificant and very sudden way, has nevertheless actually begun to arrive even at the present time; moreover, while its full manifestation will occur sometime in the future ("the close of the age"), those who *in the meantime* would be its faithful subjects must show themselves to be so by obeying the King's will as now revealed to them by Jesus.[11] Hence, Jesus' death and resurrection have been, in a profound sense, nothing more or less than *Jesus' enactment of his parables*,[12] and consequently, one might well legitimately conclude that "[Jesus] did not [merely] tell people about the kingdom, but he *was* the kingdom."[13]

Naturally, however, references to a kingdom, whether God's or anybody else's, unavoidably suggest certain questions about the nature and scope of the sovereign's power. We ourselves raised just such issues at Jesus' crucifixion, for at the cross, we questioned where God's power was—and additionally, where his justice, and where his love. Now, from the vantage point of the resurrection, we can at last plainly discern the answers to all three queries.

Where, then, was God's sure justice on the cross? In the Exodus narrative, one of God's hallmark characteristics was his unswerving fidelity to the demands of justice—from his initial intervention in fulfillment of his covenantal promises to his subsequent measure-for-measure reprisals against Pharaoh and the Egyptians.[14] Therefore, at the cross, what we should have reasonably expected was a just God acting to save the totally innocent Jesus while condemning in his place all those responsible for his fate: the envious priests and elders, the greedy Judas, the weak-willed disciples, the faithless Jewish crowds, the cowardly Pilate, and the cruel Roman troops—in short, the representatives of *all humanity*. In other words, since the whole of humankind has in one way or another participated in putting Jesus on the cross, *every human being ought to deserve to die* in Jesus' stead. Yet God let Jesus die in *their* stead! Was the Lord's concern for justice thus abandoned? Or was that concern still evident on the cross—along with other divine concerns as well?

As the Christian master story made clear from the first, Jesus is not merely one of us human beings, but a human being in whose very person and work we can come to see "God-with-us" human beings—as actively present among us human beings. From that perspective, Jesus not only embodies the full-fleshed image of God-become-man, but as significantly, he conversely displays the full-blown expression of man's being created in the image of God. Jesus is thus both paradigm-of-God and paradigm-of-man, and that is finally why he took the place on the cross rightly due all other human beings—because in the end *only he could* rightly take it. As humanity incarnate, Jesus alone could *satisfy* what justice demands; as God incarnate, he alone could *bear* what justice requires. If the cross were to show justice upheld in any other way, the vision held up would be *the world* crucified and doomed to death. For it to be saved from so horrible an end, nothing less would do than for God to accept that destiny as his own.

Consequently, in coming to see Jesus' execution as the site where God's sure justice was also executed, not only have we answered the first of our three questions, but the second one besides, for nothing could testify more convincingly to God's impassioned commitment to the world than Jesus' passion on the cross. Where was Jesus' Father's love on the cross? *There*—on the cross! What better place to see the Father's love for *all* his children than in that act of self-sacrifice done for their sake? At the cross, divinity is sacrificed so that humanity may not be; Jesus' giving up his life is the clearest sign that God has not given up on human life, and hence, the cross reveals how boundlessly determined the Creator still remains to give life to his creation. He is willing to suffer pain, torment, and humiliation, thereby sacrificing everything properly owed him as Lord—i.e., status, honor, respect—in order to save his undeserving creatures from the deadly consequences their own acts merit. Put another way, he is utterly willing to sacrifice everything at his disposal *except* his sinful creatures if only to save them *from themselves*. What greater love in all the world could there be than this?

Perhaps now we can understand why human beings have seemed strangely impotent throughout the narrative, while

God alone has appeared to be fully in command of the events that have transpired. In this story, humanity has been found so lacking that not only have its actions *not* made its situation better, but, on the contrary, they have only tended to make it worse, because the one *real* chance the world had for getting better was the very chance the world rejected when it hung Jesus on the cross.

Clearly, were Jesus' story to end with his slow and awful death, it would be yet another tragic tale of yet one more good man (indeed, the best man who ever lived—the virtual embodiment of God!) vanquished by the destructive powers of the world; however poignant his act of self-sacrificing love, it would thus have nonetheless been a sacrifice in vain. But obviously, the narrative does not end at the cross, devoid of any capacity for saving meaning, and as a result, our third and last question resurfaces: Where does God's saving power emerge in all of this?

It emerges with the risen Christ at the resurrection. For what power is demonstrated through that event of Jesus' coming back to life—never to die again[15]—but that just as the world cannot kill Jesus, it cannot kill his kind of self-sacrificing love? Such love literally has the power to overcome the worst a sin-wracked world can throw at it—envy, greed, betrayal, falsehood, and finally, even death. The power of such love is not displayed in its ability to kill those who would seek to kill us. Rather, it is revealed in its capability to empower us to enlist our lives wholeheartedly in the service of the lives of others, and even of—and perhaps most notably of—those who threaten to destroy our lives. It is the raw power of a love willing to give completely of itself to others, without setting any preconditions or requiring anything in return.

In the eyes of the Christian story, that very sort of potent love is displayed through the resurrected Jesus' return, for the resurrection shows us that nothing we can do to God—not even the attempt to crucify him—will ever succeed in permanently driving him away from us and out of our world. No matter what we may try to do to this God, he will always come back to us as powerful proof of his love for us—and his equally compelling forgiveness of us. Thus, through his decisive move to be back with his creation again, he has effected atonement—at-one-ment—with creation once and for all. From now on, no sin of ours can mean a perpetual breach with him, covenantal or otherwise, and thus our hope for salvation need never be put in doubt, not because of what *we* might do or fail to do in the future, but because of what *he* has done already. Despite our worst offenses, his startling return in Christ's resurrection is the most astonishing indication of his ever-present readiness to take the initiative in moving to heal any rifts between himself and human beings, and hence, Jesus' resurrection offers visible confirmation of God's steadfast intent to persevere with humankind, never allowing human sinfulness to result in the world's being eternally estranged from *his life-bearing presence*. God's powers are therefore quite literally *salvic* in their ability to remedy whatever woes the world may suffer—even those self-inflicted.

Thus, whatever the previous ambiguities in Matthew's narrative, the risen Christ now signals God's unambiguous declaration that we have been saved in the most elementary way of all, because we have been saved from the most fundamental threat of all—*ourselves.* In that regard, the resurrection of Jesus of Nazareth at the close of this Christian master story undeniably attests the titles given him at its start: he is *truly* called "Christ" and "Emmanuel"—God as Savior come to be with us to save us from our sins, and so save our lives as well.[16]

And therein finally lies God's—and the story's—ultimate saving power. For throughout this narrative meant to ring true to the character of human existence, people have desperately attempted, but miserably failed, to obtain one thing above all else: security for their lives.[17] In their search for such security, human beings have typically turned to such resources as material wealth, prestige, and even force. But the human being whose crucifixion we beheld relied on none of those things to save himself. Instead, he put his trust in something—Someone—else altogether, and now from the vantage point of Jesus' resurrection, we realize that such faith was justified after all. For the resurrected Jesus, alive in *body* as well as spirit, provides the most impressive kind of evidence—*physical* evidence!—that faith in God *does save* where nothing else can. Equipped with such faith, we can come to see that the One who has so miraculously transformed the cross from a symbol of death to a sign of life can likewise transform our own existence too.

Knowing that, we are able to become like the disciples at the narrative's conclusion. At last secure in the sure knowledge that God remains always truly with us no matter what travails we might encounter on our future ventures, we can set about the task he has given us. It is to be work like that which God himself has done—work whose glory is its humility, whose majesty is its ministry, and whose concern is not the self, but the other. Undertaking such a mission with and through our lives, we not only spread the word about the coming of our Lord, we simultaneously also spread out the orbit of his kingdom, until that time when its presence—and his—will be acknowledged as encompassing all the world.

Such indeed *is* good news, *the* good news of the Christian master story, whose marvelous tidings for humankind are not to be considered as too good to be true, but, on the contrary, as the gospel truth!

Notes

1. Gundry explains that in contrast to Mark's portrayal of these events happening on Sunday morning, "Matthew is pointing to Saturday evening. . . . [His wording here in 28:1] refers to the onset of evening . . . rather than to the dawn" (*Matthew: A Commentary*, p. 585). Gundry is alluding to the fact that the Jewish marking of days is from sunset to sunset; thus by a Jewish reckoning "the dawn of the first day of the week" following the Sabbath would be Saturday evening.

2. Contrast the women's *fear mixed with great joy* to the guards' *pure fear*. Moreover, in contrast to all the indications of Jesus' being alive, note the depiction of the guards as "dead men"; ibid., p. 588. At any rate, from the initial seeing of the empty tomb to the first hearing of the resurrection to the primary meeting with the risen Christ, women occupy a striking place in Jesus' story (cf. also, e.g., Matt. 26:6-13). Perhaps the heightened place of women in the narrative is so striking precisely because of the rather *déclassé* position of women in the world which Jesus enters. But then, in a sense, this may be but a further extension and deepening of an earlier Exodus motif where God's storied 'point of entry' is exactly with and through 'the underclass.' For a more detailed elaboration of some of these themes, see Elisabeth Schüssler Fiorenza's important work, *In Memory of Her* (New York: Crossroad, 1983).

3. Cf. 27:54 and the commentary *ad loc.*

4. Cf. Gundry, *Matthew: A Commentary*, pp. 542-43.

5. Cf. Stendahl, "Matthew," 695i.

6. Gundry, commenting on v. 19, remarks, "'in the name of' means 'with fundamental reference to' and distinguishes Christian baptism [which demands] allegiance to the triune God (*Matthew: A Commentary*, p. 596).

7. Significantly, for Matthew, the central issue between Jews and Christians is *not*: Torah *or* Jesus? Rather, the matter turns on who most authoritatively interprets and reveals Torah—i.e., God's desires of and for the world: Moses, the Pharisees, and the priests?—or Jesus? See also, e.g., Matt. 5:17-20; 23:1-12.

8. Cf. Gen. 22:18 and Gen. 12:3. Importantly, Israel—i.e., the Jews—are not excluded from the charge that Jesus gives. The Jews are not to be abandoned or ignored as the disciples, *who are Jews themselves*, set out on their mission. Clearly, however, the new, primary target of that divinely sanctioned errand shall now be nations other than Israel. Cf. Gundry, *Matthew: A Commentary*, p. 595.

9. See Matt. 1:1, and my comments there, and additionally, cf. Gundry, *Matthew: A Commentary*, p. 595.

10. Cf. Exod. 3:12, where prior to Moses' embarking on *his* appointed mission, God had given him similar reassurances of "I will be with you."

11. Cf. Kingsbury, *Parables*, pp. 17, 18, 20, 36, 79, 87, 128.

12. I am indebted to Professor Hans Frei for this extremely valuable insight.

13. McFague, *Speaking in Parables*, p. 82.

14. See the commentary to Exod. 2:23-25 and 9:8-12.

15. The difference between resurrection and 'mere' resuscitation.

16. Cf. Matt. 1:1, 21-23.

17. Consider, for example, how the priests, Pilate, and Peter have variously reacted when confronted by things which they have each perceived might make their own positions somehow less secure.

EPILOGUE

As we noted at the beginning of our inquiry, Christians and Jews have generally assumed that the central issues of contention dividing them were their respective acceptance or rejection of some particular piece of creed concerning, for instance, the divinity of Jesus. But, we asked, what if more fundamental than our quarrels over discrete religious doctrines were our disputes about overarching master stories, through which our various theological convictions gain their sense and from which they draw their power? Thus, we suggested that before we blindly took up the doctrinal debate once more, thereby doing continued violence to our convictions—and possibly to each other, too—we first needed to discuss with sensitivity, empathy, and above all, *clarity* the narratives underlying them, trying to see how those narratives might stand to one another. Having now attempted to give both narratives an honest and attentive hearing, we are at last in a position to sum up our conclusions as a fair and thoughtful audience.

First and last, one theme resounds throughout both the Jewish and Christian master stories. However great the disparities separating them, a common strand nevertheless unites them—the activity of a *character called God*, whose distinctive character trait is his keeping faithful to his promises to keep the world alive. Whether through Exodus' stress on his observance of the covenant made with Israel's ancestors[1] or through Matthew's emphasis on the fulfillment of the assurances made through Israel's prophets,[2] God's steadfast commitment to his creation shines through each narrative time and time again.

Ironically, though, it is that selfsame characteristic as faithful promise-keeper, about which both master stories so whole-heartedly agree, that nonetheless forms one of the prime sources of disagreement between Jews and Christians. For despite their concurrence on fidelity as being the Lord's quintessential virtue, the Exodus and Matthean narratives differ markedly—and incommensurately—in the way they depict that virtue as being most graphically revealed. At bottom, the basic point of conflict between the two stories—and the two traditions holding them—hinges on their individual perceptions of precisely *how* God manifests such unceasing devotion to human beings—and how human beings in consequence ought to display such dedicated constancy themselves, whether to the Lord or to one another.

In Exodus, whatever promised salvation is wrought by God is never worked by him alone but always *in conjunction with* and *on condition of* some complementary action by human beings. Hence, from God's first involvement with Israel's plight to his tenth plague struck on her behalf, Israel's redemption depends crucially on Israel's activity as well, be it her insistent outcry to God for succor[3] or her life-saving identification with him.[4] That motif of joint enterprise between God and human beings reaches the apex of its articulation at the story's apex, Sinai, where the divine promise held out to humanity is preceded by a stipulation demanding corresponding human assurances in kind: "Now, therefore, *if* you will obey . . . and keep My covenant . . ."[5]

To be sure, in its picturing of the fulfillment of such reciprocal pledges between God and human beings, the Exodus narrative offers no rosy portrait of the prospects for human adherence to that promise-bound relationship, but rather takes full account of human failings, flaws, and limitations.[6] And yet, despite all such shortcomings, the story never veers from its basic theme—namely, that this tale of the Lord's ongoing interaction with his people Israel offers sure evidence that history will ultimately work out if and only if God and human beings can mutually be relied upon to work things out together.

Clearly, such a scheme is not without its risks; what if, for instance, the human elements in the plan fail to perform as hoped? Even though such an eventuality remains a possibility, nevertheless, according to the Jewish master story, if human beings can depend on anything, they can depend on the trustworthy God of Israel, who, having laid down such 'ground rules for redemption,' can be trusted to follow them himself, neither altering nor undermining them midway through the game, no matter how great the stakes or how unsure the outcome. Hence, for those who have taken up the Exodus narrative in their lives, faith might be best expressed as firm reliance on the God who relies so heavily on human beings.

For those, however, who would subscribe to Matthew's narrative, a radically different appraisement is required regarding the redemptive capabilities of God and humankind. Plainly put, the latter's total lack of such capacities is matched only by the former's full command of them. Throughout Matthew's story, human beings consistently show themselves unable to do what is necessary for doing what is right; the Jews, the Romans, even Jesus' own hand-picked disciples, all fail to meet their obligations when tested,[7] and as each group lends a hand in pushing Jesus one step closer to the cross, it simultaneously seems to push increasingly away the best chance the world has for being saved. In the end, however, things manage to work out after all, not because of any human doings, but solely because of those of God, thereby revealing the Matthean account for what it truly is meant to be: a gospel story proclaiming the good news that nothing can deter the Lord from saving his creatures—not even those creatures themselves. From God's initial entry into the story at Jesus' birth to his dramatic reappearance at Christ's resurrection, the Christian story leaves no doubt of the Lord's unfaltering determination to come to the rescue of his creation.[8]

Hence, the Christian master story, like the Jewish one before it, turns on the prime characteristic of its premier character—God—and consequently, the two narratives share a profound belief in the Lord's enduring concern for the world and his continuing involvement with it. Thus, the point at issue between them is not some dispute over God's ability to save us by becoming incarnate in an individual human being, with Jews therefore denying what Christians for their part affirm. Indeed, Jews and their story would concur that in principle, at least, God *could* do such a thing.[9] Rather, the narrative-based question dividing Jews and Christians takes an importantly different form: *Would* God do such a thing?

Christians, naturally, would answer 'of course,' pointing to the Lord's hallmark trait of being utterly trustworthy to keep his promises despite the difficulties in his path and regardless of the measures necessary to fulfill his word. Moreover, Christians would doubtless add that there is one pledge in particular of which the Lord is heedful—the one he made to Abraham, promising that through Abraham's people, he would eventually bring blessing to all people. In the person of Jesus Christ, say Christians, God's unfailingly trusty character has been decisively demonstrated for all time.

And if confronted with the query, 'Would God do such a thing?' how would Jews respond? While their reply would doubtless be the opposite of that of Christians, nevertheless, their basis for it would undoubtedly be the same as that of the Christians—namely, a narrative portrayal of God as being scrupulously true to his word. If the conditions for salvation have become fixed by that Sinai covenant made between God and the people Israel, then not only have human beings become bound by that compact's terms, but the Lord himself has become likewise pledged to follow its provisos. Thus, in this arrangement yoking God and humankind as co-partners in redemption, each side has become obligated to fulfill its own part of the bargain, and obviously, the failure to do so counts

G's self-limitation - inc. mechanics as well as goal of s...

as a serious covenantal breach. But conversely, and of no less import, each side, divine as well as human, has become similarly obliged not to overstep itself by attempting to play the other's role—thus resulting in an equally dire breach of faith between them. Hence, in Jewish eyes, were the Lord to have acted in the way ascribed him by the Christian master story, he would, by his very actions, have reneged on the terms of the agreement. For in attempting to effect salvation in the person of Jesus of Nazareth, God would have in essence been playing both parts—his own and that of humanity—thereby usurping the role previously accorded, for better or for worse, to humankind alone. And in the process, he would have revealed both himself and his promises to be far from dependable, but on the contrary, inconstant and untrue.

Thus, the crux of the matter invariably comes back to the storied character *called* God as well as the storied character *of* God. From a Christian viewpoint, the character displayed in the narrative account of the life, death, and resurrection of Jesus Christ appears to be identical with the character described in Israel's earlier chronicles—that is, someone unswervingly willing and able to go to any lengths to keep his word to human beings. By contrast, according to a Jewish understanding of Israel's previous saga, the character rendered through the unilateral, wholly gracious work of Jesus Christ seems completely out of character with the Lord whom Jews have come to know through the Exodus, for that Lord, though surely determined to honor his commitments, is nonetheless also ineluctably committed to a reciprocal working relationship with human beings that makes demands on them, has expectations of them, and *counts on them* eventually to come through, regardless of whatever very real deficiencies they may possess.

In any case, however, no matter which position we take, whether Christian or Jewish, the indisputable fact remains that both these views of God's character—and characteristic way of acting in the world—rest on narrative foundations. Consequently, far more fundamental than Jews' and Christians' conflicts about religious doctrine are their clashes over narrative interpretation. For while Christians would likely claim that their story reflects the natural outgrowth, continuation, and climax of the foregoing story of God's momentous dealings with Israel, Jews, for their part, would most probably contend that, on the contrary, the Christian master story displays a serious misreading and profound distortion of that prior narrative account. Thus, no matter how much ground Jews and Christians may share, at a rock-bottom level, they still stand apart. Though the Christian master story leads its adherents to confess the deity they worship in Jesus Christ to be one with the God of Israel, Jews, responding out of *their* master story, cannot help but say that the deity Christians venerate is a different god altogether, and hence, one finally false as well.[10]

But the line of demarcation between Jews and Christians does not stop there. For as their two master stories lead to diverse conceptions of the redemptive character of God, they correspondingly give rise to disparate understandings of the character appropriate for those redeemed. How then do their core narratives portraying God's regard for human life shape the way Jews and Christians ought to regard such life themselves?

First and foremost, whether for Jews or Christians, God's saving acts performed in the service of humanity ought to call forth people whose lives themselves display just that kind of service—completely dedicated, fully involved, totally resolute. Indeed, in the closing scenes of both the Exodus and Matthean narratives, with the Lord's covenantal offer to Israel at Sinai[11] and Jesus' charge to the disciples in Galilee,[12] committed service to others is precisely what is asked of those whose own life stories have been transformed by the larger story of God's care for human beings.

However, while a *general concept* of service may stand at the heart of each of these master stories, nevertheless, the two differ significantly in their *particular conceptions* of what constitutes the substance of that service. In the context of the Exodus narrative, God's involvement springs from his covenantal obligation, while in the story of Christ, it stems

218

from his unbounded grace. Such differences ought not to be ignored or underestimated, because they supply the framework for Jews and Christians envisaging the nature and meaning of their lives.

The Exodus story of God's commitment to a mutually binding covenant between himself and Israel trains Jews to view their lives *primarily as trusts* such that life's promise can only be fulfilled if all of us—God included—can reciprocally be trusted to fulfill our promises to one another. On the other hand, Christ's passion and resurrection call for Christians to see their lives *essentially as gifts* enabling them to give just that graciously to others, neither expecting nor requiring anything in return. While the Christian's master story maps the sketch of a world redeemed, the Jew's charts an outline of a world yet to be redeemed, and thus, each narrative inevitably offers its hearers a bedrock sentiment toward life distinctly suited to its own envisioned world. For Jews, it is a sense of compelling duty forged by a pact with God at Sinai to work with him to save the world;[13] for Christians, it is a sense of overwhelming gratitude born of the salvation already achieved through Christ.[14]

There is, however, another critical respect in which their master stories give Jews and Christians their particular orientations to the world. In Exodus, the pivotal focus of God's activity is an entire people;[15] in Matthew, it is a single person.[16] In the former, therefore, virtually everything of consequence occurs through the vehicle of human community such that no one individual, whether Moses or even God, can alone effect redemption. But in the latter's account of Jesus' death and resurrection, a single individual not only can but does in fact save the world. Hence, for Jews, salvation's focal point is the community, while for Christians, it is the self.[17] And according to each narrative, what does such salvation actually save you from? On the Jewish story's understanding, from oppression that emanates from outside; on the Christian's, from affliction that originates within.

Having now therefore sought to listen to both accounts with openness and sensitivity, and having thus hopefully come to

219

see with greater insight the implications of each story for our lives, we must finally ponder which, if either, of these two master stories we ought to try to embody in our own individual life stories. But just what kinds of considerations do we need to keep in mind as we make our reasoned judgments? Though the subject is a bit complex,[18] the task of evaluating these contending stories and their often conflicting claims ultimately consists of a three-pronged assessment of their grip on truth.

First, both the Christian and Jewish master stories are portrayed as being essentially historical accounts, asking us to believe that at some specific time in some specific place certain events actually transpired. Consequently, at a fundamental level, questions about the general historicity of these narratives cannot justifiably be ignored. I say "general historicity" because while modern scholarship—and Scripture itself—may call particular details of the stories into doubt,[19] their broader story lines must nonetheless remain intact if they are to maintain their basic credibility. So, for instance, were we somehow to learn that Israel never had been enslaved in Egypt in the first place, but that the whole story had been fabricated at a much later date, then the Jewish master story—and any claims made on its behalf—would be gravely undermined. And it does not require much imagination to appreciate what serious damage might be done to the Christian story and its claims were we somehow to discover that Jesus of Nazareth did not die as a young man on a cross, but as an old man, warm at home in bed, and furthermore, that having died, he stayed dead and was never resurrected.

Yet while it is one thing to investigate a narrative's capacity to *be* true, it is another to explore its ability to *ring* true. Therefore, at a second level of appraisal, the truth of narratives is to be found not solely in their correspondence to some isolated cluster of actual persons or events,[20] but as importantly, through their reference to a whole world of possible relations, a world which the story constantly puts before our imaginations, impelling us to consider whether its depicted universe *is* reasonably imaginable given the kind of universe with which we human beings are familiar. Do the story's happenings seem at all probable or likely in light of our experience, and moreover, do such occurrences conjure up the sort of place that humankind could or would inhabit?

For example, in reading Matthew's version of the Christian master story, we might be led to say that his repeated emphasis on our own inadequacies as the root of all our suffering certainly does ring true to what we know of life. Yet even so, we might also be disposed to say that Matthew's picture of a world whose affairs are so completely under God's own sure guidance seems completely foreign and unwarranted, for from our own acquaintance with the course of world affairs, we can see no clear-cut course at all. We might even be inclined to say that such 'Mattheanisms' as "all this took place to fulfill what the Lord had spoken by the prophet" (Matt. 1:22), rather than strengthening the plausibility of Matthew's account, only weaken it by making its story line seem not genuinely believable, but instead extremely *plotted*; rather than *artfully* rendering a reality linking Jesus' story to Israel's, such pointed scriptural references perhaps end up making Matthew's narrative seem incredibly *artificial*.

In any case, however, whether for Matthew or for Exodus, before either of the two narratives can transform our present view of life, each must first resonate with at least some features of that current outlook. Hence, if the narrative's twists and turns impress us as entirely too fantastic from the standpoint we now occupy, then our ability to follow what the story has to say will likely become impaired even on a level of simply *comprehending* it in our minds—let alone on one of *enacting* it in our lives. In essence, this second step of truth assessment regarding master stories involves our reckoning whether the tale related strikes us as basically *true to life.*

Finally, there is a third—but certainly not tertiary—item we need contemplate in judging the 'truth value' of a community's master story and the potential rightness of adopting it in and for our individual life stories. For the truth of a master story hangs on more than either its giving a true portrayal of some momentously significant event in human life or its offering a true paradigm of the shape and structure of our existence; in the end, such truth depends as well on the story's providing a true guide for living such that we might *live the story out.* Consequently, at this third stage of weighing our formative communal narratives and the distinctive convictions that arise from them, we must trot out not only our little arguments for inspection, but also our little lives, for here, the best backing any of us can give to our master stories and our story-bound beliefs is through the way we back them up with the types of lives we lead.

Indeed, more often than not, it is precisely in that connection between lives and stories that each of our foundational narratives ultimately proves convincing—or unconvincing. For if we would allege any persuasive power at all for our particular tradition's root narrative, then at the very least, that story must have the power to take hold of our life and sustain it and even possibly transform it. As a result, every time Jews fail to live a life shaped deeply by Sinai's vision of mutual obligation, and every time Christans fail to live a life marked profoundly by the cross's image of unconditional self-sacrifice, whatever basic truth any of us might assert for the Jewish and/or Christian master stories stands somehow fundamentally denied. For despite what we might *say,* the way we *act* testifies that those narratives fail as truly reliable guideposts for our lives after all. And if those who supposedly espouse a particular master story nevertheless show themselves unwilling or unable to follow it truthfully and with fidelity, why should anybody else take their story seriously?

Therefore, the final validation or refutation of the Jewish and Christian master stories lies in the quality—*the character*—of Jewish and Christian life, and hence, in the last analysis, whether as Jews or Christians, the most eloquent telling of our tales of God's presence in human life inevitably takes place in the very midst of our lives themselves.

EPILOGUE

Notes

1. See Exod. 3:12-22 (and the parallel passage in Exod. 6:2-8) and my attending comments *ad loc*. Likewise, for the other various scriptural citations given in the notes below, see the accompanying commentary as well. In any case, these citations are meant to give exemplary rather than exhaustive instances of the ideas articulated in the main text of this concluding chapter.

2. Cf. Matt. 1:2-17, 22-23; 2:13-23; 26:47-56.

3. Exod. 2:23-25.

4. Exod. 12:1-28.

5. Exod. 19:5 (italics added).

6. See, e.g., Exod. 4:14-17; 5:19-23; 15:22-27.

7. Thus, note Matt. 26:36-46 and 27:20-26.

8. See Matt. 1:18-25 and 28:16-20.

9. Notice in *Church Dogmatics* how Barth, in his own way of doing narrative theology, nicely makes this point about God's wide-ranging, storied power (II, 1, pp. 524-26).

10. Such a conclusion is but a logical consequence of monotheism.

11. Exod. 19:1-6.

12. Matt. 28:16-20.

13. See Exod. 20:1-14 and especially one of the attendant footnotes there, namely, note 13.

14. See Matt. 27:54 and 28:9-10, 16-17. Clearly, a sense of gratitude for God's redemptive acts on their behalf is quite fitting for Jews also. Nevertheless, it is a story-tied sense of duty that affords Jews the most justifiable basis for responding to any question concerning their rationale for living a way of life characterized by the observance of binding covenantal obligations, i.e., the *mitsvot*.

15. Cf. Exod. 1:1; 9:1-7; 12:29-32.

16. Cf. Matt. 1:1; 3:13-17; 13:31-36.

17. It is, of course, true that Jesus calls a new community into being and that his living presence can only be known in and through that community of his followers, i.e., the Church, the *new* (or *re-newed*) Israel. Nonetheless, there is a sense in which that community comes to be formed one-by-one (e.g., the centurion at the cross, the women on the way to Galilee, the disciples in Galilee) in a way that is strikingly different from the formation of a covenant community *en masse* at Sinai. Though I am indebted to James McClendon, Stanley Hauerwas, and Robert Bilheimer for such reminders of the central value of community for the Christian story, it nevertheless seems to me that the relative significance given by that narrative to the individual on the one hand and community on the other is markedly different from that ascribed by the Jewish master story.

18. For a more detailed elaboration of this highly involved matter, see my *Theology and Narrative*, chap. 6.

19. Cf., for instance, my own comments reflecting those of Childs in n. 18 to Exod. 14:1-9 regarding the depiction of the 'ten' plagues.

20. And of course, that kind of truth, while reasonably required of such narrative genres as histories, biographies, and the like, is quite inappropriately expected from other story types such as fables, fairy tales, and other sorts of *fiction*.